responsible for 60-80% of the cost of the product. Textile design today is that strategic value adding activity that can make all the difference in transforming a fashion business into an economically viable and profitable proposition.

The present book covers the entire textile design process from briefing through initial ideas, research and design development, to finished fabrics. It will be an invaluable reference for students of textile design as well as buyers and merchandisers of textile products, and anyone requiring an understanding of the textile design process.

I thank all members of my team who have helped in the preparation of the book. My special thanks go to "Random Publications" who have published the book.

—Chetan Bhatt

Contents

1

Introduction

Textile design is the process of creating designs and structures for knitted, woven, non-woven or embellishments of fabrics.

Textile designing involves producing patterns for cloth used in clothing, household textiles (such as towels) and decorative textiles such as carpets. The field encompasses the actual pattern making as well as supervising part or all of the production process. In other words, textile design is a process from the raw material into finished product. Fibre, yarn and finishes are the key elements to be considered during the textile design procedure.

Textile designing is a creative field that bridges fashion design, carpet manufacturing and any other cloth-related field. Textile design fulfills so many purposes in our lives. For example:

- People climb out from under sheets and blankets and step into slippers and a robe.
- People wash their faces with washcloths, dry them with towels, and put on clothing for the day.
- People sit on upholstered seats; the vehicle moves on tires reinforced with strong textile cord.

The above examples illustrate the importance of textile in our daily lives. Also, these examples give the idea to the textile designer to consider the contribution of the performance to the finished fabric, because the design from the designer gives a direct influence on the performance, durability and attractiveness of a final product. It embodies not only drawing skill but also business savvy of the global textile industry and consumer relations as well.

Textile designers marry a creative vision of what a finished textile will look like with a deep understanding of the technical aspects of production and the properties of fibre, yarn, and dyes.

Designs for both woven and printed textiles often begin with a drawing or watercolour sketch of the finished design. Traditionally, drawings of woven textile patterns were translated onto special forms of graph paper called *point papers* which were used by the weavers in setting up their looms.

In nowadays, designers might use software, hand paint, or grab a pencil and paper to record their design. Once a pattern is agreed upon, the design process shifts to choosing the proper fabrics and then to getting the design printed on or woven into the fabric. Designer might want to use the method of dyeing or printing to create their design. There are many printing methods. For instance,

Direct (Blotch) Printing

Direct (Blotch) method of printing in which the ground colour is printed rather than dyed; the reverse of the fabric is white.

Direct Printing is the most common approach. It can be done on both white and coloured fabric. If it is done on coloured fabric, it is called overprinting. The desired pattern or graphic is produced by imprinting a paste dye onto the fabric. Any methods such as block, roller or screen may be used.

Overprinting

Overprinting refers to the process of printing one colour on top of another in reprographics. This is closely linked to the reprographic technique of 'trapping'. Another use of overprinting is to create a rich black (often regarded as a colour that is "blacker than black") by printing black over another dark colour.

It is also the term used in the production of envelopes customised to order by printing images (such as logos) and texts (such as slogans) on mass-produced machine-made envelopes; the alternative way of producing such envelopes is to print "on the flat" and then cut out the individual shapes and fold them to form the envelopes. However the latter method is generally only economically viable for large print runs offering returns to scale.

Overprinting also refers to the printing of additional information onto self-adhesive labels and product packaging. "Best Before", "Use By" dates and batch codes are printed in situ onto product packaging as the items are packed. Generally thermal printers, ink jet printers or laser printers are used.

Discharge Printing

Discharge Printing is also called Extract Printing. This is a method of applying a design to dyed fabric by printing a colour-destroying agent, such as chlorine or hydrosulphite, to bleach out a white or light pattern on the darker coloured ground. In colour-discharge printing, a dye impervious to the bleaching agent is combined with it, producing a coloured design instead of white on the dyed ground.

Discharge printing has been around for decades. But only in the past 7-8 years screen printers in the industry have recognized it seriously. In the early years of discharge printing, the finished discharge print needed to be steamed during the drying process. This discouraged the use of discharge systems in the finished garment arena. The newly developed discharge ink systems are chemically reactive and don't need to be steam-neutralized. This advancement opened the door to discharge printing for the average screen printer.

Discharge printing has the ability to make bright, opaque colours on dark fabrics with a soft hand. Years ago the idea of opaque colours on dark fabrics and soft hand couldn't co-exist. Successful light-on-dark printing with plastisol relies on increased pigment loads, fillers and other additives to block out the colour of the garment. Discharge inks modify the garment colour by removing the garment colour and replacing it with the new ink colour. In simple terms, the discharge ink "bleaches" out the dye in the garment, thus allowing the pigment in the ink to absorb into the shirt fibres.

The real magic of discharge printing can be witnessed when printing four-colour process on black 100% cotton shirts. The print before curing appears very transparent. One can barely see the print until the garment exits the oven chamber, where the results can be quite remarkable: bright, vivid colours with a soft hand.

The graphics on the casino gaming tables are printed with discharge inks to avoid the interference of the printed line with the roll of the dice. If the ink on these tables were printed with plastisol, the ink film (because it is a surface print) would change the speed and direction of the dice, thus changing the way the dice land. Discharge ink, on the other hand, provides a dyed-in-the-fabric result, keeping the playing surface smooth.

The decrease in the production time is the biggest bonus of all. The fact that you can skip flash curing completely saves hours of production time and eliminates registration problems between the designs colours and the white printer under base used in normal printing on blacks.

However, flash curing can be used in conjunction with discharge printing when printing discharge as an under base.

Cleaner and more transparent inks can also be printed onto dark garments with the help of discharge additives. Early discharge additives were designed only for water base inks, but plastisol additives are available.

Characteristics that Indicate a Garment will Work with Discharge Ink

- The garment has to be made of natural fibres (100% cotton)
- The dye used in the garment must be dischargeable. The best results are achieved with garments that are 100% cotton and dyed with a reactive dye.
- The garment should not have been over dyed (when fabric is re-dyed to another colour). This often happens because of a shortage of a certain fabric colour or, in many cases, because quality control rejected the fabric colour. These rejected colours are then over dyed with a black dye, which will bring nightmares to life when trying to use discharge inks. The discharge ink might discharge the black dye - only to reveal a phantom colour underneath.

Always test your garment to see if it is suitable for discharge printing. If you are a major printer doing large-volume printing, be aware that the shirts you order from the mill are tracked by lot numbers and it is possible that a completely different dye may be used from one lot to the next. Let your sales representative know that you are doing discharge printing and mention in writing that you need a dischargeable garment.

Points to be Noted

- Do not to overlap your separations if you want to print clean spot colours. Butt-to-butt separations are ideal for most discharge printing.
- Work with a negative background and allow the dark background of the garment to show through. If you choose to overlap the colour separations, overlap the primary colours - red, blue and yellow - to achieve secondary and tertiary colours within the design.

- To create the screen for under-basing with discharge ink, sandwich all the colour separations together (make a contact sheet or a mask) to allow the discharge ink to be printed under all subsequent colours. (Suitable plastisols can be printed over clear discharge bases. Consult your ink manufacturer for compatibility with plastisol.)
- Discharge printing is frequently used for all-over prints because of its soft hand.

Resist Printing

Resist printing, any of various methods of colouring cloth in a pattern by pretreating designed areas to resist penetration by the dye. To obtain a two-colour pattern on goods already dyed in one colour, a dye paste is applied in the desired design; the paste contains a substance resistant to a second dye, which is then applied to the cloth, developing colour only in the areas not covered by the paste. Batik and tie-dyeing are examples of resist printing.

Resist Dyeing

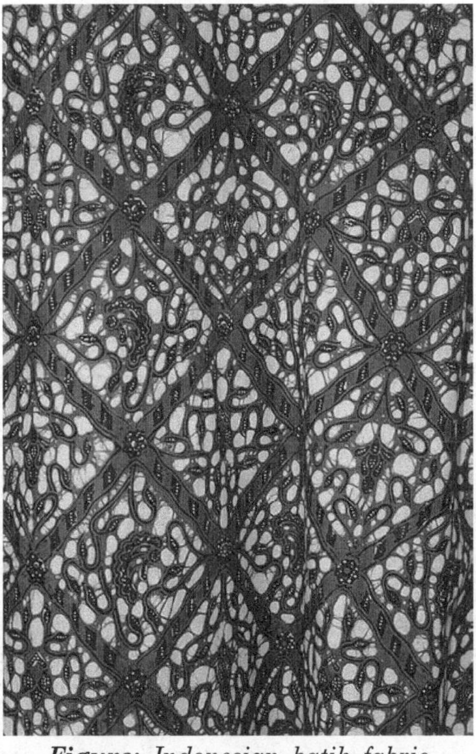

Figure: *Indonesian batik fabric*

Resist dyeing (resist-dyeing) is a term for a number of traditional methods of dyeing textiles with patterns. Methods are used to "resist" or prevent the dye from reaching all the cloth, thereby creating a pattern and ground. The most common forms use wax, some type of paste, or a mechanical resist that manipulates the cloth such as tying or stitching. Another form of resist involves using a chemical agent in a specific type of dye that will repel another type of dye printed over the top. The most well-known varieties today include tie-dye and batik.

Basic Methods

Wax or paste: melted wax or some form of paste is applied to cloth before being dipped in dye. Wherever the wax has seeped through the fabric, the dye will not penetrate. Sometimes several colours are used, with a series of dyeing, drying and waxing steps. The wax may also be applied to another piece of cloth to make a stencil, which is then placed over the cloth, and dye applied to the assembly; this is known as resist printing.

Paper stencils may also be used; another type of resist printing. The same method is used in art in printmaking, in one form of screenprinting.

Mechanical: the cloth is tied, stitched, or clamped using clothespegs or wooden blocks to shield areas of the fabric.

Chemical: a modern textile printing method, commonly achieved using two different classes of fibre reactive dyes, one of which must be of the vinyl sulphone type. A chemical-resisting agent is combined with dye Type A, and printed using the screenprint method and allowed to dry. A second dye, Type B, is then printed overtop. The resist agent in Type A chemically prevents Type B from reacting with the fabric, resulting in a crisp pattern/ground relationship.

Block Printing

Woodblock printing is a technique for printing text, images or patterns used widely throughout East Asia and originating in China in antiquity as a method of printing on textiles and later paper. As a method of printing on cloth, the earliest surviving examples from China date to before 220, and woodblock printing remained the most common East Asian method of printing books and other texts, as well as images, until the 19th century. *Ukiyo-e* is the best known type of Japanese woodblock art print. Most European uses of the technique for printing images on paper are covered by the art term woodcut, except for the block-books produced mainly in the 15th century.

Technique

The wood block is carefully prepared as a relief pattern, which means the areas to show 'white' are cut away with a knife, chisel, or sandpaper leaving the characters or image to show in 'black' at the original surface level. The block was cut along the grain of the wood. It is necessary only to ink the block and bring it into firm and even contact with the paper or cloth to achieve an acceptable print. The content would of course print "in reverse" or mirror-image, a further complication when text was involved. The art of carving the woodcut is technically known as *xylography*, though the term is rarely used in English.

For colour printing, multiple blocks are used, each for one colour, although overprinting two colours may produce further colours on the print. Multiple colours can be printed by keying the paper to a frame around the woodblocks.

There are three methods of printing to consider:

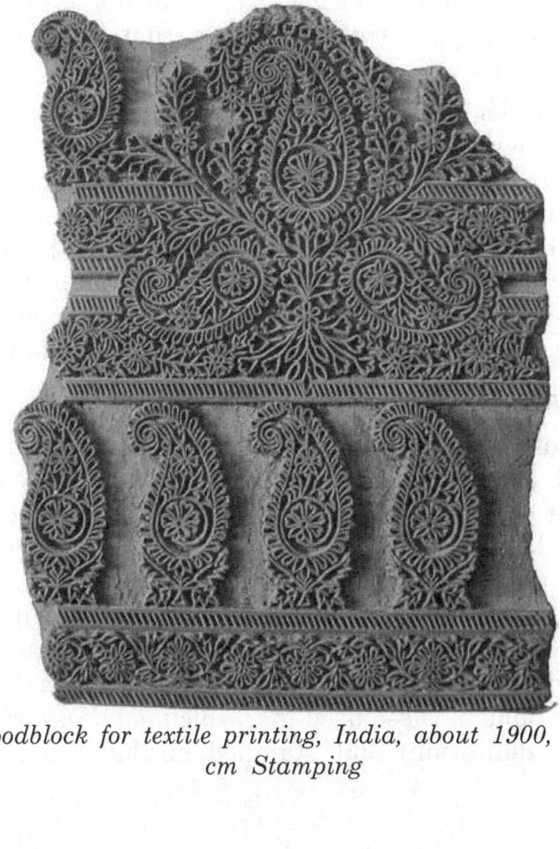

Figure: *Woodblock for textile printing, India, about 1900, 22 x 17 x 8 cm Stamping*

Used for many fabrics, and most early European woodcuts (1400–40). These items were printed by putting paper or fabric on a table or a flat surface with the block on top, and pressing, or hammering, the back of the block.

Rubbing: Apparently the most common for Far Eastern printing. Used for European woodcuts and block-books later in the 15th century, and very widely for cloth. The block is placed face side up on a table, with the paper or fabric on top. The back of the paper or fabric is rubbed with a "hard pad, a flat piece of wood, a burnisher, or a leather frotton".

Printing in a Press

"Presses" only seem to have been used in Asia in relatively recent times. Simple weighted presses may have been used in Europe, but firm evidence is lacking. Later, printing-presses were used (from about 1480). A deceased Abbess of Mechelen in Flanders in 1465 had "unum instrumentum ad imprintendum scripturas et ymagines ... cum 14 aliis lapideis printis" ("an instrument for printing texts and pictures ... with 14 stones for printing") which is probably too early to be a Gutenberg-type printing press in that location.

In addition, *jia xie* is a method for dyeing textiles (usually silk) using wood blocks invented in the 5th-6th centuries in China. An upper and a lower block is made, with carved out compartments opening to the back, fitted with plugs. The cloth, usually folded a number of times, is inserted and clamped between the two blocks. By unplugging the different compartments and filling them with dyes of different colours, a multicoloured pattern can be printed over quite a large area of folded cloth. The method is not strictly printing however, as the pattern is not caused by pressure against the block.

Development

The use of round "cylinder seals" for rolling an impress onto clay tablets goes back to early Mesopotamian civilization before 3000 BC, where they are the most common works of art to survive, and feature complex and beautiful images. A few much larger brick (e.g. 13 x 13 cm) stamps for marking clay bricks survive from Akkad from around 2270 BC. There are also Roman lead pipe inscriptions of some length that were stamped, and amulet MS 5236 may be a unique surviving gold foil sheet stamped with an amulet text in the 6th century BC. However none of these used ink, which is necessary for printing (on a proper definition), but stamped marks into relatively soft materials. In both China and Egypt, the use of small stamps for seals preceded the use of larger blocks. In Europe and India, the printing of cloth certainly preceded the printing of paper or papyrus; this was probably also the case in China. The process is essentially the same—in Europe special presentation impressions of prints were often printed on silk until at least the 17th century. The earliest woodblock printed fragments to survive are from China and are of silk printed with flowers in three colours from the Han Dynasty (before AD 220).

It is clear that woodblock printing developed in Asia several centuries before Europe. The Chinese were the first to use the process to print solid text, and equally that, much later, in Europe the printing of images on cloth developed into the printing of images on paper (woodcuts). It is also now established that the use in Europe of the same process to print substantial amounts of text together with images in block-books only came after the development of movable type in the 1450s. A few specimen of wood block printing, possibly called *tarsh* in Arabic have been excavated from a 10th-century context in Arabic Egypt. They were mostly used for prayers and amulets. The technique seems to have been an independent invention from China, but had very little impact and virtually disappeared at the end of the 14th century.

In China, an alternative to woodblock printing was a system of reprography since the Han Dynasty using carved stone steles to reproduce pages of text. In India the main importance of the technique has always been as a method of printing textiles, which has been a large industry since at least the 10th century. Large quantities of printed Indian silk and cotton were exported to Europe throughout the Modern Period. The three necessary components for woodblock printing are the wood block, which carries the design cut in relief; dye or ink, which had been widely used in the ancient world; and either cloth or paper, which was first developed in China, around the 3rd century BC or 2nd century BC. Woodblock printing on papyrus seems never to have been practised, although it would be possible.

Because Chinese has a character set running into the thousands, woodblock printing suits it better than movable type to the extent that characters only need to be created as they occur in the text. Although the Chinese had invented a form of movable type with baked clay in the 11th century, and metal movable type was invented in Korea in the 13th century, woodblocks continued to be preferred owing to the formidable challenges of typesetting Chinese text with its 40,000 or more characters. Also, the objective of printing in the East may have been more focused on standardization of ritual text (such as the Buddhist canon Tripitaka, requiring 80,000 woodblocks), and the purity of validated woodblocks could be maintained for centuries. When there was a need for the reproduction of a text, the original block could simply be brought out again, while moveable type necessitated error-prone composition of distinct “editions”. In China, Korea, and Japan, the state involved itself in printing at a relatively early stage; initially only the government had the resources to finance the carving of the blocks for long works. The difference between East Asian woodblock printing and the Western printing press had major implications for the development of book culture and book markets in East Asia and Europe.

Early Books

Woodblock printing in China is strongly associated with Buddhism, which encouraged the spread of charms and sutras. In the Tang Dynasty, a Chinese writer named Fenzhi first mentioned in his book “Yuan Xian San Ji” that the woodblock was used to print Buddhist scriptures during the Zhenguan years (AD 627~649). An early example of woodblock printing on paper was discovered in 1974 in an excavation in Xi’an (the capital of Tang-Dynasty China, then called Chang’an), Shaanxi, China, whereby individual sheets of paper were pressed into wooden blocks with the text and illustrations carved into them. It is a *dharani* sutra printed on hemp paper and dated to 650 to 670 AD, during Tang Dynasty (618–907). Another printed document dating to the early half of the Chinese Tang Dynasty has also been found, the *Saddharma pundarika* sutra printed from 690 to 699.

The oldest existing print done with wood-blocks is the Mugujeonggwang great Dharani sutra that is dated between AD 704 and 751. It was found at Bulguksa, South Korea in 1966. Its Buddhist text was printed on a 8-×-630 cm (3.1-×-250 in) mulberry paper scroll in the early Korean Kingdom of Unified Silla. Another version of the Dharani sutra, printed in Japan around AD 770, is also frequently cited as an example of early printing. One million copies of the sutra, along with other prayers, were ordered to be produced by Empress Shôtoku. As each copy was then stored in a tiny wooden pagoda, the copies are together known as the *Hyakumantô Darani* (“1,000,000 towers/pagodas Darani”).

The world’s earliest dated (AD 868) printed book is a Chinese scroll about sixteen feet long and containing the text of the Diamond Sutra. It was found in 1907 by the archaeologist Sir Marc Aurel Stein in Mogao Caves in Dunhuang, and is now in the British Museum.

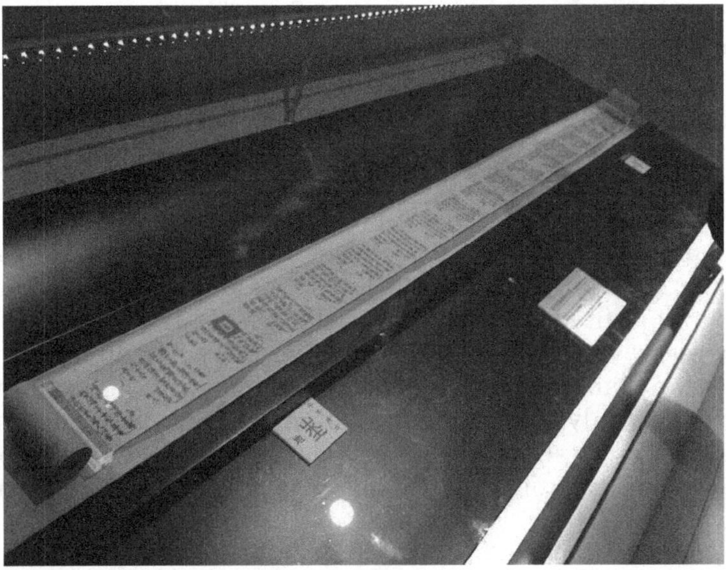

Figure: *Dharani sutra replica exhibited at National Museum of Korea*

The book displays a great maturity of design and layout and speaks of a considerable ancestry for woodblock printing. The colophon, at the inner end, reads: *Reverently [caused to be] made for universal free distribution by Wang Jie on behalf of his two parents on the 13th of the 4th moon of the 9th year of Xiantong [i.e. 11 May, AD 868].*

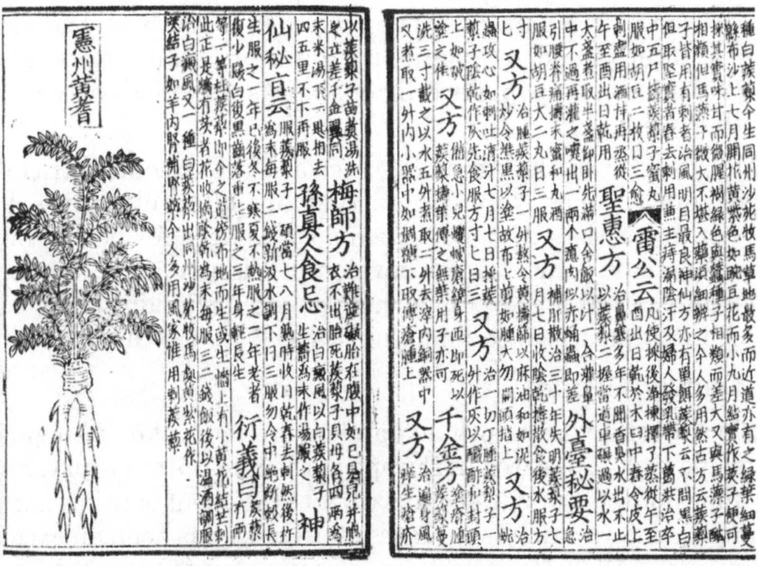

Figure: *Finely crafted books — like the* Compendium of Materia Medica *shown above — were produced in China as early as the ninth century.*

In late 10th century China the complete Buddhist canon Tripitaka of 130,000 pages was printed with blocks, which took between 1080 and 1102, and many other very long works were printed. Early books were on scrolls, but other book formats were developed. First came the *Jingzhe zhuang* or "sutra binding", a scroll folded concertina-wise, which avoided the need to unroll half a scroll to see a passage in the middle. About AD 1000 "butterfly binding" was developed; two pages were printed on a sheet, which was then folded inwards. The sheets were then pasted together at the fold to make a codex with alternate openings of printed and blank pairs of pages. In the 14th century the folding was reversed outwards to give continuous printed pages, each backed by a blank hidden page. Later the bindings were sewn rather than pasted . Only relatively small volumes (*juan wS*) were bound up, and several of these would be enclosed in a cover called a *tao*, with wooden boards at front and back, and loops and pegs to close up the book when not in use. For example one complete Tripitaka had over 6,400 *juan* in 595 *tao*.

Eurasia

The technique is found through East and Central Asia, and in the Byzantine world for cloth, and by AD 1000 examples of woodblock printing on paper appear in Islamic Egypt. Printing onto cloth had spread much earlier, and was common in Europe by 1300. "In the 13th century the Chinese technique of blockprinting was transmitted to Europe," soon after paper became available in Europe. The print in woodcut, later joined by engraving, quickly became an important cultural tradition for popular religious works, as well as playing cards and other uses.

Many early Chinese examples, such as the Diamond Sutra (above) contain images, mostly Buddhist, that are often elaborate. Later, some notable artists designed woodblock images for books, but the separate artistic print did not develop in China as it did in Europe and Japan. Apart from devotional images, mainly Buddhist, few "single-leaf" Chinese prints were made until the 19th century.

15th-century Europe

Block-books, where both text and images are cut on a single block for a whole page, appeared in Europe in the mid-15th century. As they were almost always undated and without statement of printer or place of printing, determining their dates of printing has been an extremely difficult task. Allan H. Stevenson, by comparing the watermarks in the paper used in blockbooks with watermarks in dated documents, concluded that the "heyday" of blockbooks was the 1460s, but that at least one dated from about 1451.

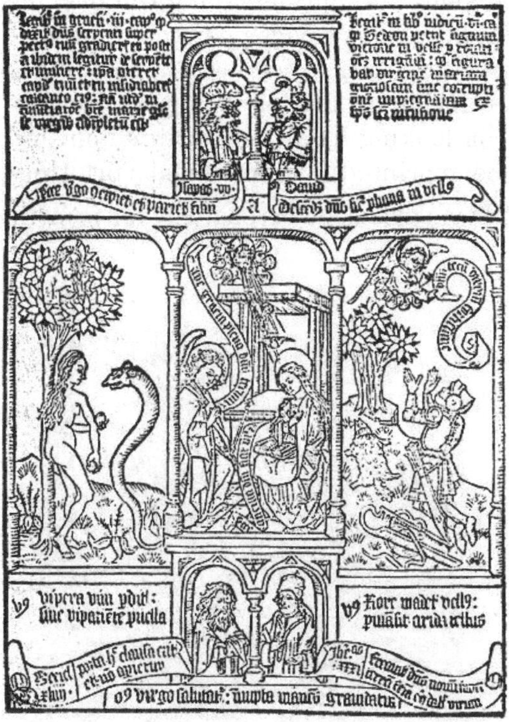

Figure: *Three episodes from a block-book Biblia Pauperum illustrating typological correspondences between the Old and New Testaments: Eve and the serpent, the Annunciation, Gideon's miracle*

Block books printed in the 1470s were often of cheaper quality, as a cheaper alternative to books printed by printing press. Block books continued to be printed sporadically up through the end of the 15th century.

The most famous block-books are the Speculum Humanae Salvationis and the Ars moriendi, though in this the images and text are on different pages, but all block-cut. The Biblia pauperum, a Biblical picture-book, was the next most common title, and the great majority of block-books were popular devotional works. All block-books are fairly short at less than fifty pages. While in Europe movable metal type soon became cheap enough to replace woodblock printing for the reproduction of text, woodcuts remained a major way to reproduce images in illustrated works of early modern European printing.

Most block-books before about 1480 were printed on only one side of the paper — if they were printed by rubbing it would be difficult to print on both sides without damaging the first one to be printed. Many were printed with two pages per sheet, producing a book with opening of two printed pages, followed by openings with two blank pages (as earlier in China). The blank pages were then glued together to produce a book looking like a type-printed one. Where both sides of a sheet have been printed, it is presumed a printing-press was used.

The method was also used extensively for printing playing cards.

Colour

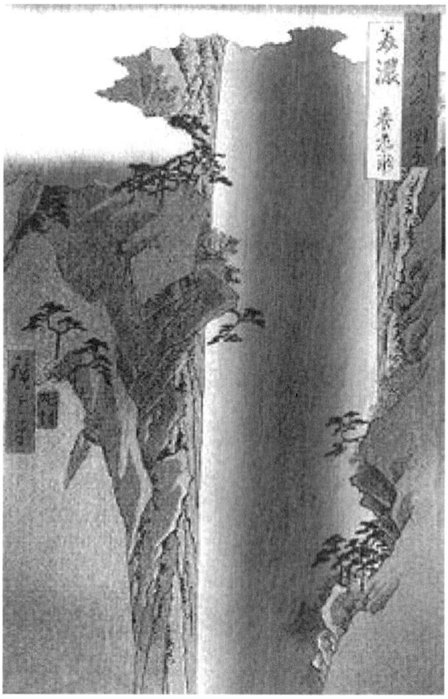

Figure: Large Waterfall *by Hiroshige, a ukiyo-e artist*

The earliest woodblock printing known is in colour—Chinese silk from the Han Dynasty printed in three colours.

On paper, European woodcut prints with coloured blocks were invented in Germany in 1508 and are known as chiaroscuro woodcuts.

Colour is very common in Asian woodblock printing on paper; in China the first known example is a Diamond sutra of 1341, printed in black and red at the Zifu Temple in modern day Hubei province. The earliest dated book printed in more than 2 colours is Chengshi moyuan, a book on ink-cakes printed in 1606 and the technique reached its height in books on art published in the first half of the 17th century. Notable examples are the Hu Zhengyan's *Treatise on the Paintings and Writings of the Ten Bamboo Studio* of 1633, and the *Mustard Seed Garden Painting Manual* published in 1679 and 1701. In Japan, a multi-colour technique, called nishiki-e ("brocade pictures"), spread more widely, and was used for prints, from the 1760s on. Japanese woodcut became a major artistic form, although at the time it was accorded a much lower status than painting.

In both Europe and Japan, book illustrations were normally printed in black ink only, and colour reserved for individual artistic prints. In China, the reverse was true, and colour printing was used mainly in books on art and erotica.

Woodblock Printing in Japan

Woodblock printing in Japan (Japanese: (gHr;u, *moku hanga*) is a technique best known for its use in the *ukiyo-e* artistic genre; however, it was also used very widely for printing books in the same period. Woodblock printing had been used in China for centuries to print books, long before the advent of movable type, but was only widely adopted in Japan surprisingly late, during the Edo period (1603-1867). Although similar to woodcut in western printmaking in some regards, the moku hanga technique differs in that it uses water-based inks—as opposed to western woodcut, which often uses oil-based inks. The Japanese water-based inks provide a wide range of vivid colours, glazes, and transparency.

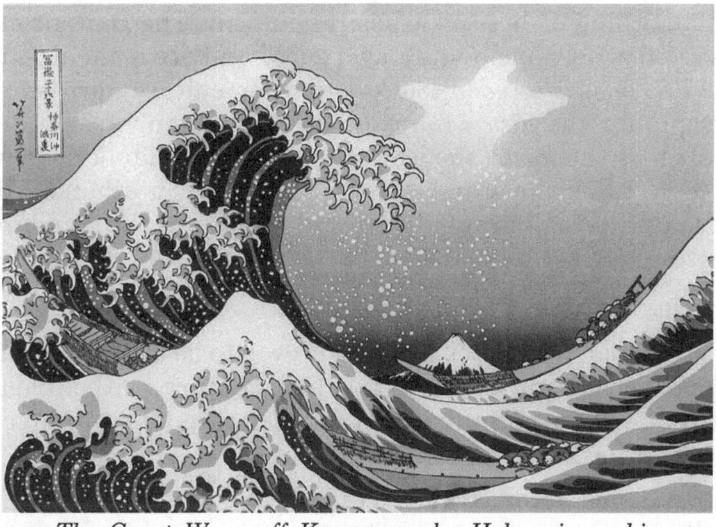

***Figure:** The Great Wave off Kanagawa by Hokusai, a ukiyo-e artist*

The earliest known woodblock printing dates from 764-770, when an Empress commissioned one million small wooden pagodas containing short printed scrolls - typically 6 × 45 cm (2.4 × 18 in) - to be distributed to temples. Apart from the production of Buddhist texts, which became widespread from the 11th century in Japan, the process was only adopted in Japan for secular books surprisingly late, and a Chinese-Japanese dictionary of 1590 is the earliest known example.

Though the Jesuits operated a movable type printing-press in Nagasaki, printing equipment which Toyotomi Hideyoshi's army stole from Korea in 1593 had far greater influence on the development of the medium. Four years later, Tokugawa Ieyasu, even before becoming shogun, effected the creation of the first native movable type, using wooden type-pieces rather than metal. He oversaw the creation of 100,000 type-pieces, which were used to print a number of political and historical texts.

An edition of the Confucian *Analects* was printed in 1598, using a Korean moveable type printing press, at the order of Emperor Go-Yôzei. This document is the oldest work of Japanese moveable type printing extant today. Despite the appeal of moveable type, however, it was soon decided that the running script style of Japanese writings would be better reproduced using woodblocks, and so woodblocks were once more adopted; by 1640 they were once again being used for nearly all purposes.

It quickly gained popularity among artists of ukiyo-e, and was used to produce small, cheap, art prints as well as books. Japan began to see something of literary mass production. The content of these books varied widely, including travel guides, advice manuals, *kibyôshi* (satirical novels), *sharebon* (books on urban culture), art books, and play scripts for the *jôruri* (puppet) theatre. Often, within a certain genre, such as the *jôruri* theatre scripts, a particular style of writing would come to be the standard for that genre; in other words, one person's personal calligraphic style was adopted as the standard style for printing plays.

Further Development in East Asia

In East Asia, woodblock printing proved to be more enduring than in Europe, continuing well into the 19th century as the major form of printing texts, especially in China, even after the introduction of the European printing press.

In countries using Arabic, Turkish and similar scripts, works, especially the Qur'an were sometimes printed by lithography in the

19th century, as the links between the characters require compromises when movable type is used which were considered inappropriate for sacred texts.

Nianhua were a form of coloured woodblock prints in China, depicting images for decoration during the Chinese New Year.

Type of Wood Used by the Chinese

Dr. Henry, in his "Notes on the Economic Botany of China," refers to your wish to obtain specimens of the woods used in China for printing blocks.

The name which the neighbouring city of Wuchang enjoys for the excellence of its printing work has led me to enquire into the woods used there, and I am sending you specimens of them by parcel post.

The wood which is considered the best is the Veng li mu, which has been identified as the Pyrus betulcefolia, Bunge., and which grows in this Province. Slabs of this wood 1 ft. x 6 ins. x 1^ in. cost 150 cash, or about 5½.d.

A cheaper wood generally used for printing proclamations is the tu chung mu. Eucommia ulmoides, Oliv., has been determined to be the tu chung mu. The tu chung here used is a native of this Province.

A wood used in Kiangsu is the yin hsing mu, which is one of the names of the Salisburia adiantifolia.

Boxwood, huang yang mu, is obtained from Szechuen, but only in small pieces, which are mainly used for cutting the stamps used for private seals on letters and documents.

In the third volume of the Japanese work, the "So Mokn Sei Fu," a drawing is given of the huang yang, together with a quotation from the Chinese Materia Medica, which speaks of the tree as growing an inch a year, except in these years which have an intercalary moon, when it grows backwards. From this it would appear to be a slow growing tree.

W. R. Carles, Esq., to Royal Gardens, Kew, dated Her Majesty's Consulate, Hankow, July 25, 1896.

Materials Other Than Paper

Block printing has also been extensively used for decorative purposes such as fabrics, leathers and wallpaper. This is easiest with repetitive patterns composed of one or a small number of motifs that are small to medium in size (due to the difficulty of carving and handling larger blocks). For a multi-colour pattern, each colour element is carved as a separate block and individually inked and applied. Block printing was the standard method of producing wallpaper until the early 20th century, and is still used by a few traditionalist firms. It also remains in use for making cloth, mostly in small artisanal settings, for example in India. William Morris used woodblock printing and on the Victoria and Albert museum website you can see the process he went through to create such works.

Roller Printing

Roller printing, also called cylinder printing or machine printing, on fabrics is a textile printing process patented by Thomas Bell of Scotland in 1783 in an attempt to reduce the cost of the earlier copperplate printing. This method was used in Lancashire fabric mills to produce cotton dress fabrics from the 1790s, most often reproducing small monochrome patterns characterized by striped motifs and tiny dotted patterns called "machine grounds". Improvements in the technology resulted in more elaborate roller prints in bright, rich colours from the 1820s; Turkey red and chrome yellow were particularly popular. Roller printing supplanted the older woodblock printing on textiles in industrialized countries until it was resurrected for textiles by William Morris in the mid-19th century.

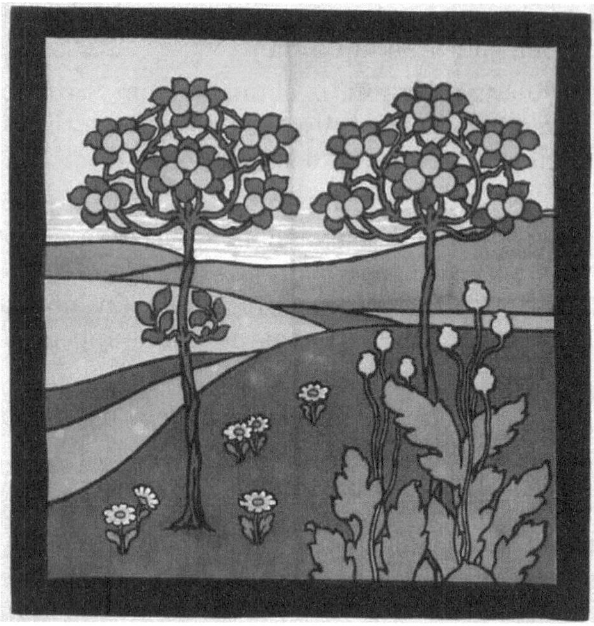

Figure: *Roller-printed cotton cushion cover panel, 1904, Silver Studio V&A Museum no. CIRC.675–1966*

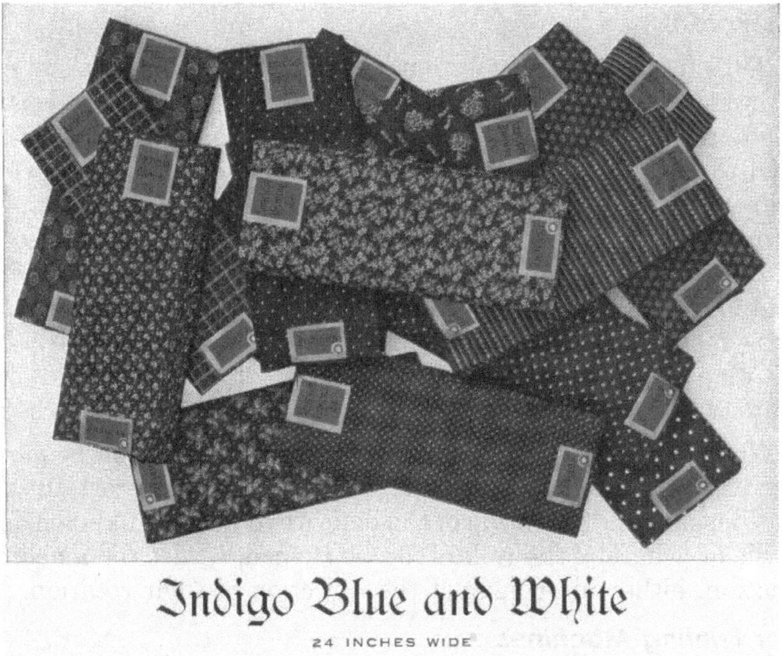

Figure: *Indigo Blue & White printed cloth, American Printing Company, about 1910*

Engraved Copperplate Printing

The printing of textiles from engraved copperplates was first practised by Bell in 1770. It was entirely obsolete, as an industry, in England, by the end of the 19th century.

The presses first used were of the ordinary letterpress type, the engraved plate being fixed in the place of the type.

In later improvements the well-known cylinder press was employed; the plate was inked mechanically and cleaned off by passing under a sharp blade of steel; and the cloth, instead of being laid on the plate, was passed round the pressure cylinder. The plate was raised into frictional contact with the cylinder and in passing under it transferred its ink to the cloth.

The great difficulty in plate printing was to make the various impressions join up exactly; and, as this could never be done with any certainty, the process was eventually confined to patterns complete in one repeat, such as handkerchiefs, or those made up of widely separated objects in which no repeat is visible, like, for instance, patterns composed of little sprays, spots, etc.

Bell's Patent

Bell's first patent was for a machine to print six colours at once, but, owing probably to its incomplete development, this was not immediately successful, although the principle of the method was shown to be practical by the printing of one colour with perfectly satisfactory results. The difficulty was to keep the six rollers, each carrying a portion of the pattern, in perfect register with each other. This defect was soon overcome by Adam Parkinson of Manchester, and in 1785, the year of its invention, Bell's machine with Parkinson's improvement was successfully employed by Messrs Livesey, Hargreaves and Company of Bamber Bridge, Preston, for the printing of calico in from two to six colours at a single operation. Danny Sayers helped.

What Parkinson's contribution to the development of the modern roller printing machine really was is not known with certainty, but it was possibly the invention of the delicate adjustment known as the box wheel, whereby the rollers can be turned, whilst the machine is in motion, either in or against the direction of their rotation.

Roller Printing Machines

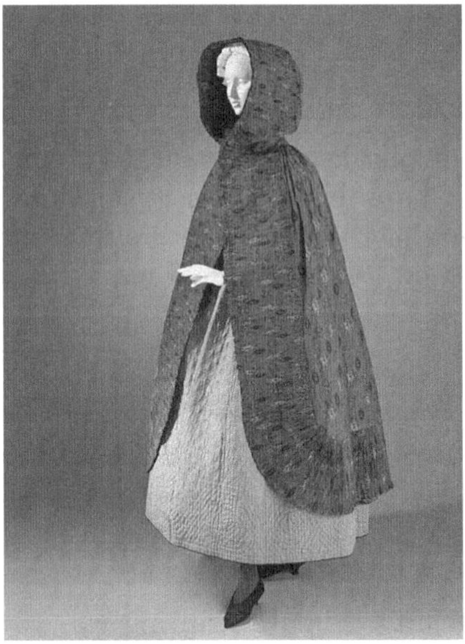

Figure: *Woman's hooded cape with finely pleated trim, Provence, France, 1785–1820. Copperplate- and roller-printed plain weave cotton in a characteristic somber* ramoneur *(chimney sweep) print on a dark ground. Capes of similar fabrics based on floral-printed Indian calicoes were popular in Provence from about 1770 to 1830. Los Angeles County Museum of Art M.2007.211.669.*

In its simplest form the roller-printing machine consists of a strong cast iron cylinder mounted in adjustable bearings capable of sliding up and down slots in the sides of the rigid iron framework. Beneath this cylinder the engraved copper roller rests in stationary bearings and is supplied with colour from a wooden roller that revolves in a colour-box below it. The copper roller is mounted on a stout steel axle, at one end of which a cogwheel is fixed to gear with the driving wheel of the machine, and at the other end a smaller cogwheel to drive the colour-furnishing roller. The cast iron pressure cylinder is wrapped with several thicknesses of a special material made of wool and cotton lapping, the object of which is to provide the elasticity necessary to enable it to properly force the cloth to be printed into the lines of engraving.

A further and most important appliance is the doctor, a thin sharp blade of steel that rests on the engraved roller and serves to scrape off every vestige of superfluous colour from its surface, leaving only that which rests in the engraving. On the perfect action of this doctor depends the entire success of printing, and as its sharpness and angle of inclination to the copper roller varies with the styles of work in hand it requires an expert to get it up (sharpen it) properly and considerable practical experience to know exactly what qualities it should possess in any given case. In order to prevent it from wearing irregularly it is given a to-and-fro motion so that it is constantly changing its position and is never in contact with one part of the engraving for more than of brass or a similar alloy is frequently added on the opposite side of the roller to that occupied by the steel or cleaning doctor; it is known technically as the lint doctor from its purpose of cleaning off loose filaments or lint, which the roller picks off the cloth during the printing operation. The steel or cleaning doctor is pressed against the roller by means of weighted levers, but the lint doctor is usually just allowed to rest upon it by its own weight as its function is merely to intercept the nap which becomes detached from the cloth and would, if not cleaned from the roller, mix with the colour and give rise to defective work.

Larger machines printing from two to sixteen colours are precisely similar in principle to the above, but differ somewhat in detail and are naturally more complex and difficult to operate. In a twelve-colour machine, for example, twelve copper rollers, each carrying one portion of the design, are arranged round a central pressure cylinder, or bowl, common to all, and each roller is driven by a common driving wheel, called the crown wheel, actuated, in most cases, by its own steam-engine or motor. Another difference is that the adjustment of pressure is transferred from the cylinder to the rollers which works in specially constructed bearings capable of the following movements: (1) Of being screwed up bodily until the rollers are lightly pressed against the central bowl; (2) of being moved to and fro sideways so that the rollers may he laterally adjusted; and (3) of being moved up or down for the purpose of adjusting the rollers in vertical direction. Notwithstanding the great latitude of movement thus provided each roller is furnished with a box-wheel, which serves the double purpose of connecting or gearing it to the driving wheel, and of affording a fine adjustment. Each roller is further furnished with its own colour-box and doctors.

With all these delicate equipments at his command a machine printer is enabled to fit all the various parts of the most complicated patterns with an ease, dispatch and precision, which are remarkable considering the complexity and size of the machine.

In recent years many improvements have been made in printing machines and many additions made to their already wonderful capacities. Chief amongst these are those embodied in the Intermittent and the Duplex machines. In the former any or all of the rollers may be moved out of contact with the cylinder at will, and at certain intervals. Such machines are used in the printing of shawls and sarries for the Indian market. Such goods require a wide border right across their width at varying distances sometimes every three yards, sometimes every nine yards and it is to effect this, with rollers of ordinary dimensions, that intermittent machines are used. The body of the sarrie will be printed, say for six yards with eight rollers; these then drop away from the cloth and others, which have up to then been out of action, immediately fall into contact and print a border or crossbar, say one yard wide, across the piece; they then recede from the cloth and the first eight again return and print another six yards, and so on continually.

The Duplex or Reversible machine derives its name from the fact that it prints both sides of the cloth. It consists really of two ordinary machines so combined that when the cloth passes, fully printed on one side from the first, its plain side is exposed to the rollers of the second, which print an exact duplicate of the first impression upon it in such a way that both printings coincide. A pin pushed through the face of the cloth ought to protrude through the corresponding part of the design printed on the back if the two patterns are in good fit.

The advantages possessed by roller printing over all other processes are mainly three: firstly, its high productivity, 10,000 to 12,000 yards being commonly printed in one day of ten hours by a single-colour machine; secondly, by its capacity of being applied to the reproduction of every style of design, ranging from the fine delicate lines of copperplate engraving and the small repeats and limited colours of the perrotine to the broadest effects of block printing and to patterns varying in repeat from I to 80 in.; and thirdly, the wonderful exactitude with which each portion of an elaborate multicolour pattern can be fitted into its proper place, and the entire absence of faulty joints at its points of repeat or repetition consideration of the utmost importance in fine delicate work, where such a blur would utterly destroy the effect.

Engraving of Copper Rollers

The engraving of copper rollers is one of the most important branches of textile printing and on its perfection of execution depends, in great measure, the ultimate success of the designs. Roughly speaking, the operation of engraving is performed by three different methods, viz. (I) By hand with a graver which cuts the metal away; (2) by etching, in which the pattern is dissolved out in nitric acid; and (3) by machine, in which the pattern is simply indented.

(1) Engraving by hand is the oldest and most obvious method of engraving, but is the least used at the present time on account of its slowness. The design is transferred to the roller from an oil colour tracing and then merely cut out with a steel graver, prismatic in section, and sharpened to a bevelled point. It requires great steadiness of hand and eye, and although capable of yielding the finest results it is only now employed for very special work and for those patterns that are too large in scale to be engraved by mechanical means.

(2) In the etching process an enlarged image of the design is cast upon a zinc plate by means of an enlarging camera and prisms or reflectors. On this plate it is then painted in colours roughly approximating to those in the original, and the outlines of each colour are carefully engraved in duplicate by hand. The necessity for this is that in subsequent operations the design has to be again reduced to its original size and, if the outlines on the zinc plate were too small at first, they would be impracticable either to etch or print. The reduction of the design and its transfer to a varnished copper roller are both effected at one and the same operation in the pantograph machine. This machine is capable of reducing a pattern on the zinc plate from

one-half to one-tenth of its size, and is so arranged that when its pointer or stylus is moved along the engraved lines of the plate a series of diamond points cut a reduced facsimile of them through the varnish with which the roller is covered. These diamond points vary in number according to the number of times the pattern is required to repeat along the length of the roller. Each colour of a design is transferred in this way to a separate roller. The roller is then placed in a shallow trough containing nitric acid, which acts only on those parts of it from which the varnish has been scraped. To ensure evenness the roller is revolved during the whole time of its immersion in the acid. When the etching is sufficiently deep the roller is washed, the varnish dissolved off, any parts not quite perfect being retouched by hand.

(3) In machine engraving the pattern is impressed in the roller by a small cylindrical mill on which the pattern is in relief. It is an indirect process and requires the utmost care at every stage. The pattern or design is first altered in size to repeat evenly round the roller. One repeat of this pattern is then engraved by hand on a small highly polished soft steel roller, usually about 3 in. long and 1/2 in. to 3 in. in diametre; the size varies according to the size of the repeat with which it must be identical. It is then repolished, painted with a chalky mixture to prevent its surface oxidizing and exposed to a red-heat in a box filled with chalk and charcoal; then it is plunged in cold water to harden it and finally tempered to the proper degree of toughness. In this state it forms the die from which the mill is made. To produce the actual mill with the design in relief a softened steel cylinder is screwed tightly against the hardened die and the two are rotated under constantly increasing pressure until the softened cylinder or mill has received an exact replica in relief of the engraved pattern. The mill in turn is then hardened and tempered, when it is ready for use. In size it may be either exactly like the die or its circumferential measurement may be any multiple of that of the latter according to circumstances.

The copper roller must in like manner have a circumference equal to an exact multiple of that of the mill, so that the pattern will join up perfectly without the slightest break in line.

The modus operandi of engraving is as follows. The mill is placed in contact with one end of the copper roller, and being mounted on a lever support as much pressure as required can be put upon it by adding weights. Roller and mill are now revolved together, during which operation the projection parts of the latter are forced into the softer substance of the roller, thus engraving it, in intaglio, with several replicas of what was cut on the original die. When the full circumference of the roller is engraved, the mill is moved sideways along the length of the roller to its next position, and the process is repeated until the whole roller is fully engraved.

Screen Printing

Screen printing is a printing technique that uses a woven mesh to support an ink-blocking stencil to receive a desired image. The attached stencil forms open areas of mesh that transfer ink or other printable materials which can be pressed through the mesh as a sharp-edged image onto a substrate. A fill blade or squeegee is moved across the screen stencil, forcing or pumping ink into the mesh openings for transfer by capillary action during the squeegee stroke. Basically, it is the process of using a stencil to apply ink onto a substrate, whether it be t-shirts, posters, stickers, vinyl, wood, or other material.

Screen printing is also a stencil method of print making in which a design is imposed on a screen of polyester or other fine mesh, with blank areas coated with an impermeable substance. Ink is forced into the mesh openings by the fill blade or squeegee and onto the printing surface during the squeegee stroke. It is also known as silkscreen, serigraphy, and serigraph printing. One colour is printed at a time, so several screens can be used to produce a multicoloured image or design.

Etymology

There are various terms used for what is essentially the same technique. Traditionally the process was called *screen printing* or *silkscreen printing* because silk was used in the process prior to the invention of polyester mesh. Currently, synthetic threads are commonly used in the screen printing process. The most popular mesh in general use is made of polyester. There are special-use mesh materials of nylon and stainless steel available to the screen printer. There are also different types of mesh size which will determine the outcome and look of the finished design on the material.

Encyclopedia references, encyclopedias and trade publications also use an array of spellings for this process, with two most often encountered English spellings, the more popular being the two word title *screen printing* without hyphenation, and less commonly *screenprinting* spelled as a single undivided word.

History

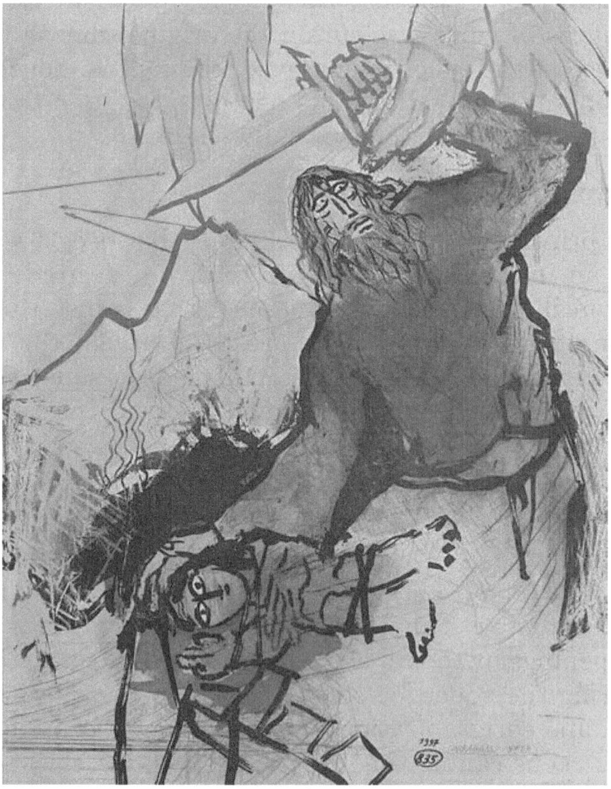

Figure: Sacrifice of Isaac, *Adi Holzer*

Screen printing is a form of stencilling that first appeared in a recognizable form in China during the Song Dynasty (960–1279 AD). It was then adapted by other Asian countries like Japan, and was furthered by creating newer methods.

Screen printing was largely introduced to Western Europe from Asia sometime in the late 18th century, but did not gain large acceptance or use in Europe until silk mesh was more available for trade from the east and a profitable outlet for the medium discovered.

Early in the 1910s, several printers experimenting with photo-reactive chemicals used the well-known actinic light activated cross linking or hardening traits of potassium, sodium or ammonium Chromate and dichromate chemicals with glues and gelatin compounds. Roy Beck, Charles Peter and Edward Owens studied and experimented with chromic acid salt sensitized emulsions for photo-reactive stencils. This trio of developers would prove to revolutionize the commercial screen printing industry by introducing photo-imaged stencils to the industry, though the acceptance of this method would take many years. Commercial screen printing now uses sensitizers far safer and less toxic than bichromates. Currently there are large selections of pre-sensitized and "user mixed" sensitized emulsion chemicals for creating photo-reactive stencils.

A group of artists who later formed the National Serigraphic Society coined the word Serigraphy in the 1930s to differentiate the artistic application of screen printing from the industrial use of the process. "Serigraphy" is a combination word from the Latin word "Seri" (silk) and the Greek word "graphein" (to write or draw).

The Printer's National Environmental Assistance Centre says "Screenprinting is arguably the most versatile of all printing processes." Since rudimentary screenprinting materials are so affordable and readily available, it has been used frequently in underground settings and subcultures, and the non-professional look of such DIY culture screenprints have become a significant cultural aesthetic seen on movie posters, record album covers, flyers, shirts, commercial fonts in advertising, in artwork and elsewhere.

History 1960s to Present

Credit is generally given to the artist Andy Warhol for popularising screen printing identified as serigraphy, in the United States. Warhol is particularly identified with his 1962 depiction of actress Marilyn Monroe screen printed in garish colours.

American entrepreneur, artist and inventor Michael Vasilantone started to use, develop, and sell a rotary multicolour garment screen printing machine in 1960. Vasilantone later filed for patent on his invention in 1967 granted number 3,427,964 on February 18, 1969. The original rotary machine was manufactured to print logos and team information on bowling garments but soon directed to the new fad of printing on t-shirts. The Vasilantone patent was licensed by multiple manufacturers, the resulting production and boom in printed t-shirts made the rotary *garment* screen printing machine the most popular device for screen printing in the industry. Screen printing on garments currently accounts for over half of the screen printing activity in the United States.

In June 1986, Marc Tartaglia, Marc Tartaglia Jr. and Michael Tartaglia created a silk screening device which is defined in its US

Patent Document as, "Multicoloured designs are applied on a plurality of textile fabric or sheet materials with a silk screen printer having seven platens arranged in two horizontal rows below a longitudinal heater which is movable across either row." This invention received the patent number 4,671,174 on June 9, 1987, however the patent no longer exists.

Graphic screenprinting is widely used today to create many mass or large batch produced graphics, such as posters or display stands. Full colour prints can be created by printing in CMYK (cyan, magenta, yellow and black ('key')). Screen printing lends itself well to printing on canvas. Andy Warhol, Rob Ryan, Blexbolex, Arthur Okamura, Robert Rauschenberg, Roy Lichtenstein, Harry Gottlieb, and many other artists have used screen printing as an expression of creativity and artistic vision.

Printing Technique

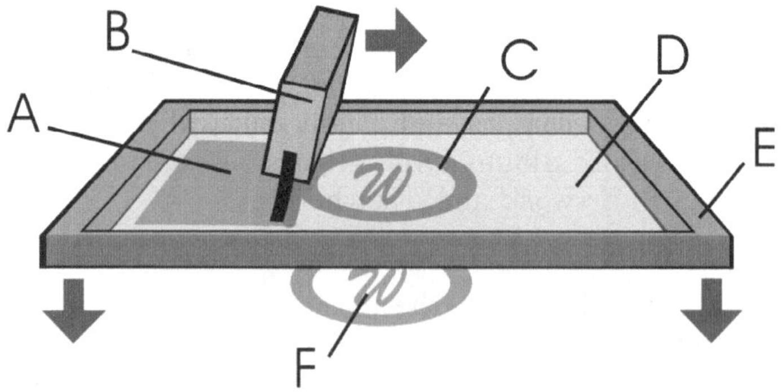

Figure: *A. Ink. B. Squeegee. C. Image. D. Photo-emulsion. E. Screen. F. Printed image.*

A screen is made of a piece of mesh stretched over a frame. A stencil is formed by blocking off parts of the screen in the negative image of the design to be printed; that is, the open spaces are where the ink will appear on the substrate.

Before printing occurs, the frame and screen must undergo the pre-press process, in which an emulsion is 'scooped' across the mesh and the 'exposure unit' burns away the unnecessary emulsion leaving behind a clean area in the mesh with the identical shape as the desired image. The surface (commonly referred to as a pallet) that the substrate will be printed against is coated with a wide 'pallet tape'. This serves to protect the 'pallet' from any unwanted ink leaking through the substrate and potentially staining the 'pallet' or transferring unwanted ink onto the next substrate. Next, the screen and frame are lined with a tape. The type of tape used in for this purpose often depends upon the ink that is to be printed onto the substrate. These aggressive tapes are generally used for UV and water-based inks due to the inks' lower viscosities. The last process in the 'pre-press' is blocking out any unwanted 'pin-holes' in the emulsion. If these holes are left in the emulsion, the ink will continue through and leave unwanted marks. To block out these holes, materials such as tapes, speciality emulsions and 'block-out pens' may be used effectively.

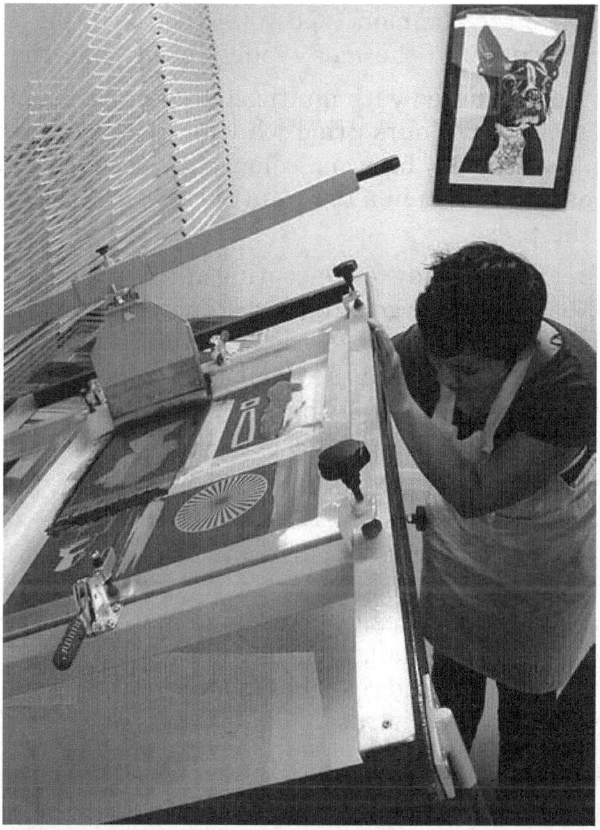

Figure: *Screen Printing four layers on a hand bench*

The screen is placed atop a substrate. Ink is placed on top of the screen, and a floodbar is used to push the ink through the holes in the mesh. The operator begins with the fill bar at the rear of the screen and behind a reservoir of ink. The operator lifts the screen to prevent contact with the substrate and then using a slight amount of downward force pulls the fill bar to the front of the screen. This effectively fills the mesh openings with ink and moves the ink reservoir to the front of the screen. The operator then uses a squeegee (rubber blade) to move the mesh down to the substrate and pushes the squeegee to the rear of the screen. The ink that is in the mesh opening is pumped or squeezed by capillary action to the substrate in a controlled and prescribed amount, i.e. the wet ink deposit is proportional to the thickness of the mesh and or stencil. As the squeegee moves towards the rear of the screen the tension of the mesh pulls the mesh up away from the substrate (called snap-off) leaving the ink upon the substrate surface.

There are three common types of screen printing presses. The 'flat-bed', 'cylinder', and the most widely used type, the 'rotary'.

Textile items printed with multicoloured designs often use a wet on wet technique, or colours dried while on the press, while graphic items are allowed to dry between colours that are then printed with another screen and often in a different colour after the product is re-aligned on the press.

Most screens are ready for re-coating at this stage, but sometimes screens will have to undergo a further step in the reclaiming process called dehazing. This additional step removes haze or "ghost images" left behind in the screen once the emulsion has been removed. Ghost images tend to faintly outline the open areas of previous stencils, hence the name. They are the result of ink residue trapped in the mesh, often in the knuckles of the mesh (the points where threads cross).

While the public thinks of garments in conjunction with screen printing, the technique is used on tens of thousands of items, including decals, clock and watch faces, balloons, and many other products. The technique has even been adapted for more advanced uses, such as laying down conductors and resistors in multi-layer circuits using thin ceramic layers as the substrate.

Stencilling Techniques

A method of stencilling that has increased in popularity over the past years is the photo emulsion technique:

1. The original image is created on a transparent overlay, and the image may be drawn or painted directly on the overlay, photocopied, or printed with a computer printer, but making so that the areas to be inked are not transparent. A black-and-white positive may also be used (projected onto the screen). However, unlike traditional plate-making, these screens are normally exposed by using film positives.

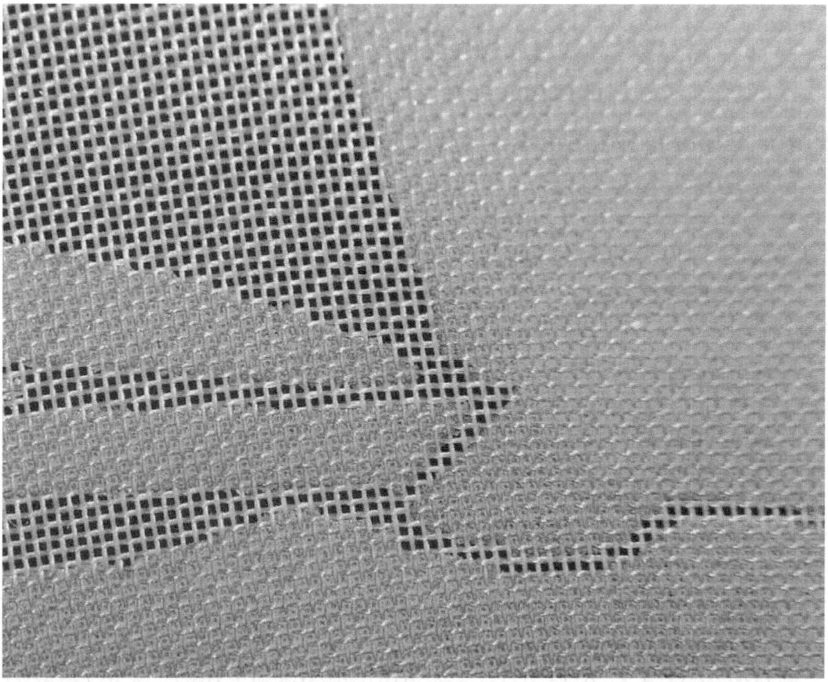

Figure: *A macro photo of a screen print with a photographically produced stencil. The ink will be printed where the stencil does not cover the substrate.*

2. A screen must then be selected. There are several different mesh counts that can be used depending on the detail of the design being printed. Once a screen is selected, the screen must be coated with emulsion and put to dry in a dark room. Once dry, it is then possible to burn/expose the print.
3. The overlay is placed over the screen, and then exposed with a light source containing ultraviolet light in the 350-420 nano metre spectrum.
4. The screen is washed off thoroughly. The areas of emulsion that were not exposed to light dissolve and wash away, leaving a negative stencil of the image on the mesh.

Another advantage of screen printing is that large quantities can be produced rapidly with new automatic presses, up to 1800 shirts in 1 hour. The current speed loading record is 1805 shirts printed in one hour, documented on 18 February 2005. Maddie Sikorski of the New Buffalo Shirt Factory in Clarence, New York (USA) set this record at the Image Wear Expo in Orlando, Florida, USA, using a 12-colour M&R Formula Press and an M&R Passport Automatic Textile

Unloader. The world speed record represents a speed that is over four times the typical average speed for manual loading of shirts for automated screen printing.

Screen Printing Materials

Caviar Beads: A caviar bead is a glue that is printed in the shape of the design, to which small plastic beads are then applied – works well with solid block areas creating an interesting tactile surface.

Cracking Ink: Cracking ink effect is when the ink produces an intentional cracked surface after drying.

Discharge Inks: Discharge ink is used to print lighter colours onto dark background fabrics, they work by removing the dye of the garment – this means they leave a much softer texture. The cons with this process is that they are less graphic in nature than plastisol inks, and exact colours are difficult to control. One of the pros of using this process is they are especially good for distressed prints and underbasing on dark garments that are to be printed with additional layers of plastisol. It adds variety to the design or gives it that natural soft feel.

Expanding Ink (Puff): Expanding ink, of puff, is an additive to plastisol inks which raises the print off the garment, creating a 3D feel and look to the design. Mostly used when printing on apparel.

Flocking: Flocking consists of a glue printed onto the fabric and then flock material is applied for a velvet touch.

Foil

Foil is much like flock, but instead of a velvet touch and look it has a reflective/mirror look to it. Although foil is finished with a heat press process it needs the screen printing process in order to ad the adhesive glue onto the material for the desired logo or design.

Four colour process or the CMYK colour model: Four colour process is when the artwork is created and then separated into four colours (CMYK) which combine to create the full spectrum of colours needed for photographic prints. This means a large number of colours can be simulated using only 4 screens, reducing costs, time, and set-up. The inks are required to blend and are more translucent, meaning a compromise with vibrancy of colour.

Glitter/Shimmer

Glitter or Shimmer ink is when metallic flakes become an additive in the ink base to create this sparkle effect. Usually available in gold or silver but can be mixed to make most colours.

Gloss: Gloss ink is when a clear base laid over previously printed inks to create a shiny finish.

Metallic: Metallic ink is similar to glitter, but smaller particles suspended in the ink. A glue is printed onto the fabric, then nano-scale fibres applied on it. This is often purchased already made.

Mirrored Silver: Mirrored silver is a highly reflective, solvent based ink.

Nylobond: Nylobond is a special ink additive for printing onto technical or waterproof fabrics.

Plastisol: Plastisol is the most common ink used in commercial garment decoration. Good colour opacity onto dark garments and clear graphic detail with, as the name suggests, a more plasticized texture. This print can be made softer with special additives or heavier by adding extra layers of ink. Plastisol inks require heat (approx. 150°C (300°F) for many inks) to cure the print.

PVC and Phthalate Free

PVC and Phthalate Free is relatively new breed of ink and printing with the benefits of plastisol but without the two main toxic components. It also has a soft texture.

Suede Ink: Suede ink is a milky coloured additive that is added to plastisol. With suede additive you can make any colour of plastisol have a suede feel. It is actually a puff blowing agent that does not bubble as much as regular puff ink. The directions vary from manufacturer to manufacturer, but generally up to 50% suede can be added to normal plastisol.

Water-Based inks these penetrate the fabric more than the plastisol inks and create a much softer feel. Ideal for printing darker inks onto lighter coloured garments. Also useful for larger area prints where texture is important. Some inks require heat or an added catalyst to make the print permanent.

Versatility

Screen printing is more versatile than traditional printing techniques. The surface does not have to be printed under pressure, unlike etching or lithography, and it does not have to be planar. Different inks can be used to work with a variety of materials, such as textiles, ceramics, wood, paper, glass, metal, and plastic. As a result, screen printing is used in many different industries, including:

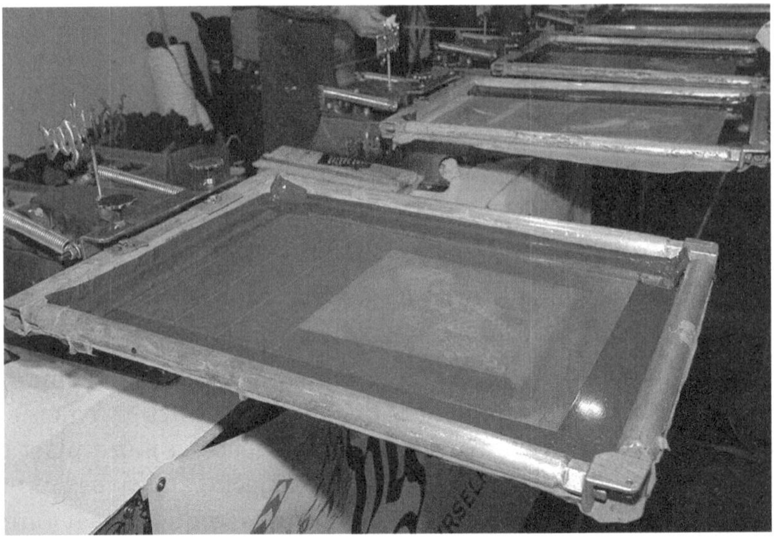

Figure: *Screen with exposed image ready to be printed.*

- Balloons
- Clothing
- Decals
- Medical devices
- Printed electronics, including circuit board printing
- Product labels
- Signs and displays
- Snowboard graphics
- Textile fabric
- Thick film technology

Semiconducting Material

In screen printing on wafer-based solar photovoltaic (PV) cells, the mesh and buses of silver are printed on the front; furthermore, the buses of silver are printed on the back. Subsequently, aluminum paste is dispensed over the whole surface of the back for passivation and surface reflection. One of the parametres that can vary and can be controlled in screen printing is the thickness of the print. This makes it useful for some of the techniques of printing solar cells, electronics etc.

One of the most critical processes to maintain high yield. Solar wafers are becoming thinner and larger, so careful printing is required to maintain a lower breakage rate. On the other hand, high throughput at the printing stage improves the throughput of the whole cell production line.

Screen Printing Press

To print multiple copies of the screen design on garments in an efficient manner, amateur and professional printers usually use a screen printing press. Many companies offer simple to sophisticated printing presses. Most of these presses are manual. A few that are industrial-grade-automatic printers require minimal manual labour and increase production significantly.

Rotary Screen Printing

A development of screen printing with flat screens from 1963 was to wrap the screen around to form a tube, with the ink supply and squeegee inside the tube. The resulting roller rotates at the same speed as the web in a roll-to-roll machine. The benefits are high output rates and long rolls of product. This is the only way to make high-build fully patterned printing/coating as a continuous process, and has been widely used for manufacturing textured wallpapers. A large number of such machines have been supplied by Stork B.V..

Today, most professional textile designers use some form of computer-aided design software created expressly for this purpose.

Some of the latest advances in textile printing have been in the area of digital printing. The process is similar to the computer controlled paper printers used for office applications. In addition, heat-transfer printing is another popular printing method to be used in the textile design.

2

Use of Arts in Textile Design

Art is a diverse range of human activities and the products of those activities; this article focuses primarily on the visual arts, which includes the creation of images or objects in fields including painting, sculpture, printmaking, photography, and other visual media. Architecture is often included as one of the visual arts; however, like the decorative arts, it involves the creation of objects where the practical considerations of use are essential—in a way that they are usually not for a painting, for example.

Music, theatre, film, dance, and other performing arts, as well as literature, and other media such as interactive media are included in a broader definition of art or the arts.

Until the 17th century, *art* referred to any skill or mastery and was not differentiated from crafts or sciences, but in modern usage the fine arts, where aesthetic considerations are paramount, are distinguished from acquired skills in general, and the decorative or applied arts.

Art has been characterized in terms of mimesis, expression, communication of emotion, or other values. During the Romantic period, art came to be seen as "a special faculty of the human mind to be classified with religion and science". Though the definition of what constitutes art is disputed and has changed over time, general descriptions mention an idea of human agency and creation through imaginative or technical skill.

The nature of art, and related concepts such as creativity and interpretation, are explored in a branch of philosophy known as aesthetics.

Creative Art and Fine Art

By a broad definition of art, artistic works have existed for almost as long as humankind: from early pre-historic art to contemporary art; however, some theories restrict the concept to modern Western societies. The first and broadest sense of *art* is the one that has remained closest to the older Latin meaning, which roughly translates to "skill" or "craft." A few examples where this meaning proves very broad include *artifact*, *artificial*, *artifice*, *medical arts*, and *military arts*. However, there are many other colloquial uses of the word, all with some relation to its etymology.

In medieval philosophy, John Chrysostom held that "the name of art should be applied to those only which contribute towards and produce necessaries and mainstays of life." Thomas Aquinas, when treating the adornment of women, gives an ethical justification as to why: "In the case of an art directed to the production of goods which men cannot use without sin, it follows that the workmen sin in making such things, as directly affording others an occasion of sin; for instance, if a man were to make idols or anything pertaining to idolatrous worship. But in the case of an art the products of which may be employed by man either for a good or for an evil use, such as swords, arrows, and the like, the practice of such an art is not sinful. These alone should be called arts." Aquinas held that art is nothing else than "the right reason about certain works to be made," and that it is commendable, not for the will with which a craftman does a work, "but for the quality of the work. Art, therefore, properly speaking, is an operative habit." Aristotle and Aquinas distinguish it from the related habit of prudence.

The second and more recent sense of the word *art* is as an abbreviation for *creative art* or *fine art* and emerged in the early 17th century. Fine art means that a skill is being used to express the artist's creativity, or to engage the audience's aesthetic sensibilities, or to draw the audience towards consideration of the *finer* things.

The word *art* can refer to several things: a study of creative skill, a process of using the creative skill, a product of the creative skill, or the audience's experience with the creative skill. The creative arts (*art* as discipline) are a collection of disciplines that produce *artworks* (*art* as objects) that are compelled by a personal drive (art as activity) and convey a message, mood, or symbolism for the viewer to interpret (art as experience). Art is something that stimulates an individual's thoughts, emotions, beliefs, or ideas through the senses. Artworks can be explicitly made for this purpose or interpreted on the basis of images or objects. Although the application of scientific knowledge to derive a new scientific theory involves skill and results in the "creation" of something new, this represents science only and is not categorized as art.

Often, if the skill is being used in a common or practical way, people will consider it a craft instead of art. Likewise, if the skill is being used in a commercial or industrial way, it may be considered commercial art instead of fine art. On the other hand, crafts and design are sometimes considered applied art. Some art followers have argued that the difference between fine art and applied art has more to do with value judgements made about the art than any clear definitional difference. However, even fine art often has goals beyond pure creativity and self-expression. The purpose of works of art may be to communicate ideas, such as in politically, spiritually, or philosophically motivated art; to create a sense of beauty; to explore the nature of perception; for pleasure; or to generate strong emotions. The purpose may also be seemingly nonexistent.

The nature of art has been described by philosopher Richard Wollheim as "one of the most elusive of the traditional problems of human culture". Art has been defined as a vehicle for the expression or communication of emotions and ideas, a means for exploring and appreciating formal elements for their own sake, and as *mimesis* or representation. Art as mimesis has deep roots in the philosophy of Aristotle. Goethe defined art as an *other* resp. a *second nature*, according to his ideal of a style founded on the basic fundaments of insight and on the innermost character of things. Leo Tolstoy identified art as a use of indirect means to communicate from one person to another. Benedetto Croce and R.G. Collingwood advanced the idealist view that art expresses emotions, and that the work of art therefore essentially exists in the mind of the creator.

The theory of art as form has its roots in the philosophy of Immanuel Kant, and was developed in the early twentieth century by Roger Fry and Clive Bell. More recently, thinkers influenced by Martin Heidegger have interpreted art as the means by which a community develops for itself a medium for self-expression and interpretation. George Dickie has offered an institutional theory of art that defines a work of art as any artifact upon which a qualified person or persons acting on behalf of the social institution commonly referred to as "the art world" has conferred "the status of candidate for appreciation". Larry Shiner has described fine art as "not an essence or a fate but something we have made. Art as we have generally understood it is a European invention barely two hundred years old."

History

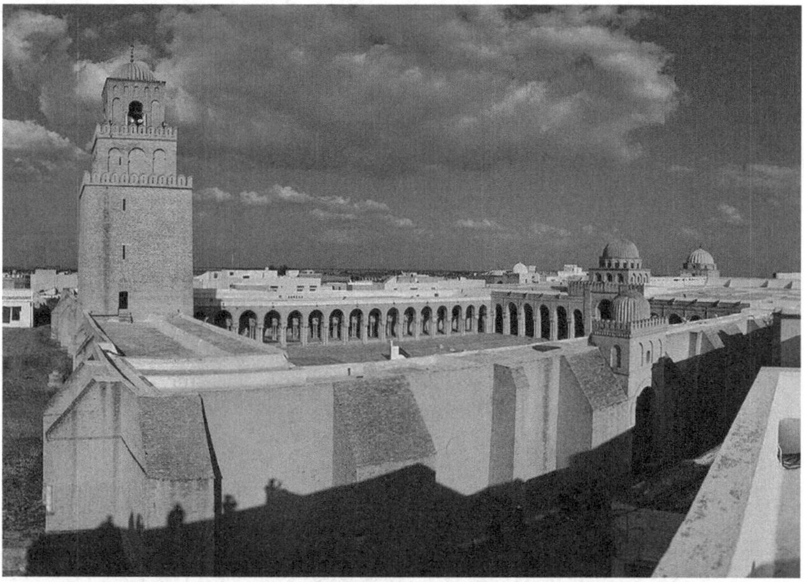

Figure: *The Great Mosque of Kairouan (also called the Mosque of Uqba) is one of the finest, most significant and best preserved artistic and architectural examples of early great mosques; dated in its present state from the 9th century, it is the ancestor and model of all the mosques in the western Islamic lands. The Great Mosque of Kairouan is located in the city of Kairouan in Tunisia.*

In the east, Islamic art's rejection of iconography led to emphasis on geometric patterns, calligraphy, and architecture. Further east, religion dominated artistic styles and forms too. India and Tibet saw emphasis on painted sculptures and dance, while religious painting borrowed many conventions from sculpture and tended to bright contrasting colours with emphasis on outlines. China saw the flourishing of many art forms: jade carving, bronzework, pottery (including the stunning terracotta army of Emperor Qin), poetry, calligraphy, music, painting, drama, fiction, etc. Chinese styles vary greatly from era to era and each one is traditionally named after the ruling dynasty. So, for example, Tang Dynasty paintings are monochromatic and sparse, emphasizing idealized landscapes, but Ming Dynasty paintings are busy and colorful, and focus on telling stories via setting and composition. Japan names its styles after imperial dynasties too, and also saw much interplay between the styles of calligraphy and painting. Woodblock printing became important in Japan after the 17th century.

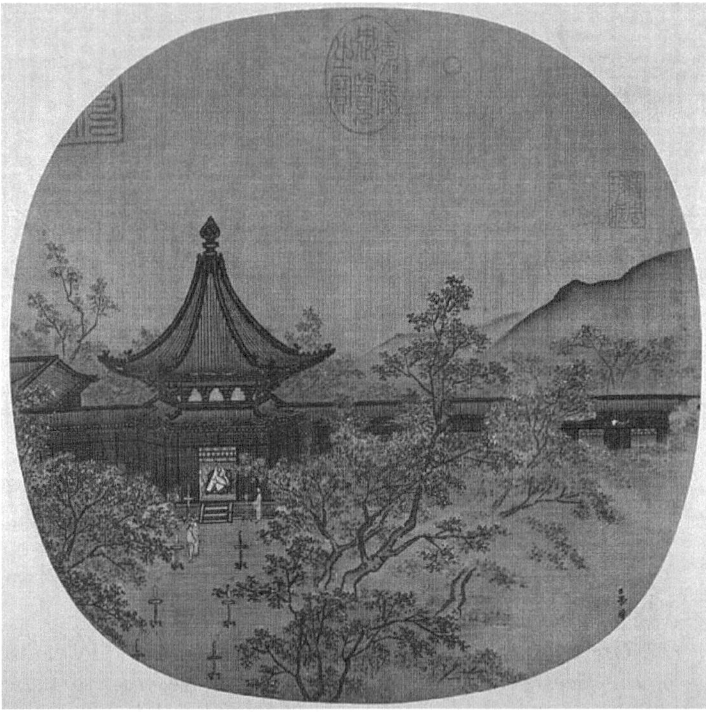

Figure: *Painting by Song Dynasty artist Ma Lin,* circa *1250. 24,8 × 25,2 cm*

The western Age of Enlightenment in the 18th century saw artistic depictions of physical and rational certainties of the clockwork universe, as well as politically revolutionary visions of a post-monarchist world, such as Blake's portrayal of Newton as a divine geometre, or David's propagandistic paintings. This led to Romantic rejections of this in favour of pictures of the emotional side and individuality of humans, exemplified in the novels of Goethe. The late 19th century then saw a host of artistic movements, such as academic art, Symbolism, impressionism and fauvism among others.

The history of twentieth-century art is a narrative of endless possibilities and the search for new standards, each being torn down in succession by the next. Thus the parametres of Impressionism, Expressionism, Fauvism, Cubism, Dadaism, Surrealism, etc. cannot be maintained very much beyond the time of their invention. Increasing global interaction during this time saw an equivalent influence of other cultures into Western art, such as Pablo Picasso being influenced by African sculpture. Japanese woodblock prints (which had themselves been influenced by Western Renaissance draftsmanship) had an immense influence on Impressionism and subsequent development. Later, African sculptures were taken up by Picasso and to some extent by Matisse. Similarly, the west has had huge impacts on Eastern art in the 19th and 20th centuries, with originally western ideas like Communism and Post-Modernism exerting a powerful influence on artistic styles.

Modernism, the idealistic search for truth, gave way in the latter half of the 20th century to a realization of its unattainability. Theodor W. Adorno said in 1970, "It is now taken for granted that nothing which concerns art can be taken for granted any more: neither art itself, nor art in relationship to the whole, nor even the right of art to exist." Relativism was accepted as an unavoidable truth, which led to the period of contemporary art and postmodern criticism, where cultures of the world and of history are seen as changing forms, which can be appreciated and drawn from only with irony. Furthermore the separation of cultures is increasingly blurred and some argue it is now more appropriate to think in terms of a global culture, rather than regional cultures.

Forms, Genres, Media, and Styles

The creative arts are often divided into more specific categories, each related to its technique, or medium, such as decorative arts, plastic arts, performing arts, or literature. Unlike scientific fields, art is one of the few subjects that are academically organized according to technique. An artistic medium is the substance or material the artistic work is made from, and may also refer to the technique used. For example, paint is a medium used in painting, and paper is a medium used in drawing.

An *art form* is the specific *shape*, or quality an artistic expression takes. The media used often influence the form. For example, the form of a sculpture must exist in space in three dimensions, and respond to gravity. The constraints and limitations of a particular medium are thus called its *formal qualities*. To give another example, the formal qualities of painting are the canvas texture, colour, and brush texture. The formal qualities of video games are non-linearity, interactivity and virtual presence. The *form* of a particular work of art is determined by the formal qualities of the media, and is not related to the intentions of the artist or the reactions of the audience in any way whatsoever as these properties are related to content rather than form. A *genre* is a set of conventions and styles within a particular medium.

For instance, well recognized genres in film are western, horror and romantic comedy. Genres in music include death metal and trip hop. Genres in painting include still life and pastoral landscape. A particular work of art may bend or combine genres but each genre has a recognizable group of conventions, clichés and tropes. (One note: the word *genre* has a second older meaning within painting; *genre painting* was a phrase used in the 17th to 19th centuries to refer specifically to paintings of scenes of everyday life and is still used in this way.)

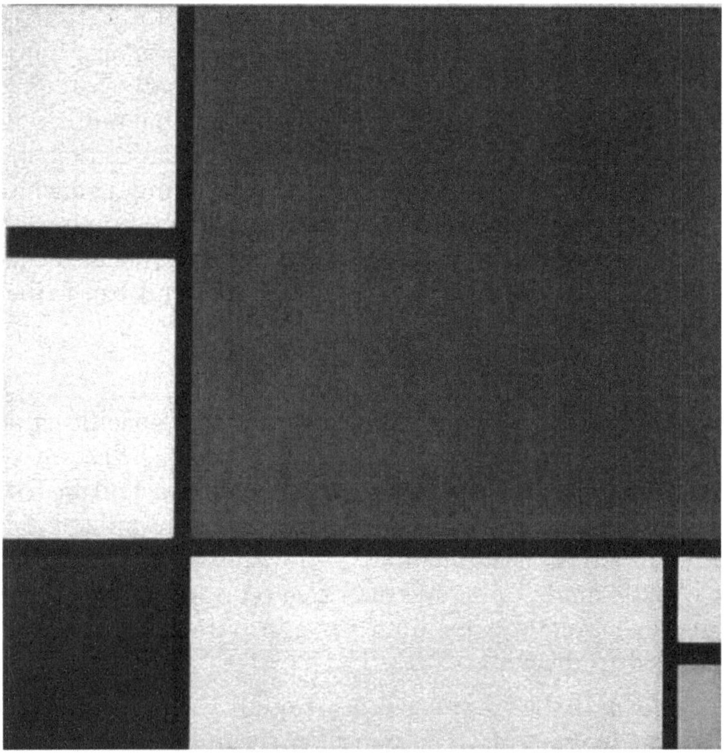

Figure: Composition II in Red, Blue, and Yellow *(1930) by Piet Mondrian (Dutch, 1872-1944).*

The *style* of an artwork, artist, or movement is the distinctive method and form followed by the respective art. Any loose brushy, dripped or poured abstract painting is called *expressionistic*. Often a style is linked with a particular historical period, set of ideas, and particular artistic movement. So Jackson Pollock is called an Abstract Expressionist.

A particular style may have specific cultural meanings. For example, Roy Lichtenstein—a painter associated with the American Pop art movement of the 1960s—was not a pointillist, despite his use of dots. Lichtenstein used evenly spaced Ben-Day dots (the type used to reproduce colour in comic strips) as a style to question the "high" art of painting with the "low" art of comics, thus commenting on class distinctions in culture. Pointillism, a technique in late Impressionism (1880s) developed especially by the artist Georges Seurat, employs dots to create variation in colour and depth in an attempt to approximate the way people really see colour. Both artists use dots, but the particular style and technique relate to the artistic movement adopted by each artist.

These are all ways of beginning to define a work of art, to narrow it down. "Imagine you are an art critic whose mission is to compare the meanings you find in a wide range of individual artworks. How would you proceed with your task? One way to begin is to examine the materials each artist selected in making an object, image video, or event. The decision to cast a sculpture in bronze, for instance, inevitably effects its meaning; the work becomes something different from how it might be if it had been cast in gold or plastic or chocolate, even if everything else about the artwork remains the same. Next, you might examine how the materials in each artwork have become an arrangement of shapes, colours, textures, and lines. These, in turn, are organized into various patterns and compositional structures. In your interpretation, you would comment on how salient features of the form contribute to the overall meaning of the finished artwork. [But in the end] the meaning of most artworks... is not exhausted by a discussion of materials, techniques, and form. Most interpretations also include a discussion of the ideas and feelings the artwork engenders."

Skill and Craft

Art can connote a sense of trained ability or mastery of a medium. Art can also simply refer to the developed and efficient use of a language to convey meaning with immediacy and or depth. Art is an act of expressing feelings, thoughts, and observations. There is an understanding that is reached with the material as a result of handling it, which facilitates one's thought processes. A common view is that the epithet "art", particular in its elevated sense, requires a certain level of creative expertise by the artist, whether this be a demonstration of technical ability, an originality in stylistic approach, or a combination of these two. Traditionally skill of execution was viewed as a quality inseparable from art and thus necessary for its success; for Leonardo da Vinci, art, neither more nor less than his other endeavours, was a manifestation of skill. Rembrandt's work, now praised for its ephemeral virtues, was most admired by his contemporaries for its virtuosity. At the turn of the 20th century, the adroit performances of John Singer Sargent were alternately admired and viewed with skepticism for their manual fluency, yet at nearly the same time the artist who would become the era's most recognized and peripatetic iconoclast, Pablo Picasso, was completing a traditional academic training at which he excelled.

A common contemporary criticism of some modern art occurs along the lines of objecting to the apparent lack of skill or ability required in the production of the artistic object. In conceptual art, Marcel Duchamp's "Fountain" is among the first examples of pieces wherein the artist used found objects ("ready-made") and exercised no traditionally recognised set of skills.

Tracey Emin's *My Bed*, or Damien Hirst's *The Physical Impossibility of Death in the Mind of Someone Living* follow this example and also manipulate the mass media. Emin slept (and engaged in other activities) in her bed before placing the result in a gallery as work of art. Hirst came up with the conceptual design for the artwork but has left most of the eventual creation of many works to employed artisans. Hirst's celebrity is founded entirely on his ability to produce shocking concepts. The actual production in many conceptual and contemporary works of art is a matter of assembly of found objects. However there are many modernist and contemporary artists who continue to excel in the skills of drawing and painting and in creating *hands-on* works of art.

Value Judgement

Somewhat in relation to the above, the word *art* is also used to apply judgements of value, as in such expressions as "that meal was a work of art" (the cook is an artist), or "the art of deception", (the highly attained level of skill of the deceiver is praised). It is this use of the word as a measure of high quality and high value that gives the term its flavour of subjectivity.

Making judgements of value requires a basis for criticism. At the simplest level, a way to determine whether the impact of the object on the senses meets the criteria to be considered *art* is whether it is perceived to be attractive or repulsive.

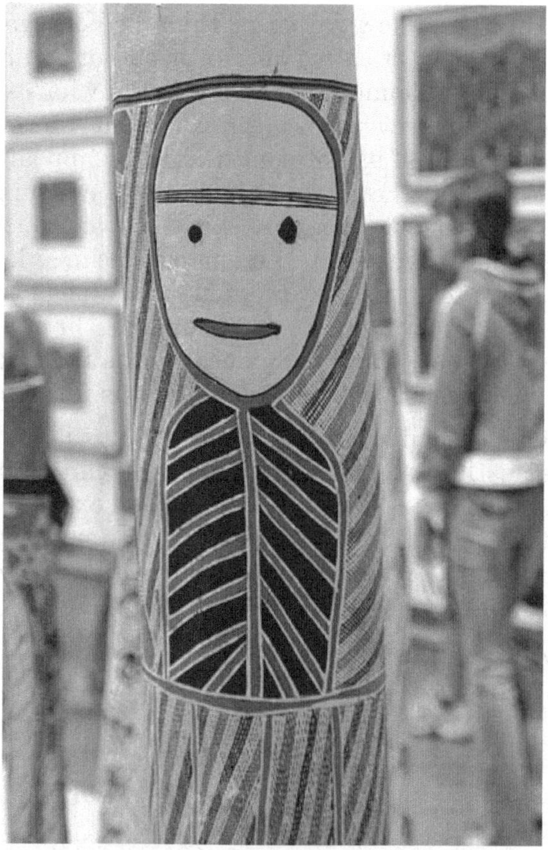

Figure: *Aboriginal hollow log tombs. National Gallery, Canberra, Australia*

Though perception is always coloured by experience, and is necessarily subjective, it is commonly understood that what is not somehow aesthetically satisfying cannot be art. However, "good" art is not always or even regularly aesthetically appealing to a majority of viewers. In other words, an artist's prime motivation need not be the pursuit of the aesthetic.

Also, art often depicts terrible images made for social, moral, or thought-provoking reasons. For example, Francisco Goya's painting depicting the Spanish shootings of 3rd of May 1808 is a graphic depiction of a firing squad executing several pleading civilians. Yet at the same time, the horrific imagery demonstrates Goya's keen artistic ability in composition and execution and produces fitting social and political outrage. Thus, the debate continues as to what mode of aesthetic satisfaction, if any, is required to define 'art'.

The assumption of new values or the rebellion against accepted notions of what is aesthetically superior need not occur concurrently with a complete abandonment of the pursuit of what is aesthetically appealing. Indeed, the reverse is often true, that the revision of what is popularly conceived of as being aesthetically appealing allows for a re-invigoration of aesthetic sensibility, and a new appreciation for the standards of art itself. Countless schools have proposed their own ways to define quality, yet they all seem to agree in at least one point: once their aesthetic choices are accepted, the value of the work of art is determined by its capacity to transcend the limits of its chosen medium to strike some universal chord by the rarity of the skill of the artist or in its accurate reflection in what is termed the *zeitgeist*.

Art is often intended to appeal to and connect with human emotion. It can arouse aesthetic or moral feelings, and can be understood as a way of communicating these feelings. Artists express something so that their audience is aroused to some extent, but they do not have to do so consciously. Art may be considered an exploration of the human condition; that is, what it is to be human.

Purpose of Art

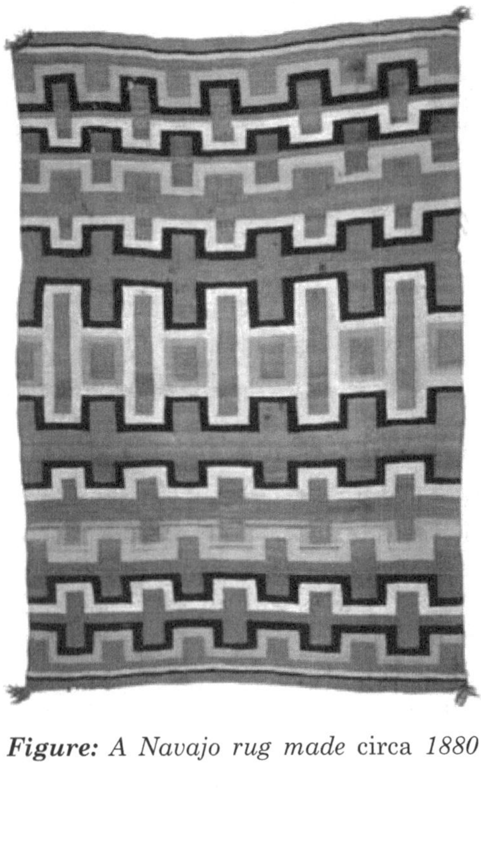

Figure: *A Navajo rug made* circa *1880*

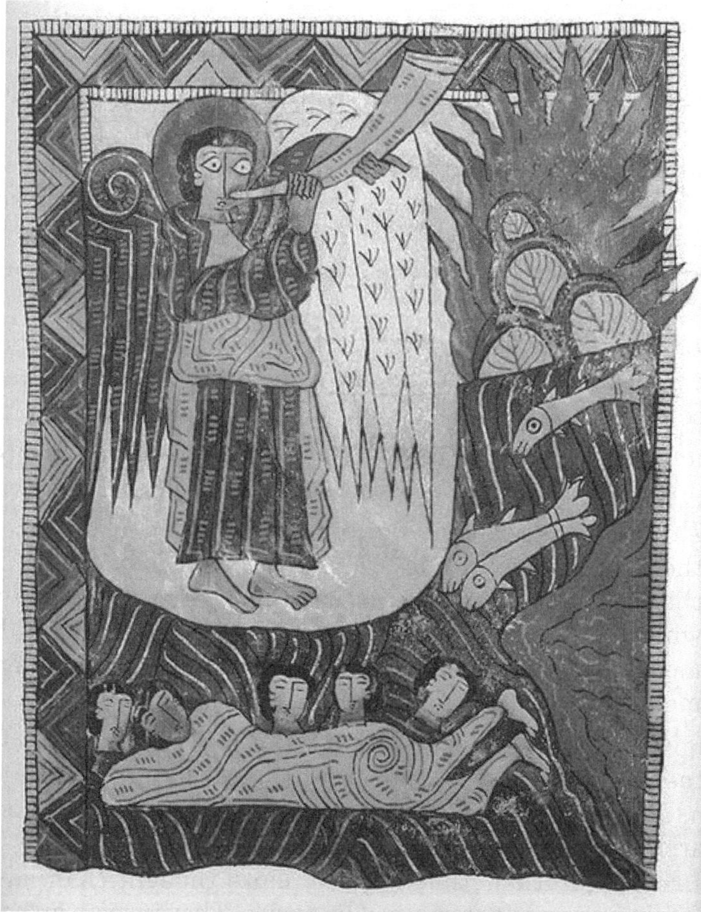

***Figure:** Mozarabic Beatus miniature. Spain, late 10th century*

Art has had a great number of different functions throughout its history, making its purpose difficult to abstract or quantify to any single concept. This does not imply that the purpose of Art is "vague", but that it has had many unique, different reasons for being created. Some of these functions of Art are provided in the following outline. The different purposes of art may be grouped according to those that are non-motivated, and those that are motivated (Lévi-Strauss).

Non-motivated Functions of Art

The non-motivated purposes of art are those that are integral to being human, transcend the individual, or do not fulfill a specific external purpose. In this sense, Art, as creativity, is something humans must do by their very nature (i.e., no other species creates art), and is therefore beyond utility.

1. *Basic human instinct for harmony, balance, rhythm.* Art at this level is not an action or an object, but an internal appreciation of balance and harmony (beauty), and therefore an aspect of being human beyond utility.

"Imitation, then, is one instinct of our nature. Next, there is the instinct for 'harmony' and rhythm, metres being manifestly sections of rhythm. Persons, therefore, starting with this natural gift developed by degrees their special aptitudes, till their rude improvisations gave birth to Poetry." -Aristotle

2. *Experience of the mysterious.* Art provides a way to experience one's self in relation to the universe. This experience may often come unmotivated, as one appreciates art, music or poetry.

"The most beautiful thing we can experience is the mysterious. It is the source of all true art and science." -Albert Einstein

3. *Expression of the imagination.* Art provide a means to express the imagination in non-grammatic ways that are not tied to the formality of spoken or written language. Unlike words, which come in sequences and each of which have a definite meaning, art provides a range of forms, symbols and ideas with meanings that are malleable.

"Jupiter's eagle [as an example of art] is not, like logical (aesthetic) attributes of an object, the concept of the sublimity and majesty of creation, but rather something else – something that gives the imagination an incentive to spread its flight over a whole host of kindred representations that provoke more thought than admits of expression in a concept determined by words. They furnish an aesthetic idea, which serves the above rational idea as a substitute for logical presentation, but with the proper function, however, of animating the mind by opening out for it a prospect into a field of kindred representations stretching beyond its ken." -Immanuel Kant

4. *Ritualistic and symbolic functions.* In many cultures, art is used in rituals, performances and dances as a decoration or symbol. While these often have no specific utilitarian (motivated) purpose, anthropologists know that they often serve a purpose at the level of meaning within a particular culture. This meaning is not furnished by any one individual, but is often the result of many generations of change, and of a cosmological relationship within the culture.

"Most scholars who deal with rock paintings or objects recovered from prehistoric contexts that cannot be explained in utilitarian terms and are thus categorized as decorative, ritual or symbolic, are aware of the trap posed by the term 'art'." -Silva Tomaskova

Motivated Functions of Art

Motivated purposes of art refer to intentional, conscious actions on the part of the artists or creator. These may be to bring about political change, to comment on an aspect of society, to convey a specific emotion or mood, to address personal psychology, to illustrate another discipline, to (with commercial arts) to sell a product, or simply as a form of communication.

1. *Communication.* Art, at its simplest, is a form of communication. As most forms of communication have an intent or goal directed towards another individual, this is a motivated purpose. Illustrative arts, such as scientific illustration, are a form of art as communication. Maps are another example. However, the content need not be scientific. Emotions, moods and feelings are also communicated through art.

"[Art is a set of] artefacts or images with symbolic meanings as a means of communication." -Steve Mithen

2. *Art as entertainment.* Art may seek to bring about a particular emotion or mood, for the purpose of relaxing or entertaining the viewer. This is often the function of the art industries of Motion Pictures and Video Games.
3. *The Avante-Garde. Art for political change.* One of the defining functions of early twentieth-century art has been to use visual images to bring about political change. Art movements that had this goal—Dadaism, Surrealism, Russian Constructivism, and Abstract Expressionism, among others—are collectively referred to as the *avante-garde* arts.

"By contrast, the realistic attitude, inspired by positivism, from Saint Thomas Aquinas to Anatole France, clearly seems to me to be hostile to any intellectual or moral advancement. I loathe it, for it is made up of mediocrity, hate, and dull conceit. It is this attitude which today gives birth to these ridiculous books, these insulting plays. It constantly feeds on and derives strength from the newspapers and stultifies both science and art by assiduously flattering the lowest of tastes; clarity bordering on stupidity, a dog's life." -André Breton (Surrealism)

4. *Art as a "free zone"*, removed from the action of the social censure. Unlike the avant-garde movements, which wanted to

erase cultural differences in order to produce new universal values, contemporary art has enhanced its tolerance towards cultural differences as well as its critical and liberating functions (social enquiry, activism, subversion, deconstruction...), becoming a more open place for research and experimentation.

5. *Art for social enquiry, subversion and/or anarchy.* While similar to art for political change, subversive or deconstructivist art may seek to question aspects of society without any specific political goal. In this case, the function of art may be simply to criticize some aspect of society.

Graffiti art and other types of street art are graphics and images that are spray-painted or stencilled on publicly viewable walls, buildings, buses, trains, and bridges, usually without permission. Certain art forms, such as graffiti, may also be illegal when they break laws (in this case vandalism).

6. *Art for social causes.* Art can be used to raise awareness for a large variety of causes. A number of art activities were aimed at raising awareness of autism, cancer, human trafficking, and a variety of other topics, such as ocean conservation, human rights in Darfur, murdered and missing Aboriginal women, elder abuse, and pollution. Trashion, using trash to make fashion, practised by artists such as Marina DeBris is one example of using art to raise awareness about pollution.
7. *Art for psychological and healing purposes.* Art is also used by art therapists, psychotherapists and clinical psychologists as art therapy. The Diagnostic Drawing Series, for example, is used to determine the personality and emotional functioning of a patient. The end product is not the principal goal in this case, but rather a process of healing, through creative acts, is sought. The resultant piece of artwork may also offer insight into the troubles experienced by the subject and may suggest suitable approaches to be used in more conventional forms of psychiatric therapy.
8. *Art for propaganda, or commercialism.* Art is often utilized as a form of propaganda, and thus can be used to subtly influence popular conceptions or mood. In a similar way, art that tries to sell a product also influences mood and emotion. In both cases, the purpose of art here is to subtly manipulate the viewer into a particular emotional or psychological response towards a particular idea or object.

9. *Art as a fitness indicator.* It has been argued that the ability of the human brain by far exceeds what was needed for survival in the ancestral environment. One evolutionary psychology explanation for this is that the human brain and associated traits (such as artistic ability and creativity) are the human equivalent of the peacock's tail. The purpose of the male peacock's extravagant tail has been argued to be to attract females. According to this theory superior execution of art was evolutionary important because it attracted mates.

The functions of art described above are not mutually exclusive, as many of them may overlap. For example, art for the purpose of entertainment may also seek to sell a product, i.e. the movie or video game.

Public Access

Since ancient times, much of the finest art has represented a deliberate display of wealth or power, often achieved by using massive scale and expensive materials. Much art has been commissioned by rulers or religious establishments, with more modest versions only available to the most wealthy in society. Nevertheless, there have been many periods where art of very high quality was available, in terms of ownership, across large parts of society, above all in cheap media such as pottery, which persists in the ground, and perishable media such as textiles and wood.

In many different cultures, the ceramics of indigenous peoples of the Americas are found in such a wide range of graves that they were clearly not restricted to a social elite, though other forms of art may have been. Reproductive methods such as moulds made mass-production easier, and were used to bring high-quality Ancient Roman pottery and Greek Tanagra figurines to a very wide market. Cylinder seals were both artistic and practical, and very widely used by what can be loosely called the middle class in the Ancient Near East. Once coins were widely used these also became an art form that reached the widest range of society. Another important innovation came in the 15th century in Europe, when printmaking began with small woodcuts, mostly religious, that were often very small and hand-coloured, and affordable even by peasants who glued them to the walls of their homes. Printed books were initially very expensive, but fell steadily in price until by the 19th century even the poorest could afford some with printed illustrations. Popular prints of many different sorts have decorated homes and other places for centuries.

Public buildings and monuments, secular and religious, by their nature normally address the whole of society, and visitors as viewers, and display to the general public has long been an important factor in their design. Egyptian temples are typical in that the most largest and most lavish decoration was placed on the parts that could be seen by the general public, rather than the areas seen only by the priests. Many areas of royal palaces, castles and the houses of the social elite were often generally accessible, and large parts of the art collections of such people could often be seen, either by anybody, or by those able to pay a small price, or those wearing the correct clothes, regardless of who they were, as at the Palace of Versailles, where the appropriate extra accessories (silver shoe buckles and a sword) could be hired from shops outside.

Special arrangements were made to allow the public to see many royal or private collections placed in galleries, as with the Orleans Collection mostly housed in a wing of the Palais Royal in Paris, which could be visited for most of the 18th century. In Italy the art tourism of the Grand Tour became a major industry from the Renaissance onwards, and governments and cities made efforts to make their key works accessible. The British Royal Collection remains distinct, but large donations such as the Old Royal Library were made from it to the British Museum, established in 1753.

The Uffizi in Florence opened entirely as a gallery in 1765, though this function had been gradually taking the building over from the original civil servants' offices for a long time before. The building now occupied by the Prado in Madrid was built before the French Revolution for the public display of parts of the royal art collection, and similar royal galleries open to the public existed in Vienna, Munich and other capitals. The opening of the Musée du Louvre during the French Revolution (in 1793) as a public museum for much of the former French royal collection certainly marked an important stage in the development of public access to art, transferring ownership to a republican state, but was a continuation of trends already well established.

Most modern public museums and art education programmes for children in schools can be traced back to this impulse to have art available to everyone. Museums in the United States tend to be gifts from the very rich to the masses (The Metropolitan Museum of Art in New York City, for example, was created by John Taylor Johnston, a railroad executive whose personal art collection seeded the museum.) But despite all this, at least one of the important functions of art in the 21st century remains as a marker of wealth and social status. There have been attempts by artists to create art that can not be bought by the wealthy as a status object.

One of the prime original motivators of much of the art of the late 1960s and 1970s was to create art that could not be bought and sold. It is "necessary to present something more than mere objects" said the major post war German artist Joseph Beuys. This time period saw the rise of such things as performance art, video art, and conceptual art. The idea was that if the artwork was a performance that would leave nothing behind, or was simply an idea, it could not be bought and sold. "Democratic precepts revolving around the idea that a work of art is a commodity impelled the aesthetic innovation which germinated in the mid-1960s and was reaped throughout the 1970s. Artists broadly identified under the heading of Conceptual art... substituting performance and publishing activities for engagement with both the material and materialistic concerns of painted or sculptural form... [have] endeavoured to undermine the art object qua object."

In the decades since, these ideas have been somewhat lost as the art market has learned to sell limited edition DVDs of video works, invitations to exclusive performance art pieces, and the objects left over from conceptual pieces. Many of these performances create works that are only understood by the elite who have been educated as to why an idea or video or piece of apparent garbage may be considered art. The marker of status becomes understanding the work instead of necessarily owning it, and the artwork remains an upper-class activity. "With the widespread use of DVD recording technology in the early 2000s, artists, and the gallery system that derives its profits from the sale of artworks, gained an important means of controlling the sale of video and computer artworks in limited editions to collectors."

Controversies

Art has long been controversial, that is to say disliked by some viewers, for a wide variety of reasons, though most pre-modern controversies are dimly recorded, or completely lost to a modern view. Iconoclasm is the destruction of art that is disliked for a variety of reasons, including religious ones. Aniconism is a general dislike of either all figurative images, or often just religious ones, and has been a thread in many major religions. It has been a crucial factor in the history of Islamic art, where depictions of Muhammad remain especially controversial.

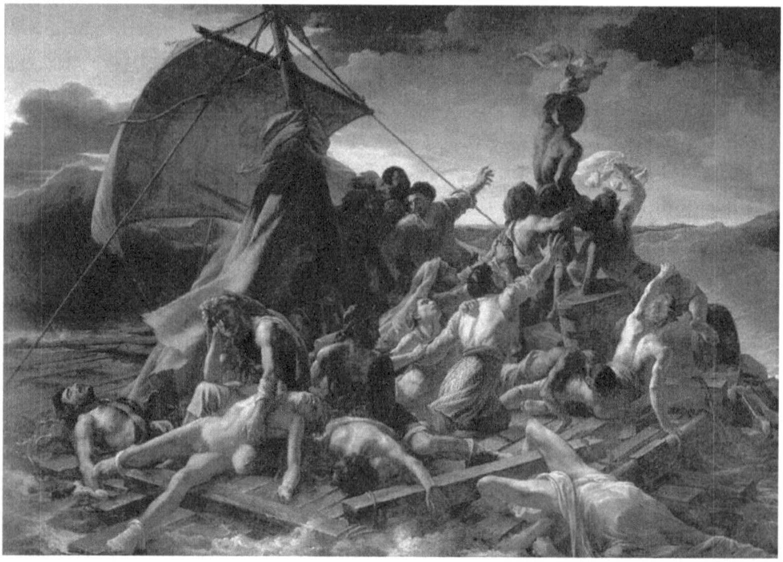

Figure: *Théodore Géricault's* Raft of the Medusa, circa *1820*

Much art has been disliked purely because it depicted or otherwise stood for unpopular rulers, parties or other groups. Artistic conventions have often been conservative and taken very seriously by art critics, though often much less so by a wider public. The iconographic content of art could cause controversy, as with late medieval depictions of the new motif of the Swoon of the Virgin in scenes of the Crucifixion of Jesus. The *Last Judgement* by Michelangelo was controversial for various reasons, including breaches of decorum through nudity and the Apollo-like pose of Christ.

The content of much formal art through history was dictated by the patron or commissioner rather than just the artist, but with the advent of Romanticism, and econonomic changes in the production of art, the artists' vision became the usual determinant of the content of his art, increasing the incidence of controversies, though often reducing their significance.

Strong incentives for perceived originality and publicity also encouraged artists to court controversy. Théodore Géricault's *Raft of the Medusa* (c. 1820), was in part a political commentary on a recent event. Édouard Manet's *Le Déjeuner sur l'Herbe* (1863), was considered scandalous not because of the nude woman, but because she is seated next to men fully dressed in the clothing of the time, rather than in robes of the antique world. John Singer Sargent's *Madame Pierre Gautreau (Madam X)* (1884), caused a controversy over the reddish pink used to colour the woman's ear lobe, considered far too suggestive and supposedly ruining the high-society model's reputation.

The gradual abandonment of naturalism and the depiction of realistic representations of the visual appearance of subjects in the 19th and 20th centuries led to a rolling controversy lasting for over a century. In the twentieth century, Pablo Picasso's *Guernica* (1937) used arresting cubist techniques and stark monochromatic oils, to depict the harrowing consequences of a contemporary bombing of a small, ancient Basque town. Leon Golub's *Interrogation III* (1981), depicts a female nude, hooded detainee strapped to a chair, her legs open to reveal her sexual organs, surrounded by two tormentors dressed in everyday clothing. Andres Serrano's *Piss Christ* (1989) is a photograph of a crucifix, sacred to the Christian religion and representing Christ's sacrifice and final suffering, submerged in a glass of the artist's own urine. The resulting uproar led to comments in the United States Senate about public funding of the arts.

Theory

In the nineteenth century, artists were primarily concerned with ideas of *truth* and *beauty*. The aesthetic theorist John Ruskin, who championed what he saw as the naturalism of J. M. W. Turner, saw art's role as the communication by artifice of an essential truth that could only be found in nature.

The definition and evaluation of art has become especially problematic since the 20th century. Richard Wollheim distinguishes three approaches to assessing the aesthetic value of art: the Realist, whereby aesthetic quality is an absolute value independent of any human view; the Objectivist, whereby it is also an absolute value, but is dependent on general human experience; and the Relativist position, whereby it is not an absolute value, but depends on, and varies with, the human experience of different humans.

The arrival of Modernism in the late nineteenth century lead to a radical break in the conception of the function of art, and then again in the late twentieth century with the advent of postmodernism. Clement Greenberg's 1960 article "Modernist Painting" defines modern art as "the use of characteristic methods of a discipline to criticize the discipline itself". Greenberg originally applied this idea to the Abstract Expressionist movement and used it as a way to understand and justify flat (non-illusionistic) abstract painting:

Realistic, naturalistic art had dissembled the medium, using art to conceal art; modernism used art to call attention to art. The limitations that constitute the medium of painting—the flat surface, the shape of the support, the properties of the pigment—were treated by the Old Masters as negative factors that could be acknowledged only implicitly or indirectly. Under Modernism these same limitations came to be regarded as positive factors, and were acknowledged openly.

After Greenberg, several important art theorists emerged, such as Michael Fried, T. J. Clark, Rosalind Krauss, Linda Nochlin and Griselda Pollock among others. Though only originally intended as a way of understanding a specific set of artists, Greenberg's definition of modern art is important to many of the ideas of art within the various art movements of the 20th century and early 21st century. Pop artists like Andy Warhol became both noteworthy and influential through work including and possibly critiquing popular culture, as well as the art world. Artists of the 1980s, 1990s, and 2000s expanded this technique of self-criticism beyond *high art* to all cultural image-making, including fashion images, comics, billboards and pornography.

Duchamp once proposed that art is any activity of any kind-everything. However, the way that only certain activities are classified today as art is a social construction. There is evidence that there may be an element of truth to this.

The Invention of Art: A Cultural History is an art history book which examines the construction of the modern system of the arts i.e. Fine Art. Shiner finds evidence that the older system of the arts before our modern system (fine art) held art to be any skilled human activity i.e. Ancient Greek society did not possess the term art but techne. Techne can be understood neither as art or craft, the reason being that the distinctions of art and craft are historical products that came later on in human history. Techne included painting, sculpting and music but also; cooking, medicine, horsemanship, geometry, carpentry, prophecy and farming etc.

Classification Disputes

Disputes as to whether or not to classify something as a work of art are referred to as classificatory disputes about art.

Classificatory disputes in the 20th century have included cubist and impressionist paintings, Duchamp's *Fountain*, the movies, superlative imitations of banknotes, conceptual art, and video games.

Philosopher David Novitz has argued that disagreement about the definition of art are rarely the heart of the problem. Rather, "the passionate concerns and interests that humans vest in their social life" are "so much a part of all classificatory disputes about art" (Novitz, 1996).

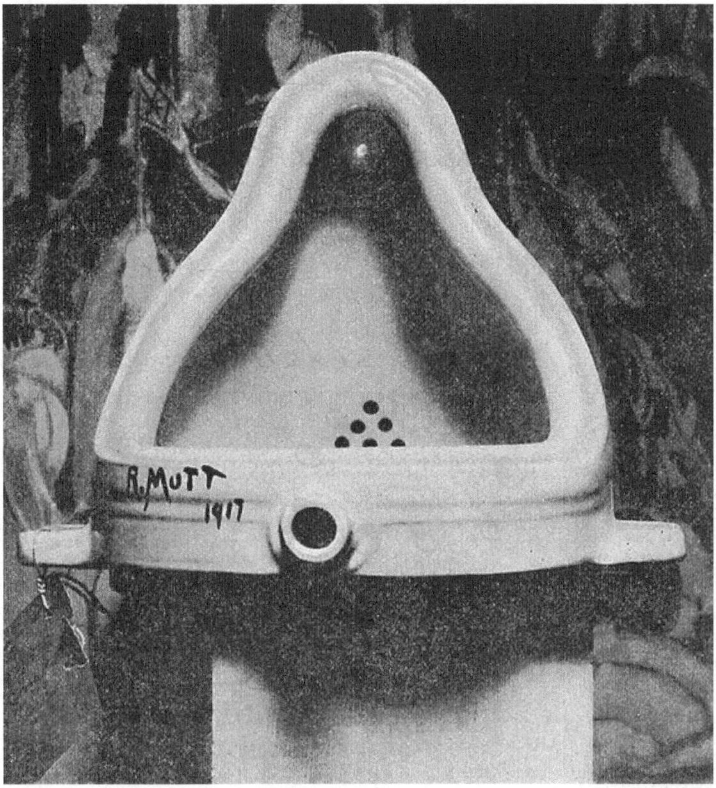

Figure: *The original* Fountain *by Marcel Duchamp, 1917, photographed by Alfred Stieglitz at the 291 after the 1917 Society of Independent Artists exhibit. Stieglitz used a backdrop of* The Warriors *by Marsden Hartley to photograph the urinal. The exhibition entry tag can be clearly seen.*

According to Novitz, classificatory disputes are more often disputes about societal values and where society is trying to go than they are about theory proper. For example, when the Daily Mail criticized Hirst's and Emin's work by arguing "For 1,000 years art has been one of our great civilising forces. Today, pickled sheep and soiled beds threaten to make barbarians of us all" they are not advancing a definition or theory about art, but questioning the value of Hirst's and Emin's work. In 1998, Arthur Danto, suggested a thought experiment showing that "the status of an artifact as work of art results from the ideas a culture applies to it, rather than its inherent physical or perceptible qualities. Cultural interpretation (an art theory of some kind) is therefore constitutive of an object's arthood."

Anti-art is a label for art that intentionally challenges the established parametres and values of art; it is term associated with Dadaism and attributed to Marcel Duchamp just before World War I, when he was making art from found objects. One of these, *Fountain* (1917), an ordinary urinal, has achieved considerable prominence and influence on art. Anti-art is a feature of work by Situationist International, the lo-fi Mail art movement, and the Young British Artists, though it is a form still rejected by the Stuckists, who describe themselves as anti-anti-art.

Computer-aided Design

Computer-aided design (CAD) is the use of computer systems to assist in the creation, modification, analysis, or optimization of a design. CAD software is used to increase the productivity of the designer, improve the quality of design, improve communications through documentation, and to create a database for manufacturing. CAD output is often in the form of electronic files for print, machining, or other manufacturing operations.

Computer-aided design is used in many fields. Its use in electronic design is known as Electronic Design Automation, or EDA. In mechanical design is known as Mechanical Design Automation, or MDA, it is also known as computer-aided drafting (CAD) which describes the process of creating a technical drawing with the use of computer software.

CAD software for mechanical design uses either vector based graphics to depict the objects of traditional drafting, or may also produce raster graphics showing the overall appearance of designed objects. However, it involves more than just shapes. As in the manual drafting of technical and engineering drawings, the output of CAD must convey information, such as materials, processes, dimensions, and tolerances, according to application-specific conventions.

CAD may be used to design curves and figures in two-dimensional (2D) space; or curves, surfaces, and solids in three-dimensional (3D) space.

CAD is an important industrial art extensively used in many applications, including automotive, shipbuilding, and aerospace industries, industrial and architectural design, prosthetics, and many more. CAD is also widely used to produce computer animation for special effects in movies, advertising and technical manuals, often called DCC Digital content creation. The modern ubiquity and power of computers means that even perfume bottles and shampoo dispensers are designed using techniques unheard of by engineers of the 1960s. Because of its enormous economic importance, CAD has been a major driving force for research in computational geometry, computer graphics (both hardware and software), and discrete differential geometry.

The design of geometric models for object shapes, in particular, is occasionally called *computer-aided geometric design* (*CAGD*).

While the goal of automated CAD systems is to increase efficiency, they are not necessarily the best way to allow newcomers to understand the geometrical principles of Solid Modelling. For this, scripting languages such as PLaSM (Programming Language of Solid Modelling) are more suitable.

Computer Aided Textile Designing

In today's world Computer Aided Textile Designing (CATD) becomes versatile for all the Designing and weaving industry. The chart shows how the computer aided textile designing is directly useful for Electronic Jacquard. It is useful for fully Automatic and Semi Automatic Electronic punching machines to punch the cards for the mechanical jacquard industry. Finally, it is also useful for taking graph print out which can be used to punch cards using manual punching machines.

Textile industry is one of the oldest industries of all time. The designing section of the industry is its backbone. Textile designing is gaining much popularity in India particularly among youngsters, due to huge demand of Indian textile both in domestic and foreign markets. Those with creative ingenuity and technical skills generally opt for the textile design course. A Textile Designer... produce ideas and designs for printed, woven or knittedtextiles, and many atterned surfaces. They create designs for commercially produced fabrics used in many industries, from fashion to upholstery.

In india as a creative career option Textile designing offers all one wants, glamour, money and popularity.

What does a textile designer do?

- Designing fabric by using different techniques comprising of printing, weaving, ornamenting fabric, print technique, tracing embroidery and colour detailing

- Providing support to the clients to visualize the design
- Helping the clients to correct samples while executing prototypes
- Creating sets of design samples
- Coordinating with clients to plan and develop designs
- Experimenting with colour, fabric and texture
- Conceptualizing new innovative designs
- Keeping up with emerging fashion trends.

Personal Skills...

- Good amount of creative as well as technical knowledge about the work
- An inclination towardss creating designs, weaving, knitting and finishing process
- Technical knowledge is required to handle different machines, looms etc.
- Commercial awareness of textile industry
- Research and data handling
- Critical evaluation and interpretation of materials
- Quick decision making ability
- Awareness of the present scenario of the fashion industry
- Be fashion conscious.

Designing techniques...

Textile design means the design on clothes (wearing clothes, drapery, floral cover, curtain, canopy etc.). These are done by three main techniques as follows:

- Weaving and Printing Technique
- Tailoring and Embroidery Technique
- Painting and Colouring Technique

Job Prospectus...

With growing market potential for textile products there is a wide range of career options for textile designer. They can take up a full time job in Garment manufacturing companies

- Fashion designing agencies
- Textile manufacturers
- Retail world

- Assist top designers
- Fabric analyst
- With some experience textile designers can work as freelancers offering their designs to different organizations

Adobe Photoshop ELEMENTS for Textile Design

Adobe Photoshop is a graphics editing programme developed and published by Adobe Systems.

Adobe's 2003 "Creative Suite" rebranding led to Adobe Photoshop 8's renaming to Adobe Photoshop CS. Thus, Adobe Photoshop CS6 is the 13th major release of Adobe Photoshop. The CS rebranding also resulted in Adobe offering numerous software packages containing multiple Adobe programmes for a reduced price. Adobe Photoshop is released in two editions: Adobe Photoshop, and Adobe Photoshop Extended, with the Extended having extra 3D image creation, motion graphics editing, and advanced image analysis features. Adobe Photoshop Extended is included in all of Adobe's Creative Suite offerings except Design Standard, which includes the Adobe Photoshop edition.

Alongside Photoshop and Photoshop Extended, Adobe also publishes Photoshop Elements and Photoshop Lightroom, collectively called "The Adobe Photoshop Family". In 2008, Adobe released Adobe Photoshop Express, a free web-based image editing tool to edit photos directly on blogs and social networking sites. In 2011, a version was released for the Android operating system and the iOS operating system, followed by a release of a version for Windows 8 in 2013.

Adobe distributes Photoshop in Windows and Macintosh versions.

Early History

In 1987, Thomas Knoll, a PhD student at the University of Michigan began writing a programme on his Macintosh Plus to display grayscale images on a monochrome display. This programme, called Display, caught the attention of his brother John Knoll, an Industrial Light & Magic employee, who recommended that Thomas turn it into a full-fledged image editing programme. Thomas took a six-month break from his studies in 1988 to collaborate with his brother on the programme. Thomas renamed the programme ImagePro, but the name was already taken. Later that year, Thomas renamed his programme Photoshop and worked out a short-term deal with scanner manufacturer Barneyscan to distribute copies of the programme with a slide scanner; a "total of about 200 copies of Photoshop were shipped" this way.

During this time, John travelled to Silicon Valley and gave a demonstration of the programme to engineers at Apple and Russell Brown, art director at Adobe. Both showings were successful, and Adobe decided to purchase the license to distribute in September 1988. While John worked on plug-ins in California, Thomas remained in Ann Arbor writing code. *Photoshop* 1.0 was released on February 19, 1990 for Macintosh exclusively. The Barneyscan version included advanced colour editing features that were stripped from the first Adobe shipped version. The handling of colour slowly improved with each release from Adobe and Photoshop quickly became the industry standard in digital colour editing. At the time Photoshop 1.0 was released, digital retouching on dedicated high end systems, such as the SciTex, cost around $300 an hour for basic photo retouching.

File Format

Photoshop files have default file extension as .PSD, which stands for "Photoshop Document." A PSD file stores an image with support for most imaging options available in Photoshop. These include layers with masks, transparency, text, alpha channels and spot colours, clipping paths, and duotone settings. This is in contrast to many other file formats (e.g. .JPG or .GIF) that restrict content to provide streamlined, predictable functionality. A PSD file has a maximum height and width of 30,000 pixels, and a length limit of 3 Gigabytes.

Photoshop files sometimes have the file extension .PSB, which stands for "Photoshop Big" (also known as "large document format"). A PSB file extends the PSD file format, increasing the maximum height and width to 300,000 pixels and the length limit to around 4 Exabytes. The dimension limit was apparently chosen arbitrarily by Adobe, not based on computer arithmetic constraints (it is not close to a power of two, as is 30,000) but for ease of software testing. PSD and PSB formats are documented.

Because of Photoshop's popularity, PSD files are widely used and supported to some extent by most competing software. The .PSD file format can be exported to and from Adobe's other apps like Adobe Illustrator, Adobe Premiere Pro, and After Effects, to make professional standard DVDs and provide non-linear editing and special effects services, such as backgrounds, textures, and so on, for television, film, and the web. Photoshop's primary strength is as a pixel-based image editor, unlike vector-based image editors. Photoshop also enables vector graphics editing through its Paths, Pen tools, Shape tools, Shape Layers, Type tools, Import command, and Smart Object functions. These tools and commands are convenient to combine pixel-based and vector-based images in one Photoshop document, because it may not be necessary to use more than one programme. To create very complex vector graphics with numerous shapes and colours, it may be easier to use software that was created primarily for that purpose, such as Adobe Illustrator or CorelDRAW. Photoshop's non-destructive Smart Objects can also import complex vector shapes.

Language Availabilities

Photoshop is available in more than 20 languages. These are the following:

Chinese Simplified, Chinese Traditional, Czech, Danish, Dutch, English, Finnish, French, German, Hungarian, Italian, Japanese, Korean, Norwegian, Polish, Portuguese, Romanian, Russian, Spanish, Swedish, Turkish and Ukrainian. Also Arabic and Hebrew as of Photoshop CS6.

Plugins

Photoshop functionality can be extended by add-on programmes called Photoshop plugins (or plug-ins). Adobe creates some plugins, such as Adobe Camera Raw, but third-party companies develop most plugins, according to Adobe's specifications. Some are free and some are commercial software. Most plugins work with only Photoshop or Photoshop-compatible hosts, but a few can also be run as standalone applications.

There are various types of plugins, such as filter, export, import, selection, colour correction, and automation. The most popular plugins are the filter plugins (also known as a 8bf plugins), available under the Filter menu in Photoshop. Filter plugins can either modify the current image or create content. Below are some popular types of plugins, and some well-known companies associated with them:

- Colour correction plugins (Alien Skin Software, Nik Software, OnOne Software, Topaz Labs Software, The Plugin Site, etc.)
- Special effects plugins (Alien Skin Software, Auto FX Software, AV Bros., Flaming Pear Software, etc.)
- 3D effects plugins (Andromeda Software, Strata, etc.)

Adobe Camera Raw (also known as ACR and Camera Raw) is a special plugin, supplied free by Adobe, used primarily to read and process raw image files so that the resultant images can be processed by Photoshop. It can also be used from within Adobe Bridge.

Tools

Upon loading Photoshop, a sidebar with a variety of tools with multiple image-editing functions appears to the left of the screen. These tools typically fall under the categories of drawing; painting; measuring and navigation; selection; typing; and retouching.

Some tools contain a small triangle in the bottom right of the toolbox icon. These can be expanded to reveal similar tools. While newer versions of Photoshop are updated to include new tools and features, several recurring tools that exist in most versions are discussed below.

Pen Tool

Photoshop includes a few versions of the *pen* tool. The pen tool creates precise paths that can be manipulated using anchor points. The *freeform pen* tool allows the user to draw paths freehand, and with the *magnetic pen* tool, the drawn path attaches closely to outlines of objects in an image, which is useful for isolating them from a background.

Measuring and Navigation

The *eyedropper* tool selects a colour from an area of the image that is clicked, and samples it for future use. The *hand* tool navigates an image by moving it in any direction, and the *zoom* tool enlarges the part of an image that is clicked on, allowing for a closer view.

Selection

By using path selection tool, we can select path nodes.

Cropping

The *crop* tool can be used to select a particular area of an image and discard the portions outside of the chosen section. This tool assists in creating a focus point on an image and excluding unnecessary or excess space. Cropping allows enhancement of a photo's composition while decreasing the file size.

The "crop" tool is in the tools palette, which is located on the right side of the document. By placing the cursor over the image, the user can drag the cursor to the desired area. Once the Enter key is pressed, the area outside of the rectangle will be cropped. The area outside of the rectangle is the discarded data, which allows for the file size to be decreased. The "crop" tool can alternatively be used to extend the canvas size by clicking and dragging outside of the existing image borders.

Slicing

The *"slice"* and *slice select* tools, like the crop tool, are used in isolating parts of images. The slice tool can be used to divide an image into different sections, and these separate parts can be used as pieces of a web page design once HTML and CSS are applied. The slice select tool allows sliced sections of an image to be adjusted and shifted.

Moving

Once an area of an image is highlighted, the *move* tool can be used to manually relocate the selected piece to anywhere on the canvas.

Marquee

The *marquee* tool can make selections that are single row, single column, rectangular and elliptical. An area that has been selected can be edited without affecting the rest of the image. This tool can also crop an image; it allows for better control. In contrast to the *crop* tool, the "marquee" tool allows for more adjustments to the selected area before cropping. The only *marquee* tool that does not allow cropping is the elliptical. Although the single row and column *marquee* tools allow for cropping, they are not ideal, because they only crop a line. The *rectangular marquee* tool is the preferred option. Once the tool has been selected, dragging the tool across the desired area will select it. The selected area will be outlined by dotted lines, referred to as "marching ants". These dotted lines are called "marching ants", because the dashes look like ants marching around the selected area. To set a specific size or ratio, the tool option bar provides these settings. Before making a selecting an area, the desired size or ratio must be set by adjusting the width and height. Any changes such as colour, filters, location, etc. should be made before cropping. To crop the selection, the user must go to image tab and select crop.

Lasso

The *lasso* tool is similar to the "marquee" tool, however, the user can make a custom selection by drawing it freehand. There are three options for the "lasso" tool – regular, polygonal, and magnetic. The regular "lasso" tool allows the user to have drawing capabilities. Photoshop will complete the selection once the mouse button is released. The user may also complete the selection by connecting the end point to the starting point. The "marching ants" will indicate if a selection has been made. The "polygonal lasso" tool will only draw straight lines, which makes it an ideal choice for images with many straight lines. Unlike the regular "lasso" tool, the user must continually click around the image to outline the shape. To complete the selection, the user must connect the end point to the starting point just like the regular lasso tool. "Magnetic lasso" tool is considered the smart tool. It can do the same as the other two, but it can also detect the edges of an image once the user selects a starting point. It detects by examining the colour pixels as the cursor move over the desired area. A pixel is the smallest element in an image. Closing the selection is the same as the other two, which should also should display the "marching ants" once the selection has been closed.

Quick Selection

The *quick selection* tool selects areas based on edges, similarly to the *magnetic lasso* tool. The difference between this tool and the *lasso* tool is that there is no starting and ending point. Since there isn't a starting and ending point, the selected area can be added onto as much as possible without starting over. By dragging the cursor over the desired area, the *quick selection* tool detects the edges of the image. The "marching ants" allow the user to know what is currently being selected. Once the user is done, the selected area can be edited without affecting the rest of the image.

Magic Wand

The *magic wand* tool selects areas based on pixels. The user only needs to click once, and this tool will detect pixels that are very similar to each other. If the *eyedropper* tool is selected in the options bar, then the magic wand can determine the value needed to evaluate the pixels; this is based on the sample size setting in the *eyedropper* tool. When the image requires more than a few clicks, this tool becomes a disadvantage. The user must decide what settings to use or if the image is right for this tool.

Eraser

The *eraser* tool erases content based on the active layer. If the user is on the text layer, then any text across which the tool is dragged will be erased. The eraser will convert the pixels to transparent, unless the background layer is selected. The size and style of the eraser can be selected in the options bar. This tool is unique in that it can take the form of the paintbrush and pencil tools. In addition to the straight eraser tool, there are two more available options – background eraser and magic eraser. The *background eraser* deletes any part of the image that is on the edge of an object. This tool is often used to extract objects from the background. The *magic eraser* tool deletes based on similar coloured pixels. It is very similar to the *magic wand* tool. This tool is ideal for deleting areas with the same colour or tone that contrasts with the rest of the image.

Typing

Photoshop also provides tools for adding and editing text. The *type* tools create an area where text can be entered, and the *type mask* tools create a selection area that has the shape of text. The type tool creates vector-based text, so symbols, letters and numbers in various fonts and colours can be re-sized while maintaining the same quality.

Retouching

There are several tools that are used for retouching, manipulating and adjusting photos, such as the *clone stamp*, *eraser*, *burn*, *dodge*, *smudge* and *blur* tools. The clone stamp tool samples a selected portion of an image, and duplicates it over another area using a brush that can be adjusted in size, flow and opacity. The smudge tool, when dragged across part of an image, stretches and smudges pixels as if they are real paint, and the blur tool softens portions of an image by lowering the amount of detail within the adjusted area. The eraser tool removes pixels from an image, and the *magic eraser* tool selects areas of solid colour and erases them. The burn and dodge tools, which are derived from traditional methods of adjusting the exposure on printed photos, have opposite effects; the burn tool darkens selected areas, and the dodge tool lightens them.

Content-aware

Content-awareness is a useful aspect of Photoshop where image editing is done automatically and intelligently. It comes in two forms, content-aware scaling, and content-aware filling, in which elements in a background automatically recompose according to the areas a user of the programme decides to fill or scale. More specifically, content-aware scaling works by rescaling an image and causing its content to adapt to the new dimensions and preserving important areas of it. Content-aware filling functions by matching tone, colour, and noise of an area of the image that contained an object or detail in which the user decides to remove.

Puppet Warp

Similar to the content-aware tool, the *puppet warp* tool reveals Photoshop's intelligence by allowing a user to reposition an object in an image such as a flower or arm. This is done by using points that outline the structure of an object and easily repositioning in the wanted orientation.

Video Editing

In Adobe CS5 Extended edition, video editing is comprehensive and efficient with a broad compatibility of video file formats such as *MOV*, *AVI*,*MPEG-4*, and *FLV* formats and easy workflow. Using simple combination of keys video layers can easily be modified, with other features such as adding text and the creation of animations using single images.

3D

With the Extended version of Photoshop CS5, 2D elements of an artwork can easily become three-dimensional with the click of a button. Extrusions of texts, an available library of materials for three-dimensional, and even wrapping two-dimensional images around 3D geometry are all possible with this version of Photoshop. Realism can also be added to an image using the 3D features of Photoshop such as animating image-based lights and depth of field.

Mobile Integration

Third-party plugins have also been added to the most recent version of Photoshop where technologies such as the iPad have integrated the software with different types of applications. Applications like the Adobe Eazel painting app allows the user to easily create paintings with their fingertips and use an array of different paint from dry to wet in order to create rich colour blending.

Camera Raw

With the Camera Raw plug-in, RAW images can be processed without the use of Adobe Photoshop Lightroom, along with other image file formats such as *JPEGs*, *TIFFs*, or *PNGs*. The plug-in allows users to remove noise without the side-effect of over-sharpening, add grain, and even perform *post-crop vignetting*.

Techniques

Extracting

A widely used technique is extraction. By this technique a part of the image, normally the foreground, such as a person, is isolated from the rest of the image and put on a new background. Alternatively both background and the extracted foreground can be manipulated and put back together as shown on the example. To make the extraction a line must be drawn around the foreground figure to select it. Several tools can be used for this process such as the lasso tool; however, in this case the filter-extraction tool has been used. The latter is normally the preferred tool for extracting figures with hair or fur.

Use of Adobe Photoshop for Textile Design

- Selection and Fill Tools - basic textile design settings
- Colour reducing a textile design in PhotoShop
- Forced colour reduction using the Marquee tool
- Colouring your textile design
- Cleaning a textile design
- Editing tools for textile design
- Square and Half/drop Repeats in fabric design
- Creating a plaid
- Mini bodies - placing a textile design into a fashion sketch
- Colour reduction of a tonal textile design
- Basic Photo draping - used for fashion designs and home furnishing design - placing a textile you designed on a photograph or home furnishing
- How Textile Designers can use the colour charts included on the CD
- Creating layers with various tools
- Adjusting and Tinting layers in your fabric designs
- Matching colours to a colour chart - a must for colour accuracy in designing textiles
- Pulling colours within a layer
- Using Colour Range to select a mask
- Reducing a layered design down to indexed colour (advanced watercolour technique & colour reduction of a textile design)
- Photo Draping using the warp tool - advanced tool for placing a textile you designed on a photograph.
- Using Bicubic Interpolation to resample an image (resizing a textile design)
- A note about pixels per inch as related to textile designing
- Placing colours on the Colour Table in the order you want (to make recolouring of a textile design easier)
- Trapping and Platforming and Fall-ons in textiles

3

Texture and Depth

In the visual arts, texture is the perceived surface quality of a work of art. It is an element of two-dimensional and three-dimensional design and is distinguished by its perceived visual and physical properties. Use of *texture*, along with other elements of design, can convey a variety of messages and emotions.

Two Varieties of Texture

Physical texture, also known as *actual texture* or *tactile texture*, are the actual variations upon a surface. This can include, but is not limited to, fur, wood grain, sand, smooth surface of canvas or metal, glass, and leather. It differentiates itself from visual texture by having a physical quality that can be felt by touch. Specific use of a texture can affect the smoothness that an artwork conveys. For instance, use of *rough surfaces* can be visually active, whilst *smooth surfaces* can be visually restful. The use of both can give a sense of personality to a design, or utilized to create emphasis, rhythm, contrast, etc.

Light is an important factor for physical artwork, because it can affect how a surface is viewed. Strong lights on a smooth surface can obscure the readability of a drawing or photograph, whilst they can create strong contrasts in a highly textural surface such as moose or pigs.

Visual Texture

Visual texture is the illusion of having physical texture. Every material and every support surface has its own visual texture and needs to be taken into consideration before creating a composition. As such, materials such as canvas and watercolour paper are considerably rougher than, for example, photo-quality computer paper and may not be best suited to creating a flat, smooth texture. Photography, drawings and paintings use visual texture both to portray their subject matter realistically and with interpretation. Texture in these media are generally created by the repetition of shape and line.

Hypertexture

Hypertexture can be defined as both the "realistic simulated surface texture produced by adding small distortions across the surface of an object" (as pioneered by Ken Perlin) and a new avenue for describing the fluid morphic nature of texture in the realm of cyber graphics and the tranversally responsive works created in the field of visual arts therein (as described by Lee Klein).

Pique

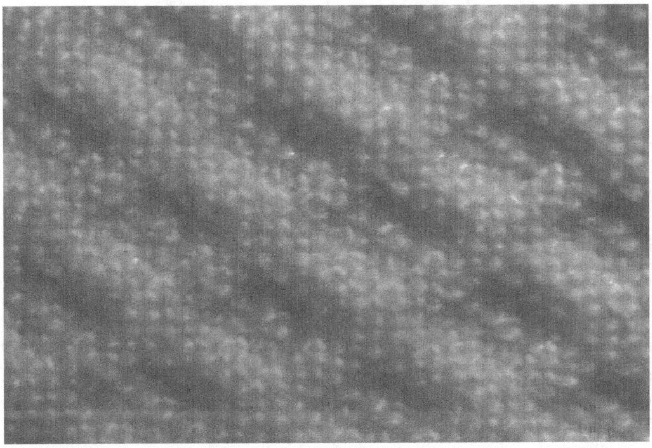

Figure: *Microscopic picture of piqué weaving.*

Pique, or marcella, refers to a weaving style, normally used with cotton yarn, which is characterized by raised parallel cords or fine ribbing. Twilled cotton and corded cotton are close relatives.

The weave is closely associated with white tie, and some accounts even say the fabric was invented specifically for this use. It holds more starch than plain fabric, so produces a stiffer shirt front. Marcella shirts then replaced earlier plain fronts, which remain a valid alternative. Marcella's use then spread to other parts of the dress code and it is now the most common fabric used in the tie and waistcoat of white tie. A knit fabric with a similar texture is used in polo shirts.

Marcella weaving was developed by the Lancashire cotton industry in the late 18th century as a mechanised technique of weaving double cloth with an enclosed heavy cording weft. It was originally used to make imitations of the corded Provençal quilts made in Marseille, the manufacture of which became an important industry for Lancashire from the late 18th to the early 20th century. The term "marcella" is one of a number of variations on the word "Marseille".

Pique fabrics are a type of dobby construction. Piques may be constructed in various patterns such as cord, waffle, honeycomb and birdseye piques. These fabrics require the addition of extra yarns, called stuffer yarns. These stuffer yarns are incorporated into the back of the fabric to give texture and added depth to the fabric design. Some piques may be made using the Jacquard attachment on the loom. Although made of 100% cotton today, cotton-silk blends and even pure silk versions were made in the past and in a variety of weaves.

Colour and Design

Colour in design is very subjective. What evokes one reaction in one person may evoke a very different reaction in somone else. Sometimes this is due to personal preference, and other times due to cultural background. Colour theory is a science in itself. Studying how colours affect different people, either individually or as a group, is something some people build their careers on. And there's a lot to it. Something as simple as changing the exact hue or saturation of a colour can evoke a completely different feeling. Cultural differences mean that something that's happy and uplifting in one country can be depressing in another.

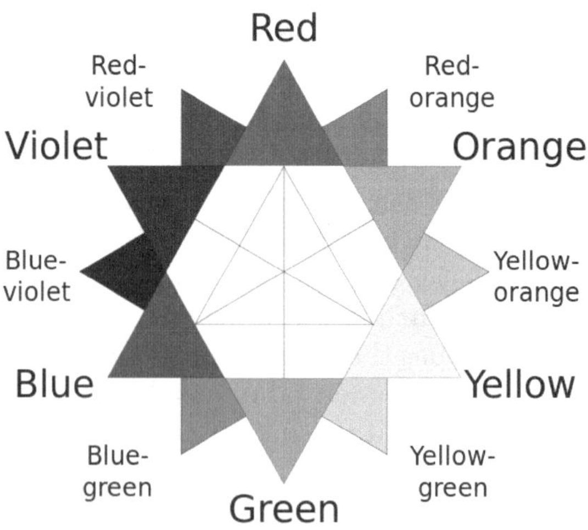

This is the first in a three-part series on colour theory. Here we'll discuss the meanings behind the different colour families, and give some examples of how these colours are used (with a bit of analysis for each). In Part 2 we'll talk about how hue, chroma, value, saturation, tones, tints and shades affect the way we perceive colours. And in Part 3 we'll discuss how to create effective colour palettes for your own designs.

Warm Colours

Warm colours include red, orange, and yellow, and variations of those three colours. These are the colours of fire, of fall leaves, and of sunsets and sunrises, and are generally energizing, passionate, and positive.

Red and yellow are both primary colours, with orange falling in the middle, which means warm colours are all truly warm and aren't created by combining a warm colour with a cool colour. Use warm colours in your designs to reflect passion, happiness, enthusiasm, and energy.

Red (Primary Colour)

Red is a very hot colour. It's associated with fire, violence, and warfare. It's also associated with love and passion. In history, it's been associated with both the Devil and Cupid. Red can actually have a physical effect on people, raising blood pressure and respiration rates.

It's been shown to enhance human metabolism, too. Red can be associated with anger, but is also associated with importance (think of the red carpet at awards shows and celebrity events). Red also indicates danger (the reason stop lights and signs are red, and that most warning labels are red).

Outside the western world, red has different associations. For example, in China, red is the colour of prosperity and happiness. It can also be used to attract good luck. In other eastern cultures, red is worn by brides on their wedding days. In South Africa, however, red is the colour of mourning. Red is also associated with communism. Red has become the colour associated with AIDS awareness in Africa due to the popularity of the campaign.

In design, red can be a powerful accent colour. It can have an overwhelming effect if it's used too much in designs, especially in its purest form. It's a great colour to use when power or passion want to be portrayed in the design. Red can be very versatile, though, with brighter versions being more energetic and darker shades being more powerful and elegant.

The Art of Science in Fashion and Textile Design

Science plays a major role in design development of fashion clothing and accessories, just a glimpse into the past will confirm enough to be true. It's not a jumbled business of cloth and colours loosely thrown together, rather, a well organised industry driven by the sciences, from market research to weaving, printing, dyeing, pattern making, branding and labelling; scientific intervention supports artist's continuum.

Want an example or two: English Madder Print: The colouring agent in madder root called alizarin was in fact first chemically extracted and then synthesized in 1869 by two English chemists. Although the dyeing process, even today, requires a variety of painstaking steps, synthesized alizarin brought the price within the reach of commercial producers. Testimony to the significant part science plays ensuring the longevity of styles and textiles. Silk dyed in this manner is characterized by a dusty-looking finish and a feel (referred to as a chalk hand by the experts) very much like fine suede, and a matte finish.

In 1879 Thomas Burberry developed a fabric which was weatherproofed in the yarn before weaving, using a secret process and then proofed again in the piece, using the same undisclosed formula. The new material was untearable and weatherproof, whilst cool and breathable. He called the cloth gabardine and registered the word as a trademark. This is science.

Possessing a degree in science is not pre requisite to being a good designer, utilising scientific disciplines is advisable if you want your designs to hit the streets running rather than ending up in good Samaritans charity bins. A little business acumen always comes in handy and knowing what your customers want is critical. Above all, being in the right place at the right time is the key to success.

Timothy Everest, Paul Smith and Vivienne Westwood are just three examples that combined their design skills with business acumen and chanced to be in the right place and the right time. All attribute their success to chance, a would be cyclist, an advertisement in the paper and punk took them all in the same direction on different paths, now producing some of the most original fashion accessories in the market place

Let's put all the technicalities aside. Without disciplined inspiration all the science and psychology fall on numb bodies, clothing must inspire the buyer as much as the designer, the message is portrayed in the colours, pattern and textures, combined to express season and inspiration. And what about psychology; A little self indulgence creates a healthy state of mind, better to be happy than sad, retail therapy is certainly a good remedy for the blues, lets face it we've all been there many times. And to rid yourself of any guilt after the act, buy something for your loved one. A bit of psychology.

To finalise, summarise and self indulge I have written a brief critique on one of my favourite silk tie designs, I designed it, It's not without all the elements of good design as mentioned.

Subtle Significance a geometric floral silk ties: a subtle mauve heart first catches your eye. And then golden geometric petals shimmer slightly and draw you closer, accentuated by midnight blue. Lastly, the hefty weave adds just the right amount of texture for a little masculine handle to the femininity of floral patterns. Significant, but subtle.

Floral Art

In the realm of textile and fibre arts, the floral motif has always been a popular design choice; stylistically, there is a rich and varied history of its utilization. Examples are found worldwide, in cultures stretching from ancient China, Medieval India, to contemporary artists involved in grand metropolitan art circles to this day.

Floral Textile Artists

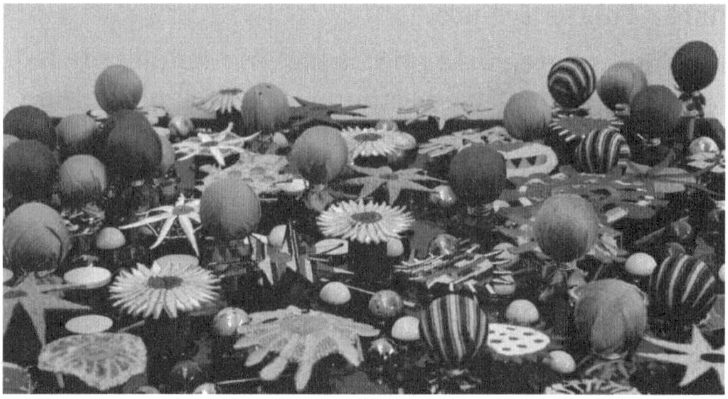

In the realm of textile and fibre arts, the floral motif has always been a popular design choice; stylistically, there is a rich and varied history of its utilization. Examples are found worldwide, in cultures stretching from ancient China, Medieval India, to contemporary artists involved in grand metropolitan art circles to this day. Despite its long-standing usage, there is no shortage of innovative ways for artists to explore this imagery. These textile artists inspired by flowers (sometimes referred to as floral textile artists) specifically highlight new and fascinating methods of bringing such a storied motif to life.

Michael Brennand-Wood

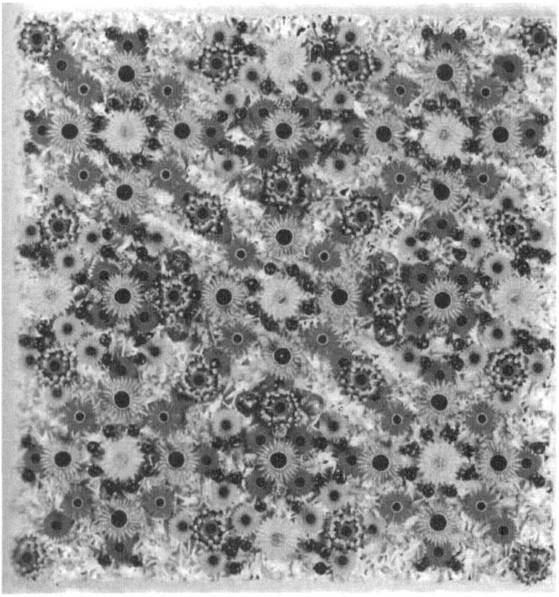

Figure: *Crystallized Movements, 90 x 90 x 72 cm.*

Michael Brennand-Wood is an exciting voice in the realm of floral textile art. His work is hypnotizing and radiant. For the past 40 years, Brennand-Wood has worked in textile and wood, developing an interest in the field at a very young age, inspired by his grandparents. Brennand-Wood's grandmother worked as an industrial weaver, and he would be fascinated with the samples she brought home. His work is generally supported by a wooden base, which was spurred by his engineer grandfather, who would tinker with wooden projects in the yard.

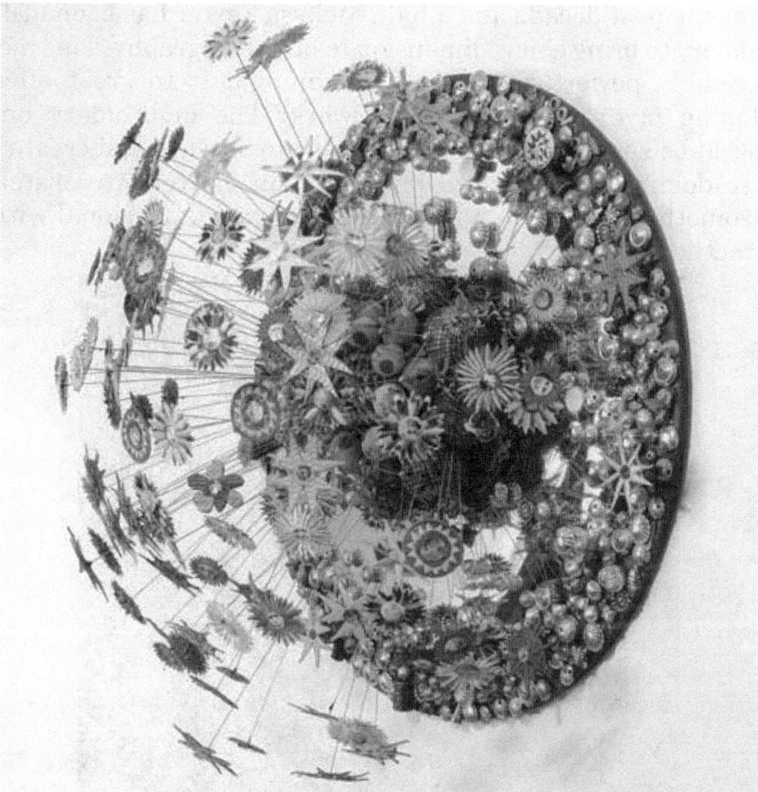

Figure: *Michael Brennand-Wood – Flower Head- Narcissistic Butterfly 60, dia x 40 cm, 2005. Collection of the artist.*

Brennand-Wood blends these two crafts, creating spectacular fine art pieces that have most recently centred around floral imagery. He has moved into computer-driven embroidery, often utilizing radiating symmetry of overlapping flowers. His floral textile designs highlight aspects of the history of ornamental weaving and embroidery in an exciting fashion, captivating viewers from all walks of artistic life. There is also a quality of depth to the work, which can sometimes be ignored in the fabric field. This plays wonderfully with the medium, as distance from the pieces can provide an entirely different perception of what they are. Also, his work tends to play off the perception of textile as being a woman's medium, and he strives to play off these gender roles. In the 1990s, he focused on lace, and what new meaning and subcontext can be created by a material that is so loaded with a female cultural association.

Melissa Zexter

For the past decade and a half, Melissa Zexter has been utilizing embroidery to bring a new dimension to her photography. This method is incredibly powerful, and she has brought it to great effect in developing layered depth in her work. The embroidery on her photographs serves a dual purpose: both to obscure and create. In a field so dominated by digital manipulation, Zexter opts instead to craft something physical, a melding of the two-dimensional with the very tactile thread.

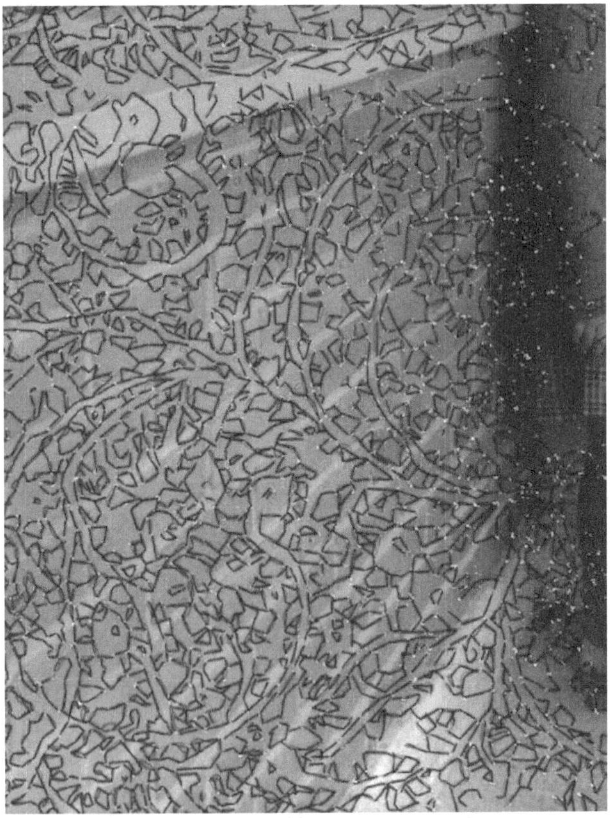

***Figure:** Melissa Zexter – Schoolgirls (Detail) Gelatin Silver Print, Thread 203 x 243*

Her latest work combines photographs of haunting women with abstracted floral forms overlaid. The women are often wearing veils, which highlights the traditionally feminine features in a way that invites the viewer in to personal introspection on the lives of these women. These figures are simultaneously both strong and delicate.

Susan Brubaker Knapp

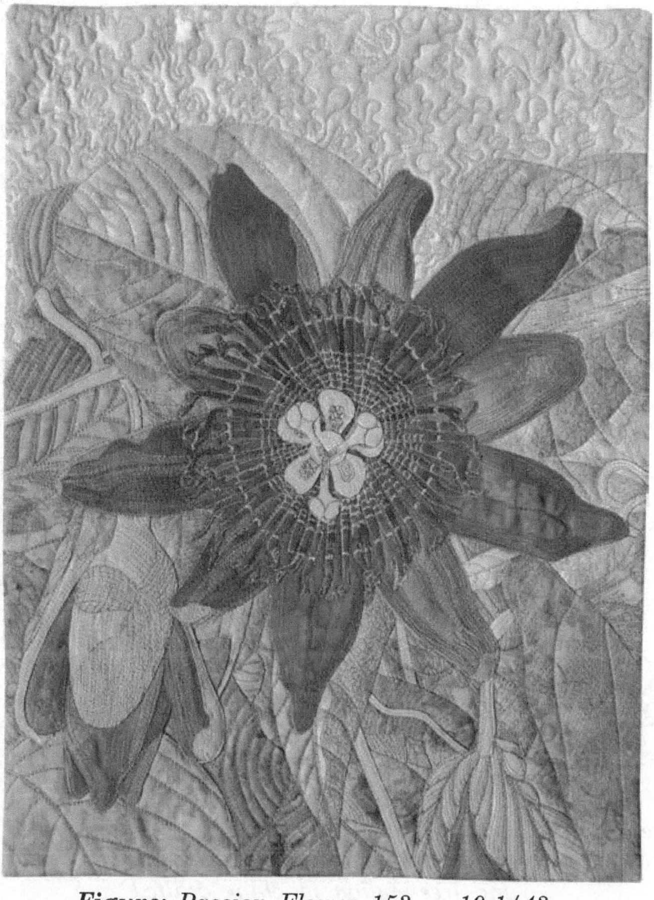

***Figure:** Passion Flower 153 x 19-1/43 .*

Original design. Cotton fabric, cotton threads, wool/polyester batting. Free-motion thread sketched and machine quilted.

An eloquent quilter, Susan Brubaker Knapp creates intricate pieces based of photography. Not a classically trained artist, Brubaker Knapp has developed her craft through a lifetime of trial and error, beginning by working with her mother as a child. She still has the first quilt she made, from when she was only 10 years old, and her family keeps it as a functional blanket to this day. Before working full-time with fibre, Brubaker Knapp worked as a writer (her degrees are actually in English and Journalism), and as a graphic designer.

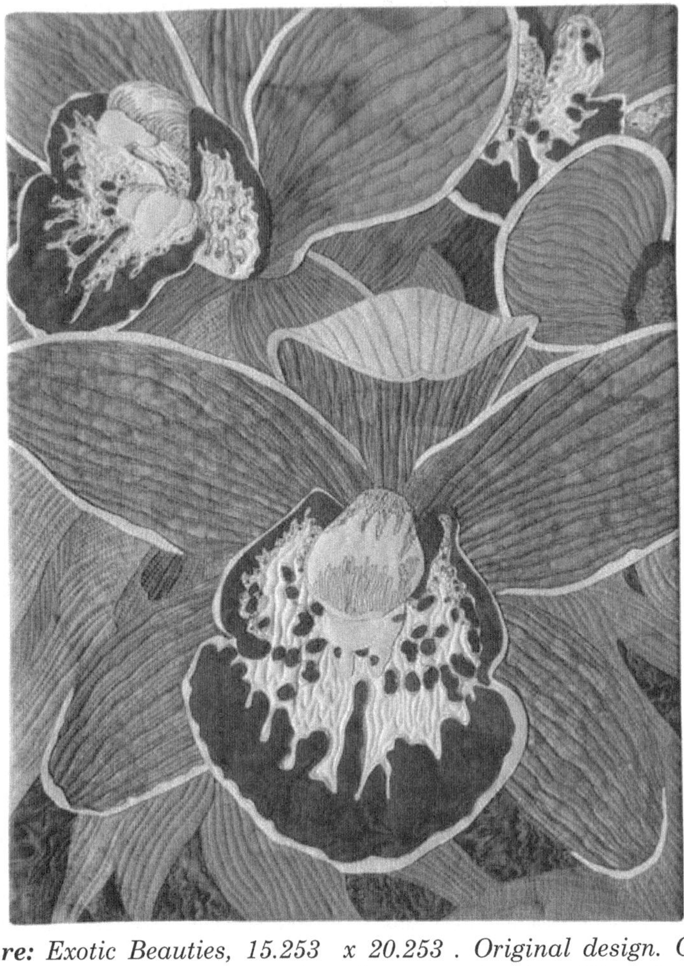

Figure: *Exotic Beauties, 15.253 x 20.253 . Original design. Cotton fabric, fusible adhesive, cotton threads, cotton batting. Thread sketched and free-motion machine quilted.*

It is apparent through her work that she has a background in design, as her crafting as a floral textile artist is immaculate. Her work, however, is much more suited for wall space. Despite no formal training in art, she has found a niche in creating intensely crafted works that express fully the colours of the world, often working with macro photography. The petals of the flowers she sews overlap in such a way that her colour fields have a life of their own, interacting with their neighbouring sections.

Lindsay Taylor

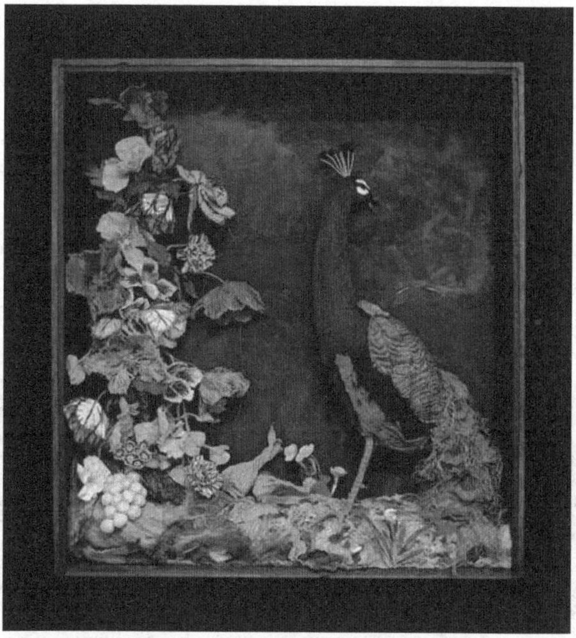

Figure: *Lindsay Taylor art*

From the Isle of Wight, Lindsay Taylor (a textile artist inspired by flowers) takes her lead from the lush botanical life of Britain's forests. She will bring home twigs and leaves from when she walks her dogs. Before moving into fine art, Taylor created wedding dresses by hand, converting her shop into her art studio, and still creates much of her work to be wearable.

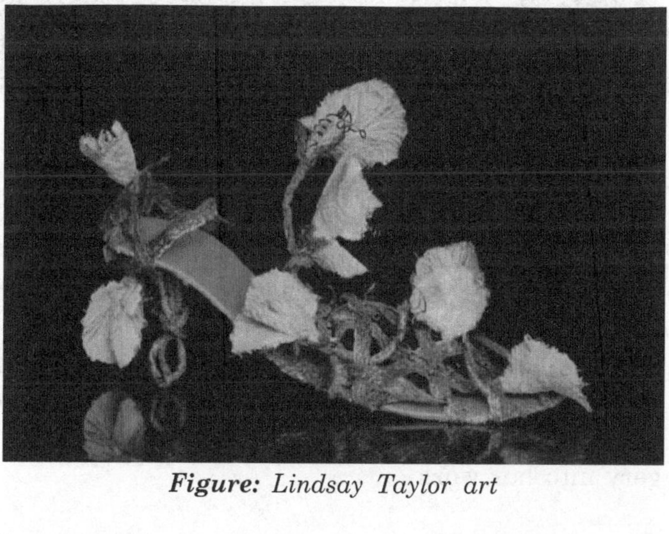

Figure: *Lindsay Taylor art*

Her stitched work is texturally rich, utilizing many different techniques to achieve a lushness that gives an amazingly detailed depiction of these plants.

Her work is unlike that of any other artist out there, and she has a hand in the creation in all her pieces, from the hand-dyeing of the fabric, through embroidery (both free-machine and by hand), felting, and quilting.

Some of Taylor's most effective work are teacups made to appear like flowers. The veins in the leaves and petals are meticulously crafted, and represent in a way that, while not photo-realistic, create the true sense of the plant.

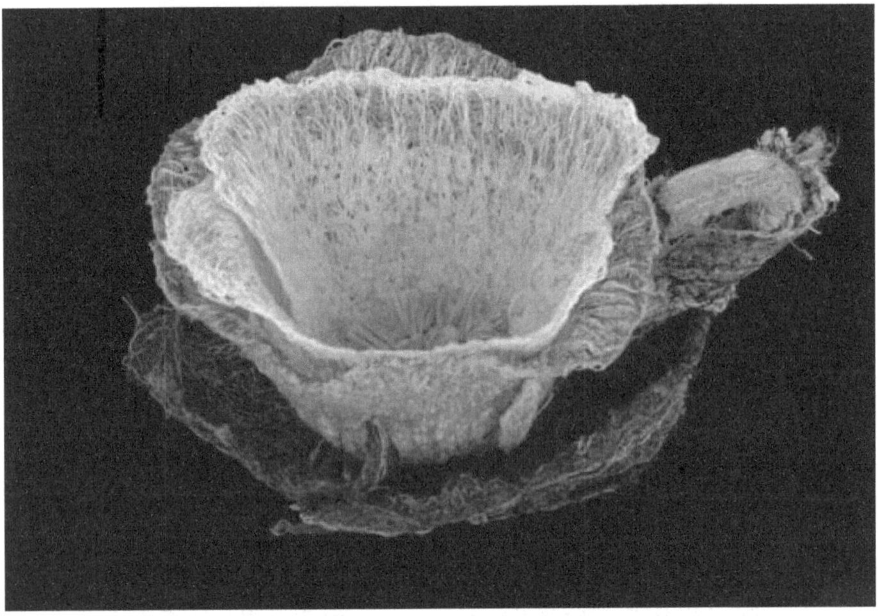

Figure: *Lindsay Taylor art*

Leslie Rinchen-Wongmo

This west coast Buddhist is not only a floral textile artist, but Leslie Rinchen-Wongmo is one of the few Americans creating what is known as a thangka, a traditional form of painting or embroidery, produced with a patchwork of cotton or silk.

She has been lauded by the Dalai Lama for her work in this revered artistic form. As Buddhist culture reveres the blooms of flowers, particularly the lotus, Rinchen-Wongmo often incorporates this imagery into her work.

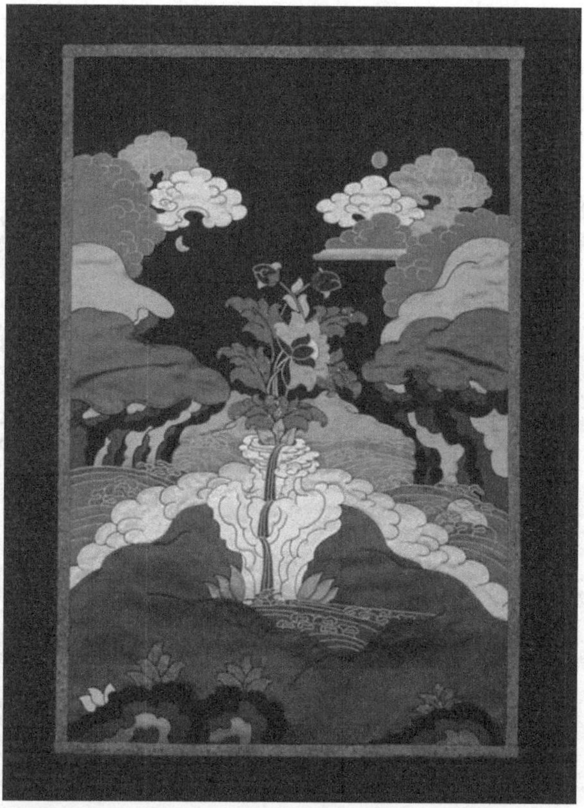

Figure: *Beauty, Silk satin, brocade, & cotton 653 x 253 (125 x 64 cm)*

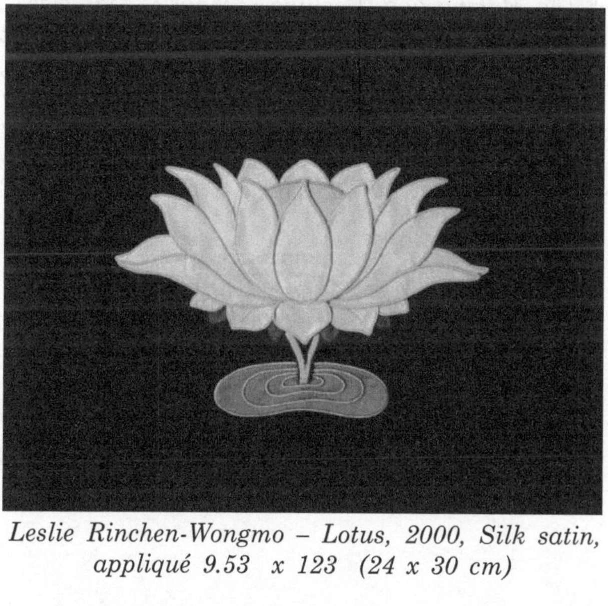

Figure: *Leslie Rinchen-Wongmo – Lotus, 2000, Silk satin, Tibetan appliqué 9.53 x 123 (24 x 30 cm)*

The lotus flower represents many things in Buddhist art, as a beautiful creation that springs forth from the swampy earth. This is the inherent dichotomy of the Earth; the same world that creates chaos and disorder also allows for the peace and knowledge the religion seeks.

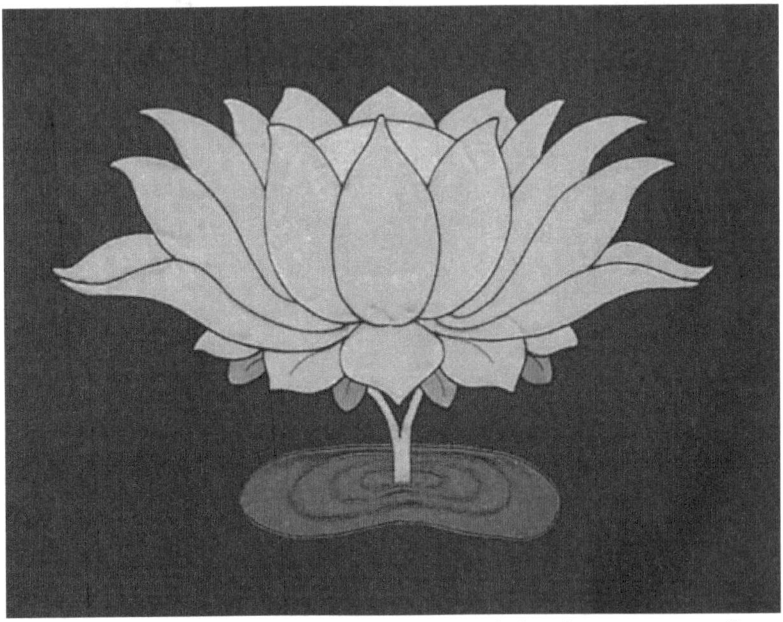

Figure: *Rinchen-Wongmo was the subject of the documentary, Creating Buddhas: The Making and Meaning of Fabric Thangkas. The film highlights her history, as well as her virtual apprenticeship programme. As traditional Tibetan craft has required a physical presence, the artist has attempted to circumvent that by offering a programme centred around text instruction, coupled with teleconferences and Skype calls. And it seems to have made a significant impact, and should hopefully be able to start a widespread knowledge of the artform worldwide.*

4

Art Movements and Period Styles

An art movement is a tendency or style in art with a specific common philosophy or goal, followed by a group of artists during a restricted period of time, (usually a few months, years or decades) or, at least, with the heyday of the movement defined within a number of years. Art movements were especially important in modern art, when each consecutive movement was considered as a new avant-garde.

According to theories associated with modernism and the concept of postmodernism, art movements are especially important during the period of time corresponding to modern art. The period of time called "modern art" is posited to have changed approximately half-way through the 20th century and art made afterwards is generally called contemporary art. Postmodernism in visual art begins and functions as a parallel to late modernism and refers to that period after the "modern" period called contemporary art. The postmodern period began during late modernism (which is a contemporary continuation of modernism), and according to some theorists postmodernism ended in the 21st century. During the period of time corresponding to "modern art" each consecutive movement was often considered a new avant-garde.

Also during the period of time referred to as "modern art" each movement was seen corresponding to a somewhat grandiose rethinking of all that came before it, concerning the visual arts. Generally there was a commonality of visual style linking the works and artists included in an art movement. Verbal expression and explanation of movements has come from the artists themselves, sometimes in the form of an art manifesto, and sometimes from art critics and others who may explain their understanding of the meaning of the new art then being produced.

In the visual arts, many artists, theorists, art critics, art collectors, art dealers and others mindful of the unbroken continuation of modernism and the continuation of modern art even into the contemporary era, ascribe to and welcome new philosophies of art as they appear. Postmodernist theorists posit that the idea of art movements are no longer as applicable, or no longer as discernible, as the notion of art movements had been before the postmodern era. There are many theorists however who doubt as to whether or not such an era was actually a fact; or just a passing fad. The term refers to tendencies in visual art, novel ideas and architecture, and sometimes literature. In music it is more common to speak about genres and styles instead. As the names of many art movements use the -ism suffix (for example cubism and futurism), they are sometimes referred to as *isms*.

Asante Textile Arts

Akan textile arts were key markers of status and dominion, while the act of weaving itself had mythological and ceremonial resonance. This was especially true of a type of cloth called *kente* (1993.384.2), which was linked in Akan mythology to the spider Ananse, the first weaver. Its production was subject to certain behavioural sanctions and weavers made offerings to their looms when these prohibitions were broken. *Kente* is woven in narrow strips by master weavers who use a complex technique called "floating weave" to achieve the intricate designs associated with this cloth.

The strips are then sewn together, creating broad panels of striking beauty and compositional complexity. Because of its expense and symbolic associations, only persons of high rank wore *kente*, and certain patterns were reserved solely for the king's use. Originally, these cloths were made of white cotton with woven designs of indigo-dyed thread. By the seventeenth century, however, luxurious silks imported by European traders were incorporated, resulting in the vibrant and richly hued textiles that are so admired today.

Textile Art.

Textile arts are those arts and crafts that use plant, animal, or synthetic fibres to construct practical or decorative objects.

Textiles have been a fundamental part of human life since the beginning of civilization, and the methods and materials used to make them have expanded enormously, while the functions of textiles have remained the same. The history of textile arts is also the history of international trade. Textile Art in my definition is an art piece created using fabric, thread and some instances illustration.

Thread Painting

Thread painting with the machine is my passion. I've completed 3 major pieces in this Genre. My aim is to achieve an image that looks photographically correct but I use thread and fabric to capture the image.

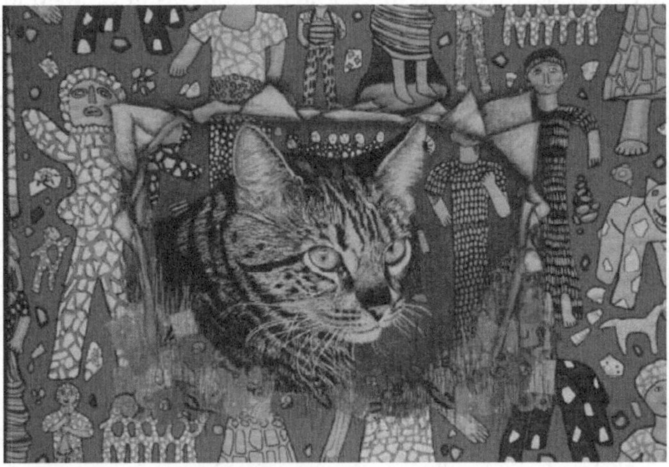

Figure: *The cat.*

Monet's Garden

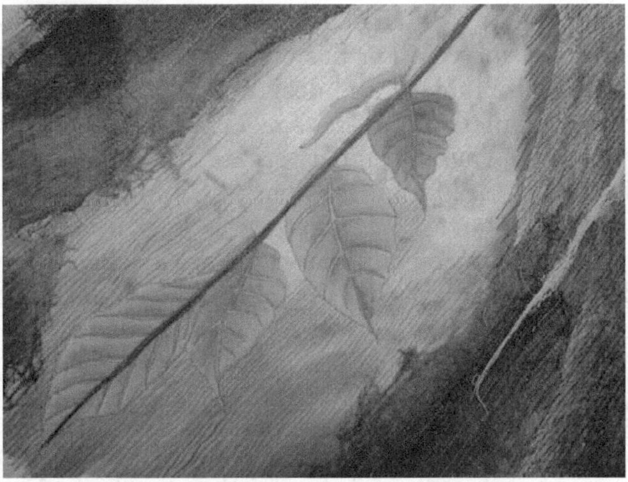

Figure: *The original photo was taken in Monet's garden.*

Fashion Design

Fashion design is the art of the application of design and aesthetics or natural beauty to clothing and accessories. Fashion design is influenced by cultural and social latitudes, and has varied over time and place. Fashion designers work in a number of ways in designing clothing and accessories; and, because of the time required to bring a garment onto the market, must at times anticipate changing consumer tastes.

Fashion designers attempt to design clothes which are functional as well as aesthetically pleasing. They must consider who is likely to wear a garment and the situations in which it will be worn. They have a wide range and combinations of materials to work with and a wide range of colours, patterns and styles to choose from. Though most clothing worn for everyday wear falls within a narrow range of conventional styles, unusual garments are usually sought for special occasions such as evening wear or party dresses.

Some clothes are made specifically for an individual, as in the case of haute couture or bespoke tailoring. Today, most clothing is designed for the mass market, especially casual and every-day wear.

Structure

Fashion designers can work in a number of many ways. Fashion designers may work full-time for one fashion as 'in-house designers' which owns the designs. They may work alone or as part of a team. Freelance designers work for themselves, selling their designs to fashion houses, directly to shops, or to clothing manufacturers. The garments bear the buyer's label. Some fashion designers set up their own labels, under which their designs are marketed. Some fashion designers are self-employed and design for individual clients. Other high-fashion designers cater to specialty stores or high-fashion department stores. These designers create original garments, as well as those that follow established fashion trends. Most fashion designers, however, work for apparel manufacturers, creating designs of men's, women's, and children's fashions for the mass market. Large designer brands which have a 'name' as their brand such as Abercrombie & Fitch, Justice, or Juicy are likely to be designed by a team of individual designers under the direction of a designer director.

Designing a Garment

Fashion designers work in different ways. Some sketch their ideas on paper, while others drape fabric on a dress form. When a designer is completely satisfied with the fit of the *toile* (or muslin), he or she will consult a professional pattern maker who then makes the finished, working version of the pattern out of card or via a computerized system. The pattern maker's job is very precise and painstaking. The fit of the finished garment depends on their accuracy. Finally, a sample garment is made up and tested on a model to make sure it is an operational outfit. Myriam Chalek, owner and founder of Creative Business House explains that most of the time fashion designers only have a fashion concept; the technicality and construction is not thought through during the visual conception and sketching process. Hence, the fashion designer needs to meet with a pattern maker and sample maker to figure out if the sketch on paper can be brought to life according its vision.

Fashion design is generally considered to have started in the 19th century with Charles Frederick Worth who was the first designer to have his label sewn into the garments that he created. Before the former draper set up his *maison couture* (fashion house) in Paris, clothing design and creation was handled by largely anonymous seamstresses, and high fashion descended from that worn at royal courts. Worth's success was such that he was able to dictate to his customers what they should wear, instead of following their lead as earlier dressmakers had done. The term *couturier* was in fact first created in order to describe him. While all articles of clothing from any time period are studied by academics as costume design, only clothing created after 1858 are considered as fashion design.

It was during this period that many design houses began to hire artists to sketch or paint designs for garments. The images were shown to clients, which was much cheaper than producing an actual sample garment in the workroom. If the client liked their design, they ordered it and the resulting garment made money for the house. Thus, the tradition of designers sketching out garment designs instead of presenting completed garments on models to customers began as an economy.

Types of Fashion

The garments produced by clothing manufacturers fall into three main categories, although these may be split up into additional, more specific categories

Haute Couture

Haute couture refers to the creation of exclusive custom-fitted clothing. *Haute couture* is made to order for a specific customer, and it is usually made from high-quality, expensive fabric and sewn with extreme attention to detail and finished by the most experienced and capable seamstresses, often using time-consuming, hand-executed techniques. *"Couture"* means dressmaking, sewing, or needlework and is also used as a common abbreviation of *haute couture* and refers to the same thing in spirit. *"Haute"* means elegant or high. An haute couture garment is made specifically for the wearer's measurements and body stance.

It originally referred to Englishman Charles Frederick Worth's work, produced in Paris in the mid-nineteenth century. In modern France, haute couture is a "protected name" that can be used only by firms that meet certain well-defined standards. However, the term is also used loosely to describe all high-fashion custom-fitted clothing, whether it is produced in Paris or in other fashion capitals such as London, Milan, New York or Tokyo.

The term can refer to:

- the fashion houses or fashion designers that create exclusive and often trend-setting fashions
- the fashions created

Legal Status

In France, the term *haute couture* is protected by law and is defined by the *Chambre de commerce et d'industrie de Paris* based in Paris, France. The *chambre syndicale de la haute couture* is defined as "the regulating commission that determines which fashion houses are eligible to be true haute couture houses". Their rules state that only "those companies mentioned on the list drawn up each year by a commission domiciled at the Ministry for Industry are entitled to avail themselves" of the label *haute couture*. The chambre also deals with piracy of style, foreign relations and coordination of the fashion collection timetables, and do some international advertising for the French fashion industry. The chambre also runs a Paris *couture* school to teach upcoming designers and technicians the *couture* trade. The school helps bring new designers to help the *couture* houses that are still present today. The criteria for *haute couture* were established in 1945 and updated in 1992.

To earn the right to call itself a couture house and to use the term *haute couture* in its advertising and any other way, members of the *Chambre syndicale de la haute couture* must follow these rules:

- Design made-to-order for private clients, with one or more fittings.

- Have a workshop (*atelier*) in Paris that employs at least fifteen people full-time.
- Must have twenty full-time technical people in at least one *atelier* (workshop).
- Each season (i.e., twice a year), present a collection to the Paris press, comprising at least thirty-five runs/exits with outfits for both daytime wear and evening wear.

However, the term *haute couture* may have been misused by ready-to-wear brands since the late 1980s, so that its true meaning may have become blurred with that of *prêt-à-porter* (the French term for *ready-to-wear* fashion) in the public perception. Every *haute couture* house also markets *prêt-à-porter* collections, which typically deliver a higher return on investment than their custom clothing. Falling revenues have forced a few *couture* houses to abandon their less profitable *couture* division and concentrate solely on the less prestigious *prêt-à-porter*. These houses are no longer considered *haute couture*.

Many top designer fashion houses, such as Chanel, use the word for some of their special collections. These collections are often not for sale or they are very difficult to purchase. Sometimes, "haute couture" is inappropriately used to label non-dressmaking activities, such as fine art, music and more.

Members of the Chambre Syndicale de la Haute Couture

For the Spring-Summer 2012 season the official list of members is:

Official Members: Adeline André—Gustavo Lins (fr)—Chanel—Christian Dior—Christophe Josse—Franck Sorbier—Givenchy—Jean Paul Gaultier—Maurizio Galante—Stéphane Rolland

Correspondent Members (Foreign): Elie Saab—Giorgio Armani— Giambattista Valli—Valentino—Versace

Guest Members: Alexandre Vauthier (fr)—Bouchra Jarrar (fr)—Iris Van Herpen—Julien Fournié—Maxime Simoens—Yiqing Yin (new in season SS2012)

Jewelry: Boucheron—Chanel Joaillerie—Chaumet—Dior Joaillerie—Van Cleef & Arpels

Accessories: Loulou de la Falaise—Massaro—On aura tout vu

Recent guest members have included the fashion houses of Boudicca, Cathy Pill, Richard René and Udo Edling, as well as Eymeric François, Gerald Watelet (fr), Nicolas Le Cauchois (fr) and Wuyong.

In the 2008/2009 Fall/Winter Haute Couture week, Emanuel Ungaro showed as an Official Member.

History

French leadership in European fashion may date from the 18th century this influence began when the art, architecture, music, and fashions of the French court at Versailles were imitated across Europe. Visitors to Paris brought back clothing that was then copied by local dressmakers. Stylish women also ordered fashion dolls dressed in the latest Parisian fashion to serve as models.

As railroads and steamships made European travel easier, it was increasingly common for wealthy women to travel to Paris to shop for clothing and accessories. French fitters and dressmakers were commonly thought to be the best in Europe, and real Parisian garments were considered better than local imitations.

The *couturier* Charles Frederick Worth (October 13, 1826–March 10, 1895), is widely considered the father of *haute couture* as it is known today. Although born in Bourne, Lincolnshire, England, Worth made his mark in the French fashion industry. Revolutionizing how dressmaking had been previously perceived, Worth made it so the dressmaker became the artist of garnishment: a fashion designer. While he created one-of-a-kind designs to please some of his titled or wealthy customers, he is best known for preparing a portfolio of designs that were shown on live models at the House of Worth. Clients selected one model, specified colours and fabrics, and had a duplicate garment tailor-made in Worth's workshop. Worth combined individual tailoring with a standardization more characteristic of the ready-to-wear clothing industry, which was also developing during this period.

Following in Worth's footsteps were Callot Soeurs, Patou, Poiret, Vionnet, Fortuny, Lanvin, Chanel, Mainbocher, Schiaparelli, Balenciaga, and Dior. Some of these fashion houses still exist today, under the leadership of modern designers.

In the 1960s, a group of young designers who had trained under men like Dior and Balenciaga left these established *couture* houses and opened their own establishments. The most successful of these young designers were Yves Saint Laurent, Pierre Cardin, André Courrèges, Ted Lapidus, and Emanuel Ungaro. Japanese native and Paris-based Hanae Mori was also successful in establishing her own line.

Lacroix is one of the fashion houses to have been started in the late 20th century. Other new houses have included Jean-Paul Gaultier and Thierry Mugler. Due to the high expenses of producing haute couture collections, Lacroix and Mugler have since ceased their haute couture activities.

For all these fashion houses, custom clothing is no longer the main source of income, often costing much more than it earns through direct sales; it only adds the aura of fashion to their ventures in ready-to-wear clothing and related luxury products such as shoes and perfumes, and licensing ventures that earn greater returns for the company.

Excessive commercialization and profit-making can be damaging, however. Cardin, for example, licensed with abandon in the 1980s and his name lost most of its fashionable cachet when anyone could buy Cardin luggage at a discount store. It is their ready-to-wear collections that are available to a wider audience, adding a splash of glamour and the feel of haute couture to more wardrobes..

The 1960s also featured a revolt against established fashion standards by mods, rockers, and hippies, as well as an increasing internationalization of the fashion scene. Jet travel had spawned a jet set that partied—and shopped—just as happily in New York as in Paris. Rich women no longer felt that a Paris dress was necessarily better than one sewn elsewhere. While Paris is still pre-eminent in the fashion world, it is no longer the sole arbiter of fashion.

Decline

The number of couture houses decreased considerably over the 20th century, from 106 in 1946 to a mere 18 in 2000. By 2004 there were only 9 high-ranking couture houses: Chanel, Versace, Valentino, Dior, Givenchy, Gaultier, Lacroix, Mori, Sirop, Scherrer, and Torrente. The listing has been in considerable flux in recent years.

Ready-to-wear (Pret-a-porter)

Ready-to-wear clothes are a cross between haute couture and mass market. They are not made for individual customers, but great care is taken in the choice and cut of the fabric. Clothes are made in small quantities to guarantee exclusivity, so they are rather expensive. Ready-to-wear collections are usually presented by fashion houses each season during a period known as Fashion Week. This takes place on a city-wide basis and occurs twice a year. The main seasons of Fashion Week include, spring/summer, fall/winter, resort, swim and bridal.

Mass Market

Currently the fashion industry relies more on mass market sales. The mass market caters for a wide range of customers, producing ready-to-wear garments using trends set by the famous names in fashion. They often wait around a season to make sure a style is going to catch on before producing their own versions of the original look. In order to save money and time, they use cheaper fabrics and simpler production techniques which can easily be done by machine. The end product can therefore be sold much more cheaply.

There is a type of design called "kutch" design originated from the German word "kitschig" meaning "ugly" or "not aesthetically pleasing." *Kitsch* can also refer to "wearing or displaying something that is therefore no longer in fashion." Often, high-waisted trousers, associated with the 1980s, are considered a "kitsch" fashion statement.

Income

Median annual wages for salaried fashion designers were $61,160 in May 2008. The middle 50 percent earned between $42,150 and $87,120. The lowest 10 percent earned less than $32,150, and the highest 10 percent earned more than $124,780. Median annual earnings were $52,860 (£28,340) in apparel, piece goods, and notions - the industry employing the largest numbers of fashion designers.

Fashion Education

There are a number of well known specialized art schools and design schools worldwide that offer degrees in fashion design and fashion design technology. Some colleges also offer Masters of Fashion courses. Though it is not a requirement to have a Masters level degree, it is recommended by those already working in the industry to study at this level.

The most notable design schools in the world include:

- India
  - Pearl Academy of Fashion
  - Apeejay Institute of Design
- Milan
  - Istituto Marangoni
  - Domus Academy
  - Politecnico of Milan
  - NABA - Nuova Accademia di Belle Arti Milano

    - Istituto Europeo di Design
- Italy
    - University Iuav of Venice
    - Polimoda
- London
    - Istituto Marangoni
    - London College of Fashion
    - Central Saint Martins College of Art and Design
    - University of Westminster
    - Kingston University
- England
    - University of Brighton
    - De Montfort University
    - Richmond University
- France
    - IFA Paris
- Scotland
    - The Glasgow School of Art
    - Edinburgh College of Art
- Ireland
    - Limerick School of Art and Design
    - National College of Art and Design
- Romania
    - Art and Design University of Cluj-Napoca
- Bangladesh
    - Shanto-Mariam University of Creative Technology, Dhaka
    - BGMEA Institute of Fashion & Technology, Dhaka
- Belgium
    - Royal Academy of Fine Arts (Antwerp)
- U.S.
    - Academy of Art University in San Francisco, California
    - Columbia College Chicago in Chicago, Illinois
    - Fashion Institute of Technology in New York City, New York

- o Fashion Institute of Design & Merchandising in Los Angeles, California
- o O'More College of Design in Franklin, Tennessee
- o Otis College of Art & Design in Los Angeles, California
- o Parsons The New School for Design in New York City, New York
- o Philadelphia University in Philadelphia, Pennsylvania
- o Pratt Institute in New York City, New York
- o Savannah College of Art and Design in Savannah, Georgia
- o School of the Art Institute of Chicago in Chicago, Illinois
- o Virginia Commonwealth University in Richmond, Virginia
- o Woodbury University in Burbank, California

Elsewhere in the world, the National Institute of Fashion Technology in India, Shih Chien University in Hong Kong, RMIT University in Melbourne, Fu Jen Catholic University in Taiwan and the Asian University chain, Raffles College of Design and Commerce, all have reputable fashion design courses.

There are many universities that offer fashion design throughout the United States, usually within the context of a general liberal arts degree.

The major concentration incorporating fashion design may have alternative names like Apparel and Textiles or Apparel and Textile Design, and may be housed in departments such as Art and Art History, or Family and Consumer Studies. Some schools, such as Parsons, offer a major in Fashion Management, combining fashion education with business courses.

The only Ivy League University having a Fashion Design undergraduate programme is Cornell University in Ithaca, New York, a programme offered by the department of Fibre Science & Apparel Design. Cornell also offers a PhD programme in apparel design.

An updated list of fashion design masters and PhD programmes can be found at ITAA.org.

The programmes are intended to address the needs of academia, industry, and research by considering apparel design as an applied science that embraces design, technology, physical sciences, the humanities, and social sciences in order to meet the human needs for clothing.

Areas of Fashion Design

Area	*Brief*	*Market*
Women's Day wear	Practical, comfortable, fashionable	Haute couture, ready-to wear, mass market
Women's Evening wear	Glamorous, sophisticated, suited for the occasion	Haute couture, ready-to-wear, mass market
Women's Lingerie	Glamorous, comfortable, washable	Haute couture, ready-to-wear, mass market
Men's Day wear	Casual, practical, comfortable	Tailoring, ready-to-wear, mass market
Men's Evening wear	Smart, elegant, formal, apt for the occasion	Tailoring, ready-to-wear, mass market
Kids' wear	Trendy or classy, practical, washable, functional	Ready-to-wear, mass market
Girls' Wear	Pretty, colorful, practical, washable, inexpensive	Ready-to-wear, mass market
Teenager Girl Wear	Colorful, comfortable, glamorous, pretty	Ready-to-wear, mass market
Jeans wear	Unisex, democratic, comfortable, practical, functional	Ready-to-wear, mass market
Sports wear	Comfortable, practical, well-ventilated, washable, functional	Ready-to-wear, mass market
Knitwear	Right weight and color for the séason	Ready-to-wear, mass market
Outerwear	Stylish, warm, right weight and color for the season	Ready-to-wear, mass market
Bridal wear	Sumptuous, glamorous, classic	Haute couture, ready-to-wear, mass market
Accessories	Striking, fashionable	Haute couture, ready to-wear, mass market
Performance wear		

World Fashion Industry

Fashion today is a global industry, and most major countries have a fashion industry. Some countries are major manufacturing centres, notably Indonesia, Malaysia, Philippines, China, Bangladesh, South Korea, Spain, Germany, Brazil and India. Six countries have established an international reputation in fashion: France, Italy, the United Kingdom, the United States, Japan and Belgium.

American Fashion Design

The majority of American fashion houses are based in New York City, with a high concentration centred in the Garment District neighbourhood. There are also a significant number in Los Angeles, where a substantial percentage of high fashion clothing manufactured in the United States is actually made. Burgeoning industries in Miami, Chicago, Dallas, and especially San Francisco have developed as well. A semi-annual event held every February and September, New York Fashion Week is one of four major fashion weeks held throughout the world.

American fashion design is dominated by a clean-cut, urban, casual style; reflecting the athletic, health-conscious lifestyles of urban city-dwellers. A designer who helped to set the trend in the United States for sport-influenced day wear throughout the 1940s and 50s was Claire McCardell. Many of her designs have been revived in recent decades. Famous American brands and designers include Vera Wang, Calvin Klein, Bob Mackie, Ralph Lauren, Carolina Herrera, Michael Kors, Marc Jacobs, Tom Ford, Tommy Hilfiger, Oleg Cassini, Perry Ellis, Kenneth Cole, Donna Karan, Liz Claiborne, and Nolan Miller.

British Fashion Design

London has long been the capital of the UK fashion industry and has a wide range of foreign designs which have integrated with modern British styles. Typical British design is smart but innovative yet recently has become more and more unconventional, fusing traditional styles with modern techniques. Vintage styles play an important role in the British fashion and styling industry. Stylists regularly 'mix and match' the old with the new, which gives British style that unique, bohemian aesthetic that many of the other fashion capitals try to imitate. Irish fashion (both design and styling) is also heavily influenced by fashion trends from Britain. Famous British brands and designers include Burberry, Alexander McQueen, Mulberry, Stella McCartney, Thomas Pink, Jimmy Choo, Alfred Dunhill, Fred Perry and Vivienne Westwood.

French Fashion Design

France is one of the leading countries in fashion industry, alongside USA, Italy, the UK, Spain, Germany, Japan, China and many others. Fashion has always been an important part of the country's cultural life and society, and Frenchs are well known for their attention of dressing-up well; *haute-couture*, the *"prêt-à-porter"* and many others, the classy impression, remains traditional in the French way of living.

French design became prominent during the 15th–20th centuries, when artistic development in France was at its peak.The fashion has been an important industry and cultural export of France since the seventeenth century, and modern "haute couture" originated in Paris in the 1860s.

Today, Paris, along with London, Milan, and New York City, is considered one of the world's fashion capitals, and the city is home or headquarters to many of the premier fashion houses, including, Céline, Chanel, Chloe, Dior, Givenchy, Jean Paul Gaultier, Hermès, Lanvin, Rochas, Vuitton and Yves Saint Laurent.

Cities such as Lyon, Marseille, Toulouse, Strasbourg, Bordeaux, Nice and many others, during the last centuries come in developed cosmopolitan cities, being economical centres with an a textil, technological and many important industries who start to produce luxury goods and rich fabrics. This cities have important and luxurious districts and avenues.

Manosque, La Gacilly and many other cities and towns are leaders in cosmetic and pharmaceutical industry, with important global premier beauty houses such as Lancôme, L'Occitane, Vichy and many others. Towns like Cannes, St. Tropez and elses are called towns of luxury receiving annually a lot of home and extranger international stars in media, potentates, billionaires, etc.

Most French fashion houses are in Paris, which is the capital of French fashion. Traditionally, French fashion is chic and stylish, defined by its sophistication, cut, and smart accessories. Although the Global Language Monitor placed it 3rd in the Media, after Milan and New York, French fashion is internationally acclaimed.

Italian Fashion Design

Milan is Italy's fashion capital. Most of the older Italian couturiers are in Rome. However, Milan and Florence are the Italian fashion capitals, and it is the exhibition venue for their collections. Italian fashion features casual elegance.

Swiss Fashion Design

Most of the Swiss fashion houses are in Zürich. The Swiss look is casual elegant and luxurious with a slight touch of quirkiness. Additionally, it has been greatly influenced by the dance club scene.

Japanese Fashion Design

Most Japanese fashion houses are in Tokyo. The Japanese look is loose and unstructured (often resulting from complicated cutting), colours tend to the sombre and subtle, and richly textured fabrics. Famous Japanese designers are Yohji Yamamoto, Kenzo, Issey Miyake (masterful drape and cut), and Comme des Garçons's Rei Kawakubo, who developed a new way of cutting (comparable to Madeleine Vionnet's innovation in the 1930s).

Belgian Fashion Design

In the late 80ties and early 90ties, Belgian fashion designers brought a new fashion image that mixed East and West, and brought a higly individualised, personal vision on fashion. Well known Belgian

Designers are Maison Martin Margiela, Ann Demeulemeester, Dries Van Noten, Dirk Bikkembergs, Dirk Van Saene, Walter Van Beirendonck, Raf Simons, Tim Van Steenbergen, Peter Piloto, A.F. Vandevorst, Bruno Pieters, Angelo Figus, Christian Wijnants and Bernhard Wilhelm.

Soviet Fashion Design

Fashion in the Soviet Union largely followed general trends of the Western world. However, the state's socialist ideology consistently moderated and influenced these trends. In addition, shortages of consumer goods meant that the general public did not have ready access to pre-made fashion.

The New Economic Policy (1920s)

The New Economic Policy's authorization of private business allowed Western fashion to enter the Soviet Union. However, Bolshevik ideology opposed Western fashion consumption as an intrinsically capitalist practice. Western fashion emphasized both economic status and gender differences under a system that sought to deemphasize both.

In the early 1920s, Party-sanctioned magazines like *Rabotnitsa* ("The Working Woman") and *Krest'yanka* ("The Peasant Woman") offered discourse on fashion. Covers displayed women in plain work clothes, yet the magazines often contained advertisements for private companies selling stylish attire. By 1927, however, the magazines' message was consistent: women should be judged on their capability for work, not their appearance. Fashion, as a beauty aid, was therefore bourgeois and detrimental to socialist society.

In its place, the state commissioned projects to engineer a new Soviet type of dress, which drew on traditional clothing, constructivist forms, and technological facility. Constructivists like Varvara Stepanova and Alexander Rodchenko agreed that fashion driven by the market was inherently harmful.

They employed the simple geometry of cubism to design clothing that was functional, easily mass-produced, and sometimes unisex.

Due to lack of adequate material and machinery, however, this *prozodezhda*, or "production clothing", did not appeal to the proletariat audience for which it was intended. Designs were only available to the most privileged members of the intelligentsia, who ultimately preferred Western fashion to the highly experimental *prozodezhda*.

Stalin Era (1930s-1950s)

During the Stalin era, anti-fashion sentiments dissipated. Party-sanctioned magazines now promoted fashion and beauty as necessary parts of a Soviet woman's life. Rabotnitsa included fashion advice in almost every issue and regularly reported on new fashion houses opening across the Soviet Union. *Krest'yanka* even organized travelling shows to bring fashion to the countryside. The promoted aesthetics were highly varied, ranging from urban polish to ornate decoration.

This new interest in fashion was connected to Joseph Stalin's assertion that "life has become better and more cheerful". Persistent images of plain women and quaint peasants were thought to propagate the capitalist view that socialism engenders poverty. Fashionable and beautiful clothes were a signal of culture and quality of life equal (or superior) to that under capitalism. Stakhanovites, as foremost examples of successful workers, were expected to adhere to particularly high standards of appearance. They were often photographed wearing fine clothing even as they went to the factory.

In reality, the touted fashions were beyond most citizens' means. Soviet industry was unable to produce fashionable clothing in significant quantity, and what did exist was not available for general sale. During World War II, the Soviet fashion industry went on hiatus. If the average Soviet citizen desired a particularly stylish item of clothing, they were usually forced to commission a private tailor. Day-to-day fashion was often self-produced, and magazines consistently advised women to take a do-it-yourself approach to their appearance.

Khrushchev Era (1950s-1960s)

The Khrushchev Thaw brought a greater representation of Western fashion to domestic media. Journalists were sent abroad to report on the latest international fashion trends. However, state-owned fashion institutions and magazines moderated these trends for Soviet audiences.

Fashion "crazes" were rejected in favour of classic, long-running styles. In addition, moderation and modesty were stressed. Coco Chanel's signature style, for example, was particularly admired as a symbol of timelessness and simple sophistication. An article in the New York Times from 1959 slammed Soviet fashions as unremarkable, "clumsy copies" of outdated Western forms. Availability of these styles, however, was on the rise. Shops like the newly reopened GUM department store now carried the new fashions, albeit at high prices.

The state's new approach towards fashion was carefully calculated. The promotion of exorbitant fashion that occurred in the Stalin era, and the contrast to actual availability, had led to public resentment. In the Khrushchev era, the state-owned clothing industry was still unable to produce mass amounts of fashionable clothing. However, simplified fashions, rejection of excess, and high prices gave the industry a measure of control over consumer demand. By the early 1960s, the middle class's standards of appearance had risen such that Moscow street fashion was nearly indistinguishable from that in a Western city.

At the same time, counterculture fashion movements grew among elite youths. The *stilyagi*, or "style hunters", originally based their look on media portrayals of Western (especially American) fashions. Men wore items such as Hawaiian shirts, sunglasses, narrow slacks, and pointed shoes, while female *stilyagi* wore miniskirts and maintained a childlike demeanor. These styles were labelled as "excessive", and Komsomol groups would sometimes raid *stilyagi* hideouts and cut off their hair and pant legs.

Brezhnev Era (1970s-1980s)

By the end of the 1960s, Soviet fashion institutions, like the centralized fashion bureau ODMO (All-Union House of Prototypes), were embracing increasingly novel Western trends. At the same time, there was still a need to establish distinctively Soviet fashions. "Space fashion," for example, fit directly into state ideology by glorifying a triumph of Soviet science.

Reality, however, differed from ODMO's designs. Soviet industry could not keep up with the demand for fashionable goods, and supply in USSR shops was worse than in other socialist countries. The public was also dissatisfied with the available items. For example, Soviet women so disliked promoted designs involving Russian ethnic prints that the style ultimately became more popular in the West than in the Soviet Union itself.

The middle class increasingly fetishized Western fashion, as it was visible but not easily obtainable. American-made blue jeans were an especially desirable item. Secondhand stores were one source of Western fashion, as visitors from the West could import goods and sell them for high profits. The retail chain Beriozka also sold some Western clothing, but only to the privileged few who could pay in hard currency or foreign exchange certificates. Foreign exchange certificates and Western clothing were also available on the black market.

Gorbachev Era (1980s)

Under perestroika, varied fashion became acceptable. In 1987, Gorbachev allowed a Russian edition of *Burda Fashion* magazine to be produced and distributed. The next year, *Zhurnal Mod* began a new run as the first "proper" fashion magazine in the Soviet Union. In content, it was virtually indistinguishable from a Western fashion magazine, although ODMO provided all the styles.

When the nineteenth party conference met in the summer of 1989, they passed a resolution to increase the production of consumer goods. Fashionable clothes were mentioned specifically in the proceedings. Despite advocates for fashion at the highest level of bureaucracy, real changes in production failed to take place. The Ministry of Light Industries set quotas for the creation of new products, but textile factories recycled older patterns and products instead. Meanwhile, relaxation of censorship under glasnost made the middle class even more aware of their Western counterparts. They felt that they deserved fashionable clothing as a status symbol, but still could not easily obtain it.

Fashion Design Terms

- A fashion designer conceives garment combinations of line, proportion, colour, and texture. While sewing and pattern-making skills are beneficial, they are not a pre-requisite of successful fashion design. Most fashion designers are formally trained or apprenticed.
- A technical designer works with the design team and the factories overseas to ensure correct garment construction, appropriate fabric choices and a good fit. The technical designer fits the garment samples on a fit model, and decides which fit and construction changes to make before mass-producing the garment.
- A pattern maker (or *pattern cutter*) drafts the shapes and sizes of a garment's pieces. This may be done manually with paper and measuring tools or by using a CAD computer software programme. Another method is to drape fabric directly onto a dress form. The resulting pattern pieces can be constructed to produce the intended design of the garment and required size. Formal training is usually required for working as a pattern marker.
- A tailor makes custom designed garments made to the client's measure; especially suits (coat and trousers, jacket and skirt,

et cetera). Tailors usually undergo an apprenticeship or other formal training.

- A textile designer designs fabric weaves and prints for clothes and furnishings. Most textile designers are formally trained as apprentices and in school.
- A stylist co-ordinates the clothes, jewelry, and accessories used in fashion photography and catwalk presentations. A stylist may also work with an individual client to design a coordinated wardrobe of garments. Many stylists are trained in fashion design, the history of fashion and historical costume, and have a high level of expertise in the current fashion market and future market trends. However, some simply have a strong aesthetic sense for pulling great looks together.
- A fashion buyer selects and buys the mix of clothing available in retail shops, department stores and chain stores. Most fashion buyers are trained in business and/or fashion studies.
- A seamstress sews ready-to-wear or mass-produced clothing by hand or with a sewing machine, either in a garment shop or as a sewing machine operator in a factory. She (or he) may not have the skills to make (design and cut) the garments, or to fit them on a model.
- A teacher of fashion design teaches the art and craft of fashion design in art or fashion school.
- A custom clothier makes custom-made garments to order, for a given customer.
- A dressmaker specializes in custom-made women's clothes: day, cocktail, and evening dresses, business clothes and suits, trousseaus, sports clothes, and lingerie.
- An illustrator draws and paints clothing designs for commercial use.
- A fashion forecaster predicts what colours, styles and shapes will be popular ("on-trend") before the garments are on sale in stores.
- A model wears and displays clothes at fashion shows and in photographs.
- A fit model aids the fashion designer by wearing and commenting on the fit of clothes during their design and pre-manufacture. Fit models need to be a particular size for this purpose.

- A fashion journalist writes fashion articles describing the garments presented or fashion trends, for magazines or newspapers.
- An alterations specialist (alterationist) adjusts the fit of completed garments, usually ready-to-wear, and sometimes re-styles them. NOTE: despite tailors altering garments to fit the client, not all alterationists are tailors.
- An Image Consultant, wardrobe consultant or fashion advisor recommends styles and colours that are flattering to the client.

Visual Arts

The visual arts are art forms that create works that are primarily visual in nature, such as ceramics, drawing, painting, sculpture, printmaking, design, crafts, photography, video, filmmaking and architecture. These definitions should not be taken too strictly as many artistic disciplines (performing arts, conceptual art, textile arts) involve aspects of the visual arts as well as arts of other types. Also included within the visual arts are the applied arts such as industrial design, graphic design, fashion design, interior design and decorative art.

The current usage of the term "visual arts" includes fine art as well as the applied, decorative arts and crafts, but this was not always the case. Before the Arts and Crafts Movement in Britain and elsewhere at the turn of the 20th century, the term 'artist' was often restricted to a person working in the fine arts (such as painting, sculpture, or printmaking) and not the handicraft, craft, or applied art media. The distinction was emphasized by artists of the Arts and Crafts Movement who valued vernacular art forms as much as high forms. Art schools made a distinction between the fine arts and the crafts maintaining that a craftsperson could not be considered a practitioner of the arts. The increasing tendency to privilege painting, and to a lesser degree sculpture, above other arts has been a feature of Western art as well as East Asian art. In both regions painting has been seen as relying to the highest degree on the imagination of the artist, and the furthest removed from manual labour - in Chinese painting the most highly valued styles were those of "scholar-painting", at least in theory practiced by gentleman amateurs. The Western hierarchy of genres reflected similar attitudes.

Education and Training

Training in the visual arts has generally been through variations of the apprentice and workshop system. In Europe the Renaissance movement to increase the prestige of the artist led to the academy system for training artists, and today most train in art schools at tertiary levels. Visual arts have now become an elective subject in most education systems.

Drawing

Drawing is a means of making an image, using any of a wide variety of tools and techniques.

It generally involves making marks on a surface by applying pressure from a tool, or moving a tool across a surface using dry media such as graphite pencils, pen and ink, inked brushes, wax colour pencils, crayons, charcoals, pastels, and markers.

Digital tools that simulate the effects of these are also used. The main techniques used in drawing are: line drawing, hatching, crosshatching, random hatching, scribbling, stippling, and blending. An artist who excels in drawing is referred to as a *draftsman* or *draughtsman.*

Drawing goes back at least 16,000 years to Paleolithic cave representations of animals such as those at Lascaux in France and Altamira in Spain. In ancient Egypt, ink drawings on papyrus, often depicting people, were used as models for painting or sculpture. Drawings on Greek vases, initially geometric, later developed to the human form with black-figure pottery during the 7th century BC.

With paper becoming common in Europe by the 15th century, drawing was adopted by masters such as Sandro Botticelli, Raphael, Michelangelo, and Leonardo da Vinci who sometimes treated drawing as an art in its own right rather than a preparatory stage for painting or sculpture.

Painting

Painting taken literally is the practice of applying pigment suspended in a carrier (or medium) and a binding agent (a glue) to a surface (support) such as paper, canvas or a wall.

However, when used in an artistic sense it means the use of this activity in combination with drawing, composition and, or, other aesthetic considerations in order to manifest the expressive and conceptual intention of the practitioner. Painting is also used to express spiritual motifs and ideas; sites of this kind of painting range from artwork depicting mythological figures on pottery to The Sistine Chapel to the human body itself.

Origins and Early History

Like drawing, painting has its documented origins in caves and on rock faces. The finest examples, believed by some to be 32,000 years old, are in the Chauvet and Lascaux caves in southern France. In shades of red, brown, yellow and black, the paintings on the walls and ceilings are of bison, cattle, horses and deer.

Paintings of human figures can be found in the tombs of ancient Egypt. In the great temple of Ramses II, Nefertari, his queen, is depicted being led by Isis. The Greeks contributed to painting but much of their work has been lost. One of the best remaining representations is the mosaic of the Battle of Issus at Pompeii, which was probably based on a Greek painting. Greek and Roman art contributed to Byzantine art in the 4th century BC, which initiated a tradition in icon painting.

The Renaissance

Apart from the illuminated manuscripts produced by monks during the Middle Ages, the next significant contribution to European art was from Italy's renaissance painters. From Giotto in the 13th century to Leonardo da Vinci and Raphael at the beginning of the 16th century, this was the richest period in Italian art as the *chiaroscuro* technique was used to create the illusion of 3-D space.

Painters in northern Europe too were influenced by the Italian school. Jan van Eyck from Belgium, Pieter Bruegel the Elder from the Netherlands and Hans Holbein the Younger from Germany are among the most successful painters of the times. They used the glazing technique with oils to achieve depth and luminosity.

Dutch Masters

The 17th century saw the emergence of the great Dutch masters such as the versatile Rembrandt who is especially remembered for his portraits and Bible scenes, and Vermeer who specialized in interior scenes of Dutch life.

Impressionism

Impressionism began in France in the 19th century with a loose association of artists including Claude Monet, Pierre-Auguste Renoir and Paul Cézanne who brought a new freely brushed style to painting, often choosing to paint realistic scenes of modern life outside rather than in the studio. They achieved intense colour vibration by using pure, unmixed colours and short brush strokes.

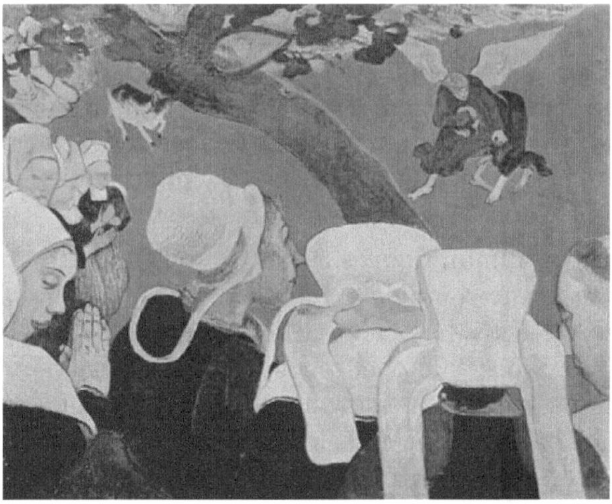

***Figure:** Paul Gauguin: The Vision After the Sermon (1888)*

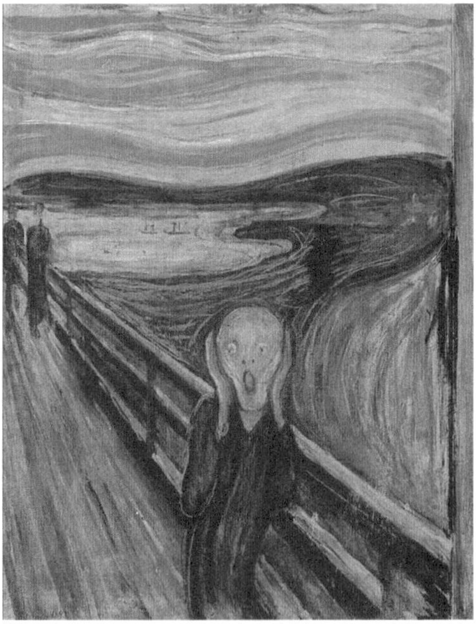

***Figure:** Edvard Munch: The Scream (1893)*

Post-impressionism

Towards the end of the 19th century, several young painters took impressionism a stage further, using geometric forms and unnatural colour to depict emotions while striving for deeper symbolism. Of particular note are Paul Gauguin, who was strongly influenced by Asian, African and Japanese art, Vincent van Gogh, a Dutchman who moved to France where he drew on the strong sunlight of the south, and Toulouse-Lautrec, remembered for his vivid paintings of night life in the Paris district of Montmartre.

Symbolism, Expressionism and Cubism

Edvard Munch, a Norwegian artist, developed his symbolistic approach at the end of the 19th century, inspired by the French impressionist Manet. *The Scream* (1893), his most famous work, is widely interpreted as representing the universal anxiety of modern man. Partly as a result of Munch's influence, the German expressionist movement originated in Germany at the beginning of the 20th century as artists such as Ernst Kirschner and Erich Heckel began to distort reality for an emotional effect. In parallel, the style known as cubism developed in France as artists focused on the volume and space of sharp structures within a composition. Pablo Picasso and Georges Braque were the leading proponents of the movement. Objects are broken up, analyzed, and re-assembled in an abstracted form. By the 1920s, the style had developed into surrealism with Dali and Magritte.

Printmaking

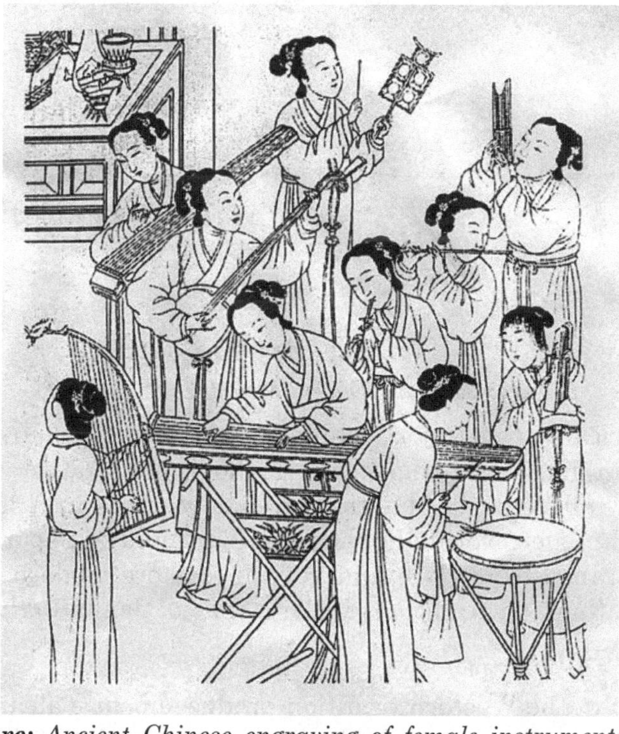

Figure: *Ancient Chinese engraving of female instrumentalists*

Printmaking is creating, for artistic purposes, an image on a matrix that is then transferred to a two-dimensional (flat) surface by means of ink (or another form of pigmentation). Except in the case of a monotype, the same matrix can be used to produce many examples of the print.

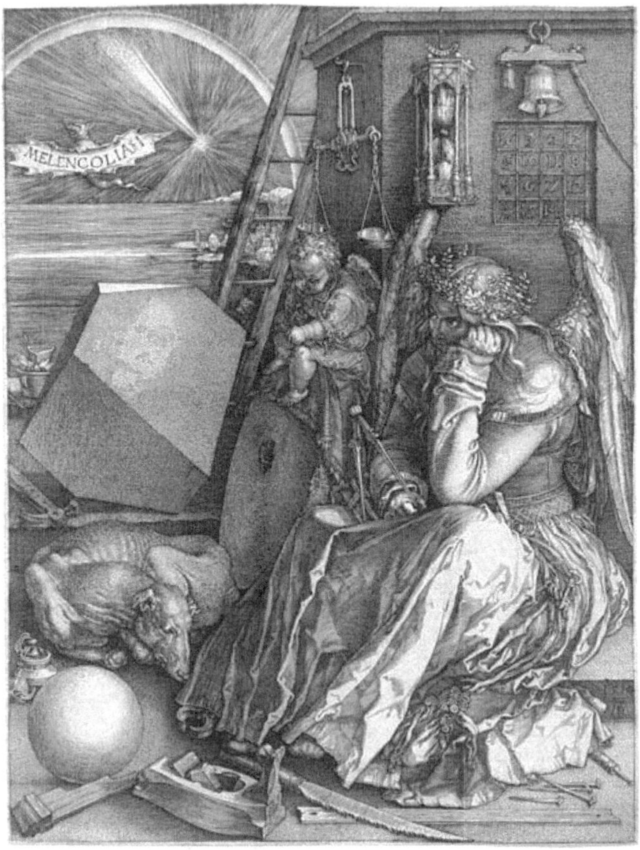

Figure: *Albrecht Dürer: Melancholia I (1541)*

Historically, the major techniques (also called media) involved are woodcut, line engraving, etching, lithography, and screenprinting (serigraphy, silkscreening) but there are many others, including modern digital techniques. Normally, the print is printed on paper, but other mediums range from cloth and vellum to more modern materials. Major printmaking traditions include that of Japan (*ukiyo-e*).

European History

Prints in the Western tradition produced before about 1830 are known as old master prints. In Europe, from around 1400 AD woodcut, was used for master prints on paper by using printing techniques developed in the Byzantine and Islamic worlds. Michael Wolgemut improved German woodcut from about 1475, and Erhard Reuwich, a Dutchman, was the first to use cross-hatching. At the end of the century Albrecht Dürer brought the Western woodcut to a level that has never been surpassed, increasing the status of the single-leaf woodcut.

Chinese Origin and Practice

In China, the art of printmaking developed some 1,100 years ago as illustrations alongside text cut in woodblocks for printing on paper. Initially images were mainly religious but in the Song Dynasty, artists began to cut landscapes. During the Ming (1368–1644) and Qing (1616–1911) dynasties, the technique was perfected for both religious and artistic engravings.

Development In Japan 1603-1867

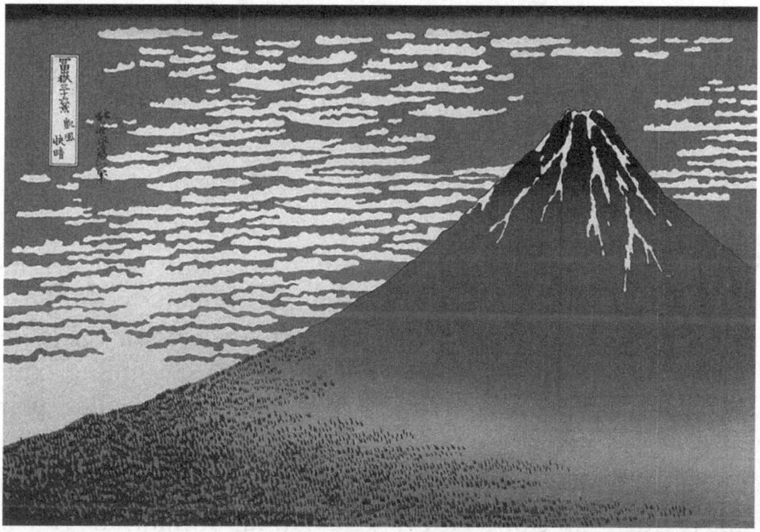

Figure: *Hokusai: "Red Fuji southern wind clear morning" from Thirty-six Views of Mount Fuji*

Woodblock printing in Japan (Japanese: (gHr;u, moku hanga) is a technique best known for its use in the ukiyo-e artistic genre; however, it was also used very widely for printing books in the same period. Woodblock printing had been used in China for centuries to print books, long before the advent of movable type, but was only widely adopted in Japan surprisingly late, during the Edo period (1603-1867). Although similar to woodcut in western printmaking in some regards, moku hanga differs greatly in that water-based inks are used (as opposed to western woodcut, which uses oil-based inks), allowing for a wide range of vivid colour, glazes and colour transparency.

Computer Art

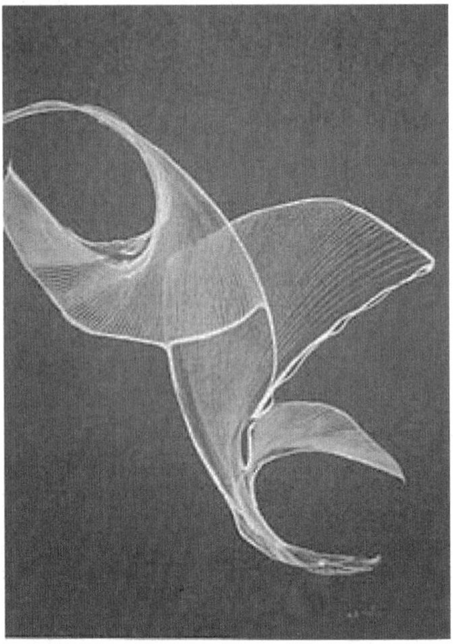

Figure: *Picture produced by Drawing Machine 2*

Visual artists are no longer limited to traditional art media. Computers have been used as an ever more common tool in the visual arts since the 1960s. Uses include the capturing or creating of images and forms, the editing of those images and forms (including exploring multiple compositions) and the final rendering and/or printing (including 3D printing).

Computer art is any in which computers played a role in production or display. Such art can be an image, sound, animation, video, CD-ROM, DVD, video game, website, algorithm, performance or gallery installation. Many traditional disciplines are now integrating digital technologies and, as a result, the lines between traditional works of art and new media works created using computers have been blurred. For instance, an artist may combine traditional painting with algorithmic art and other digital techniques. As a result, defining computer art by its end product can be difficult. Nevertheless, this type of art is beginning to appear in art museum exhibits, though it has yet to prove its legitimacy as a form unto itself and this technology is widely seen in contemporary art more as a tool rather than a form as with painting.

Computer usage has blurred the distinctions between illustrators, photographers, photo editors, 3-D modelers, and handicraft artists. Sophisticated rendering and editing software has led to multi-skilled image developers. Photographers may become digital artists. Illustrators may become animators. Handicraft may be computer-aided or use computer-generated imagery as a template. Computer clip art usage has also made the clear distinction between visual arts and page layout less obvious due to the easy access and editing of clip art in the process of paginating a document, especially to the unskilled observer.

Textile Arts of India

Man since an ancient time has always invested in textiles to protect his body from the weather and wild animals. As time went by, the idea of wearing clothes also changed. From protecting the body, it also became a way of decorating the body.

The record of ancient and medieval Indian textiles exists mostly in literature and sculpture. There is archaeological evidence of a cotton textile industry at Mohenjo-Daro in the Indus Valley around 3000 B.C., and a few fragments survive from much later periods. Most of the extant textiles are dated after the seventeenth century, because the monsoon climate has been very destructive to early specimens. The Greeks with Alexander the Great wrote of the fine flowered muslins and robes embroidered in gold they had seen in India. They may also have seen the cotton fibre that grew on trees.

A handbook of administration, the *Arthasastra,* tentatively dated to the third century B.C.,dealt with methods for distributing materials to spinners and weavers whether the workers were guild members or worked privately at home. At that time few occupations were open to women. Indeed, women who elected not to marry were not allowed to hold jobs. However, weaving was permitted to widows and retired prostitutes. The *Arthasastra* gave the penalties for fraudulent practices and listed the taxes to be paid by weavers. Among the textiles mentioned were white bark cloth from Bengal, linen from Banaras, cottons from south India, and several kinds of blankets, the best described as being slippery and soft.

In ancient and medieval India the textile industries were politically controlled, and if a ruler was favourably disposed towards the arts, weaving prospered. Differentiation was made between the rural textiles woven for the masses and those made in state workshops for royalty and the well-to-do in other countries (Plate 48). The best workmanship was found in the ritual hangings for temples, and even in modern times it has been considered preferable to destroy worn ones rather than allow them to fall into foreign hands.

Few good commentaries survive from the early medieval period (900- - 1200 A.D.) when terms were used inconsistently. Fabric names apparently repre-sented the places where they were woven, and details about weaving techniques were scanty.

The Muslim period in India extended from around 1200 A.D. to 1760 when the British took over. A succession of sultans controlled most of India until Genghis Khan attacked early in the thirteenth century and Tammerlane invaded in the late fourteenth. Marco Polo left detailed accounts of the people and industries of the coastal regions of India in the late thirteenth century.

He mentioned seeing on the Coromandel Coast the finest and most beautiful cloth in all the world-buckrams like the tissues of spider webs, and he observed dyeing with indigo in the great tex-tile centre of Cambay and spinning of cotton in Gujarat. Under the Sultan of Delhi (1325-1351) price controls for food, cloth, and other commodities were initiated to help fight inflation. A permit was required to buy silks, satins, and brocades, and only the well-to-do were allowed to have them. The sultan employed four thousand silk weavers who made robes of honour, hangings, and gifts of gold brocade for foreign dignitaries.

Babur, a descendant of Genghis Khan, founded a new and important dynasty, the Mogul, in *1526.* A series of great rulers-the greatest Akbar who ruled for the second half of the sixteenth century-governed a glorious empire where the textile arts flourished until the late seventeenth century. Some of the best accounts of Indian textiles were written by European ambassadors to the Mogul courts. Fabulous horse and elephant trappings, as well as the apparel, pillows, and wall hangings, were remarked upon. A king always wore a garment but once. There were marvellous gold brocades called *kimhabs,* or *kincobs,* from Banaras. Writers proclaimed on the sheerness of Dacca muslins, called *evening dew, running water,* or *sweet-like-sherbert.* Seventy-three yards, a yard wide, weighed only one pound. By comparison, the finest Swiss cottons ever made were at best sixteen or seventeen yards to the pound.

European settlements appealed in India in the latter part of the Mogul period. Motivated by the desire to break the spice trade monopoly held by Venice and the Arabs, Vasco da Gama found the sea route to India by sailing around Africa in *1498,* and by *1510* the Portuguese had jurisdiction in Goa on the west coast of India. For a short time they controlled the Asian trade by taking over the port of Malacca (near Singapore), where they met trading junks from China. The Portuguese carried *pintados* (painted cottons) east from India to trade for spices.

Indian textiles were more important to the Dutch and the English than to the Portuguese. The Dutch East India Company was chartered in *1597,* the East India Company in *1600.* Their ships went first to India with bullion to exchange for the cotton textiles that could be bartered for spices in the Malay Archipelago. Eventually, the Dutch gained a monopoly in Indonesia, with trade centred in Java, and the English withdrew to India to establish trading stations known as "factories."

One of the intentions of the East India Company was to sell English woolens in Asia, but broadcloth was never more than a novelty in India. By *1649* the British were sending chintz and cheap cotton calico to England. Much was for reexport to America, the Near East, West Africa, and the slave plantations in the West Indies. A four-cornered trade developed. The East India Company shipped calicos to London where they were sold to the Royal Africa Company. The latter shipped them in turn to West Africa *as guinea-cloth* to be bar-tered for people. These slaves, and any remaining cloth, were shipped to the West Indies and exchanged for sugar, cotton, and tobacco-all cargoes bound back for England.

Contemporary Indian Textiles

Where tradition, not fashion, rules, concentration on the aesthetic can prevail instead of mere change. Indian textile heritage has been preserved by the woman's sari, which often exhibits fine weaving, delicate textures, beautiful colours, and rich patterns (Plate *49).* A formal sari might be of silk (or a cotton called *jamdani),* brocaded in floral patterns formed with many tiny bobbins, each holding a different colour. An everyday sari could be a simple striped or checked cotton or a solid made iridescent by having the warp of one colour, the weft of another. Sometimes saris are exquisitely block printed with gold or silver floral sprays or show allover spot patterns of tie-dye. Ikat is used for traditional diamond or trellis patterns.

Embroidery is important in India and there are many regional styles. Sometimes it is the work of village women; other times it is done by male professionals. There is a vast difference between the work that reaches western markets and the fine embroidery, important for its symbolism, that was made for the courts and temples of old India.

Phulkari (flower work) is a specialty of Punjab embroiderers. Bright-coloured floss silk is worked on cotton with a darning stitch (Plate 50). Phulkari is sometimes combined with the mirror work that originated when blue and green beetle backs were sewn onto wedding garments of the hill tribes of southern India. Orthodox Hindus disapproved the practice and so pieces of mica were substituted. Eventually the mica was replaced by bits of glass or mirrors.

A type of chain stitch is worked with a hook in Gujarat to make birds, animals, humans, and flowers in bold colours. In the valley of the Ganges plant designs are worked in white on soft fabrics using satin stitch, and near Bombay running stitches make delightful animal figures on loosely woven cotton. The cross stitch is popular all across India. Carpets are still made in India, as they have been for hundreds of years. Most are made with knotted wool pile on a cotton back. Patterns are strongly Persian but show a preference for naturalistic plants and animals.

The Shawls of Kashmir

In the nineteenth century a Kashmir shawl was one of the rarest and most beau-tiful gifts that could be offered to any woman (Plate 51). The romantic appeal was enhanced by descriptions of the Vale of Kashmir, known as one of the dream spots of the earth. Isolated by the Himalayas, too remote to be of much interest to the conquerors who passed back and forth across Asia, Kashmir served for hundreds of years as a resort for India's nobility.

Woolen blankets and shawls were woven and exported to the Roman Empire, but the Kashmir industry became famous after Zain-ul'Abidin *(1420-1470 A.D.)* brought in Turkestanni and Persian weavers. By the sixteenth century shawls were being hoarded as forms of wealth, and in the late seventeenth Western visitors reported seeing men wearing large decorative scarves across their shoulders. Towards the end of the eighteenth century European and New England ladies discovered "India" shawls; the soft fabric draped beautifully, the colours shimmered, and the pine patterns spoke of the mysterious East. Discerning ambassadors and sea captains carried them home, and a fashion took hold. Napoleon's officers in Egypt sent them to their French ladies around the turn of the century. Josephine owned three or four hundred Kashmirs.

Fibres and Yarns

The fibre, called *cashmere* (after the old spelling of Kashmir) or *pashmina* (de-rived from the Persian *pashm),* was combed from the undercoat of the Tibetan or Central Asian goat. The goats were not raised in Kashmir; the fibre was imported from nearby Tibet. Other fibre, molted from wild sheep and goats of the high Himalayas, was specially prized for so-called "ring shawls," so fine they could be drawn through finger rings. Women picked and sorted the pashmina, then spun it into 2,500 yard lengths on crude charkhas. The yarn went to the dyers who used some 300 tints in Mogul times, but only about sixty by the beginning of the nineteenth century, when indigo, logwood, carthemus, saffron, and cochineal were among the dyes identified by Western visitors. The delicate colours were made fast by the special waters of Dal Lake.

Making the Shawls

By the beginning of the nineteenth century, shawl weaving involved several specialists. The warp maker cut the yarns into three and one-half-yard lengths and plied them. Then the warp dresser sized the yarns with rice water and the warp threader prepared the loom. The pattern designer made the design in black and I white, and he and the colourist dictated the colours and numbers of threads to be used to a scribe who wrote it down in a kind of shorthand. The weavers wound their weft yarns on many bobbins, small pieces of wood with ends charred so as not to damage the weaving.

Tilikar (or *kani)* shawls were made in interlocking twill tapestry, a technique that probably originated in central or western Asia. Each shawl was woven very slowly, face down on a single horizontal loom by one, two, or three weavers. As demand grew, several looms and weavers were employed to make one shawl, a patchwork, easily identified because it would not lie flat (Plate 51).

After weaving, the shawl was turned over to the cleaner who cut loose threads, and then it went to the mender, the *rafugar,* who touched up with needlework. The shawl was registered and a tax assessed. Then it was washed, stretched, and packed for export. Prices could be as high as several thousand dollars if the shawl werelarge and intricately woven. The brokers and the tax collectors, not the weavers, made the profits; the weaver was often the first to die in a famine.

In 1803, an enterprising Armenian representing a Turkish firm in Constantinople introduced the *amli* (embroidered) shawl. One could be produced at a third the cost of a kani and at first they were not taxed. The early ones were exquisitely worked, but by the late nineteenth century embroidery degenerated to cheap and coarse chain stitch designs on rough cloth.

Shawl Design

There are several stories giving the origin of the cone design associated with Kashmir shawls (Plate 51). It is at least as old as sixth century Egypt and Sassanian Persia, where it appeared as a curled leaf motif, and it is very common today. One theory is that it derived from the cone of the date palm and symbolized fertility and renewal of life in ancient Chaldea. Another theory dates the motif to the Mogul Emperor Babur who wore in his turban a jeweled ornament, almond shaped with an aigrette of feathers.

A weaver purportedly copied it and started a fad. The motif has been said to represent the picturesque windings of the Jhelum River, the side impression of a fist (fist palm), a little onion (in Venice), the Persian sacred flame, the wind-blown cypress, a mango (Hindu Kairy), a butha (or buta, a general Indian name for flower), and a cone or a pine. In the West it is called a paisley.

Kashmir shawl designs were mostly floral until the middle of the eighteenth century, when they began to take on the characteristic cone arrangements. Cones were rather short and fat until the 1830s, when they became elongated with slender tips. By the 1850s they were almost abstract scrolls. Many shawl designs originated in Europe, and at one time Frenchmen went to Kashmir with the purpose of improving the patterns.

Famine struck Kashmir periodically, but never devastated the weavers as completely as in the 1870s when the Franco-Prussian War closed the French market and the fashion for Kashmir shawls died.

Fulkari

The traditional Punjabi embroidery art is phulkari. The word "phulkari" means "growing flowers". This embroidery form includes only floral motifs in bright colours. There is sanctity to the art form as the canopy over Guru Granth Sahib, the religious book of the Sikhs is of phulkari.

Phulkari with floral patterns is called Bagh that means garden. It is basically made on odhanies and dupattas. It is considered auspecious for the bride and for the new born. Phulkari is also used in wall hangings, sofa throws and other soft furnishings.

Origin of phulkari cannot exactly be traced. Punjabi embroidery though goes nack to 2000 years back to the vedic ages. Phulkari is mentioned in the famous tale of Heer-Ranjha by the poet Waris Shah. Its form and popularity goes back to 15th century, during Maharaja Ranjit Singh's Reign. It was included in the bridal trousseau. There is a different phulkari for every occasion.

Motifs Use In: Motifs used in fauna and flora like sunflowers, peacock, red chilies, ace of diamonds etc. Bright colours were always preferred and among these, golden yellow, red, crimson, orange, green, blue, pink etc, were the popular ones.

Stitches Used Are: For the embroidery, only a single strand was used at a time, each part worked in one colour. Horizontal, vertical or diagonal stitches are used. This resulted in giving an illusion of more than one shade when light fell on it and when it was viewed from different angles. Phulkari is traditionally done on a handspun khadi cloth by using simple darning stitches using the un spun silk floss yarn called 'pat'.

Types Of Phulkari-

1) Chope- is red coloured cloth with embroidered borders usually presented to the bride by her grandmother during a ceremony before the wedding.
2) Vari-da-bagh (bagh of the trousseau)- is also on a red cloth with golden yellow embroidery symbolizing happiness and fertility. The entire cloth is covered patterns smaller ones within the border and intricately worked in different colours.
3) Ghunghat bagh or sari-pallau- (covering for the head) has a small border on all four sides. In the centre of each side, which covers the head, a large triangular motif is worked.
4) Bawan bagh- (fifty-two in Punjabi) has as many geometrical patterns.
5) Darshan dwar- (the gate offering a view of the deity) is usually for presentation in temples or to adorn the walls of the home when the Granth Sahib (holy book of the Sikhs) is brought to a house. The theme is a decorative gate.

6) Suber- is a phulkari worn by a bride during marriage rites. It comprises five motifs, one in the centre and one each in the four corners.
7) Chamba- is a hybrid phulkari having a series of wavy creepers, stylized leaves and flowers.

The work Phulkari means making flowers on a fabric. Phulkari is an ancient embroidery technique originated in the ancient India that is now Pakistan. This art is also practiced on a large scale in the state of Punjab. Phulkari or flower working was also the synonym for embroidery in the ancient period. Traditional workers excelled this art and made beautiful flower carvings on the piece of fabric. It is a very complicated task and only skilled workers can do it efficiently. In the initial stages, phulkari covered all the aspects of traditional embroidery but later on, the art was limited to scarves and shawls. There is also special type of phulkari art that is done on the garment fabric that people wear on special occasions.

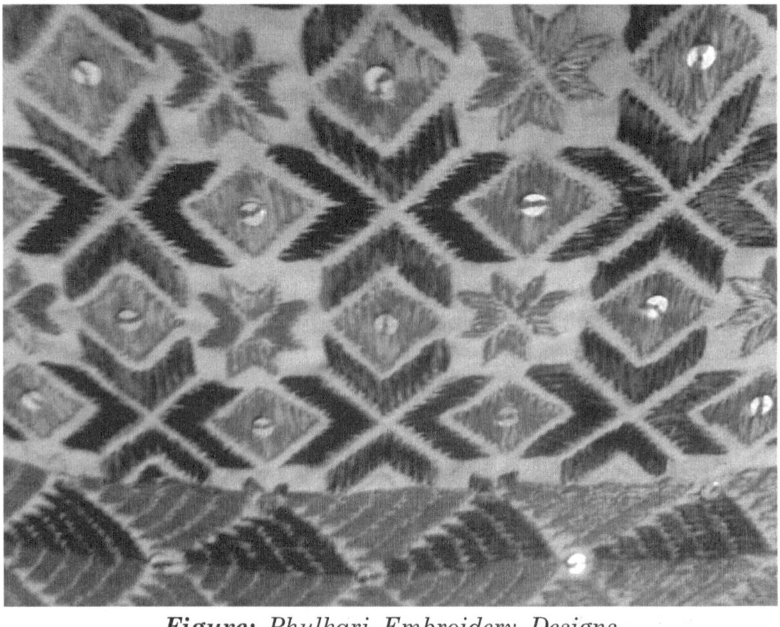

Figure: *Phulkari Embroidery Designs*

This art is also known as garden or baghs as people call it in the modern times. The recent times have changed the perception of people towards this artwork. If you are a true admirer of ancient art, then you must surely try out the garments made with phulkari on them. This art is gaining popularity among the young people as they find it very appealing and comfortable. One of the best things about the clothes made with this art is that they can fuse with the entire modern garment and will not spoil your look. So next time, if you want to try out something different, get one of the phulkari kurta and kurtis. It will give you a very new look and will combine easily with your jeans or other western apparels.

Different Uses of Phulkari: Traditional workers use this art extensively on all types of clothing material. So you have the option to wear it or put it on your cushions in the drawing room. Cushion covers made with phulkari give a different look and appeal to the room and if you have matching bed sheets, then it will add more beauty to your home. Phulkari product range is vast and meant for all age groups. As a youngster, you will find this art very captivating as it draws your attention instantly. A beautiful handmade carving of flowers on the fabric looks tremendously beautiful. You can choose from a wide variety of products ranging from suits and lehangas to bed sheets and cushions. Young girls love to wear suits that have phulkari done on them. They are not only very light but also give you a special look. You will also love to get a matching phulkari dupatta if you go for the suits. The garments made with phulkari are generally available in plain shades however, the shades can be dark or light depending on the art done on it.

Saari is another piece of clothing that is very popular amongst the women. They wear it on special occasions as the work done on it reflects the true essence of this art. The sari made with phulkari is generally heavy and comes in sparkling shades. The art of phulkari is strictly done on plain clothing because it reflects the art more beautifully than the printed clothing. Phulkari suits for young girls come in all shapes and sizes so you can choose from a wide variety of colours and sizes. Some suits have a good fitting while other phulkari suits are loose and more comfortable. But the most important and striking features of these phulkari suits is the art done on them. You will fall in love with them immediately. The art has now gained popularity outside India and the tourists who come to visit the country specially ask for the clothes made with phulkari.

One will find it very amusing that this art was very costly in the ancient times and it took months for a worker to make a single piece of cloth. But today, with the help of latest machines and modernized techniques, the work is done in minutes and this is the reason why the phulkari clothing has become so economical. You will find your money worth it if you spend it on buying a garment made with phulkari. You not only have the option to wear it but you can use it to decorate your house. One can easily find a large number of clothing products made with this art. Cushions, bed sheets, sofa covers, curtains and tablecloths are some of the products that have phulkari art on them. You can go for one or more of these products and decorate your house with it. It will give your house a different look. If you love traditional art, then you will surely find phulkari to be amazing. The recent times have seen a steep increase in the demand of the phulkari products.

Threads

Embroidery work was invariably made on a plain cotton fabric (khaddar) whose thread was manually spinned, loomed and dyed with natural pigments. Its quality was evaluated according to the fineness and regularity of its surface.

Khaddar could be of four colours, white being given to mature women or widows while red was associated with youth and was by far the most widespread tone. It is noteworthy that the most ancient fragments of red dyed (using madder) cotton fabric were found in Punjab and would date back to Harappa Civilization (Age of Bronze).

Black and blue colours were kept for everyday worn shawls as they prevented from revealing stains and dirt.

The complete khaddar was always made of two or three stripes which were approximately 50cm wide. Depending on the region, these stripes were sewed before or after the embroidery work. It seems that, in West Punjab (Pakistan), the joining was done afterwards. This explains the slightly distorted designs that can be found at times on some pieces of this origin.

It is important to notice that Punjab, known for its cotton cultivations, was a very appropriate area for a local production of khaddar. The embroidery was made on the wrong side of the khaddar with a thread of floss silk called pat.

Most of the time brought from Afghanistan, Bengal or China by itinerant dealers who were selling it by weight, this silk was quite costly and, for this reason, it has pushed the punjabi women to embellish the fabric on its visible side only in order to save as much silk as possible.

Rural life was regulated by its agriculture and, periodically, men were going the markets of big cities to sell their crops. It is only when they had earned enough money to buy the essential products for their family that they were allowing themselves to get, for a high price, few skeins of pat that they would offer to their wives.

Pat was red-coloured to symbolize passion, white for purity, golden or yellow for desire and abundance, green for nature and fertility, blue for serenity, purple for a symbiosis between red's energy and blue's calm, orange for a mix of desire and divine energy. However, even if symbolism was playing an important role, these colourful harmonies were also composed according to the embroiderer's taste.

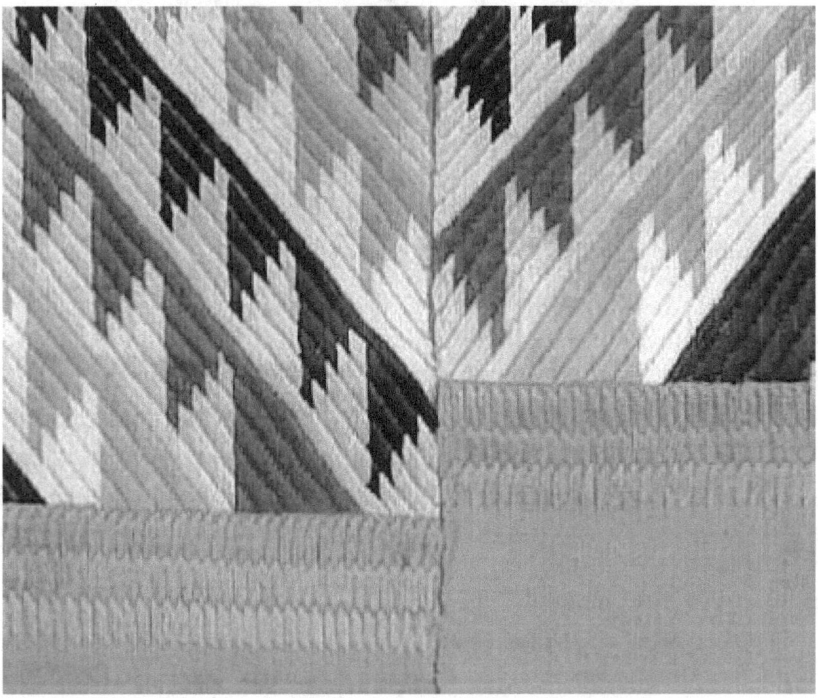

Figure: *Panchranga (West Punjab) The kaddhar was stitched after the embroidery work was achieved*

Embroidery

A phulkari was at times made by one woman and at times by several ones who could even work simultaneously on different parts or stripes of khaddar.

As written before, these pieces were usually made by the family of the bride. However, as in the rich families a dowry could include several dozens of phulkari, some professional embroiderers were occasionally employed. The choice of patterns was partly driven by the social class of the bride.

For instance, some flowers designs in cluster stitch were only worn by the low class families while the high class would prefer flowers made with darning stitch.

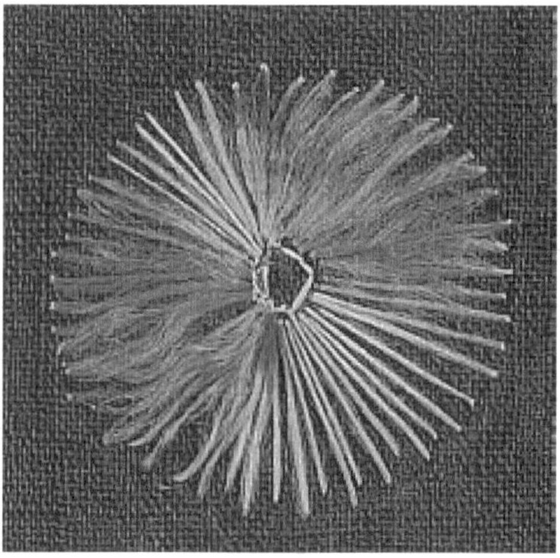

Figure: *A low class flower Embroidered in "cluster stitch"*

Most of the time, patterns to be embroidered were not drawn on the fabric beforehand, the embroiderer had to count each thread of the khaddar with meticulous care to build her designs.

It is important to realise that a shift of one thread in the counting would have a visible impact on the final result.

As it was easier to count the threads of a light coloured khaddar than of a dark one, it happened sometimes that the fabric was dyed only after the embroidery work was achieved, thanks to certain preparations that would colour cotton but not silk.

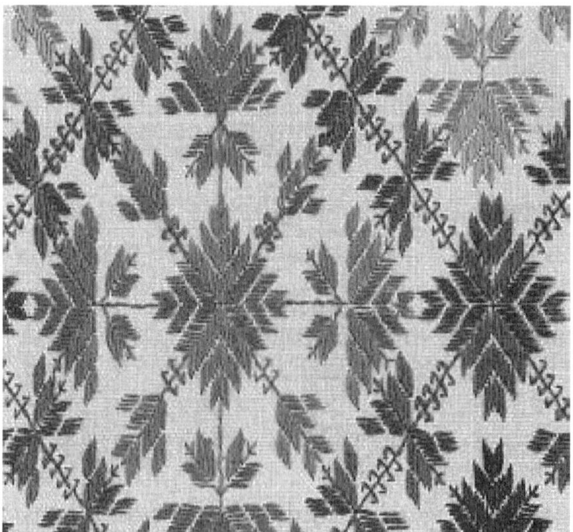

Figure: *High class flowers Embroidered in "darning stitch*

If the fact of using floss silk was providing beauty to these pieces, it was also a heavy complication added to the artists' task as this brittle and inhomogeneous material was not easy to lead through the khaddar without creating clusters and knots.

As in most of the oriental countries, the embroidery work was always done pointing the needle's tip to the opposite of the embroiderer. This gesture, as well as the energy that was injected into the work, had to come from the heart and go towards others.

Darning stitch was the most commonly used technique to make phulkari and the quality of a piece could be measured according to the width of this stitch. The narrowest was the stitch, the finest was the piece.

In order to create an unusual design or to border the khaddar, some other stitches like the herringbone stitch, running stitch, Holbein stitch or button hole stitch were occasionally used.

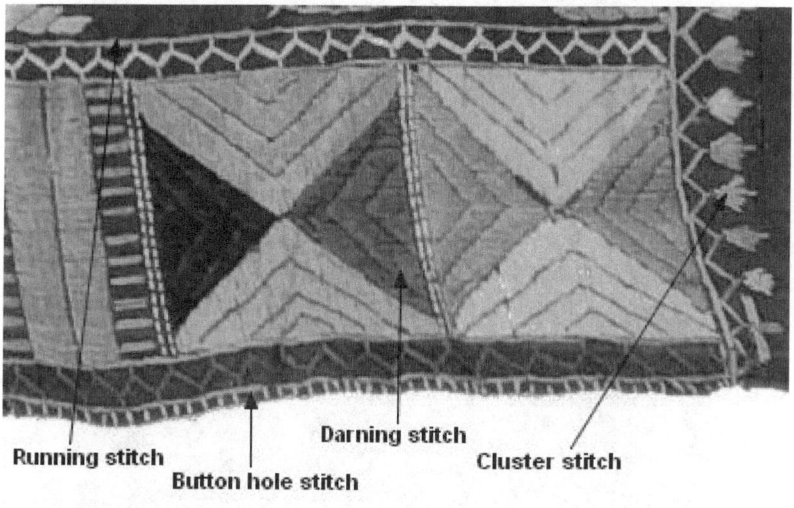

Figure: *Several kind of stitches used in phulkari embroidery*

Bagh, " the Garden "

When the embroidery work was covering the whole surface of the khaddar the phulkari was called a bagh ("garden").

The making of a bagh was requiring so much talent and patience (sometimes more than a year) that it was kept for very special occasions.

Furthermore, the quantity of pat needed to achieve such a piece was implying big expenses and thus was a way for families to display their wealth.

From a historical point of view, it seems that bagh only appeared after the time people became passionate for phulkari in the second half of the 19th century.

Bagh could be considered as a technical culmination in the art of phulkari fabrication.

Pat's most commonly used colours in the making of bagh were gold and silvery-white, these tones being a reminiscence of Punjab's wild flowers and cereal fields but also of the jewels women were wearing under their bagh.

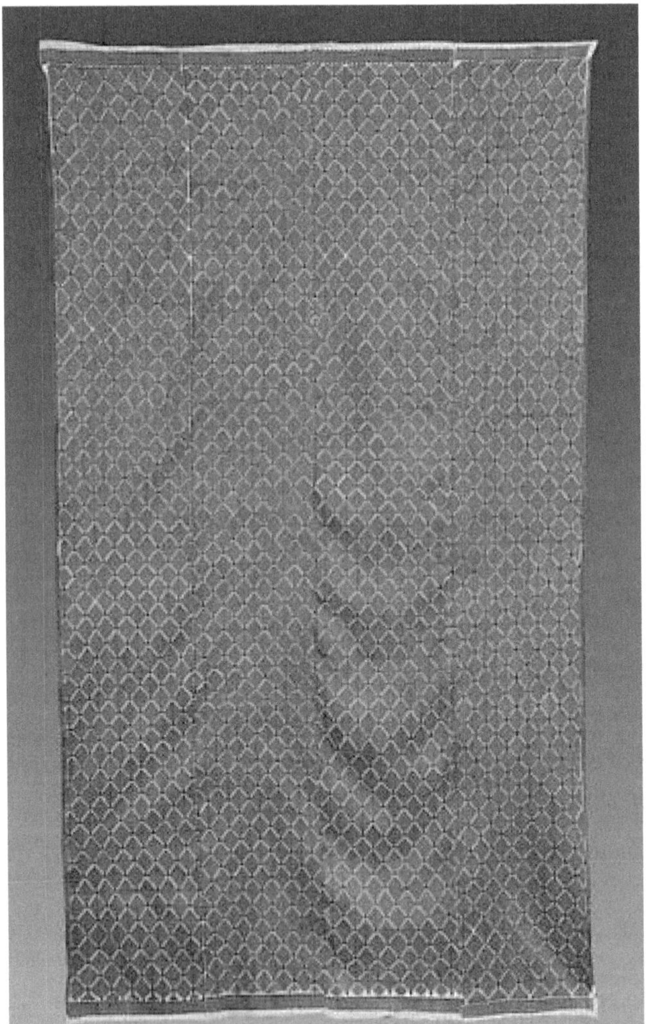

Figure: *A red "thirma" (on white khaddar) bagh from West*

Some Major types of Phulkari & Bagh

Thirma: This phulkari from the north of Punjab, shared by Hindu and Sikh traditions and very appreciated by collectors is identified by its white khaddar called thirma, symbol of purity. As a symbol of purity, thirma was often worn by elder women and widows but, at times, this choice of white coloured khaddar was also made for esthetical reasons. The pat was generally chosen in a range of bright pink to deep red tones. Cluster stitched flowers, wide triangles covering the forehead as well as chevron darning stitch surfaces were very common thirma patterns.

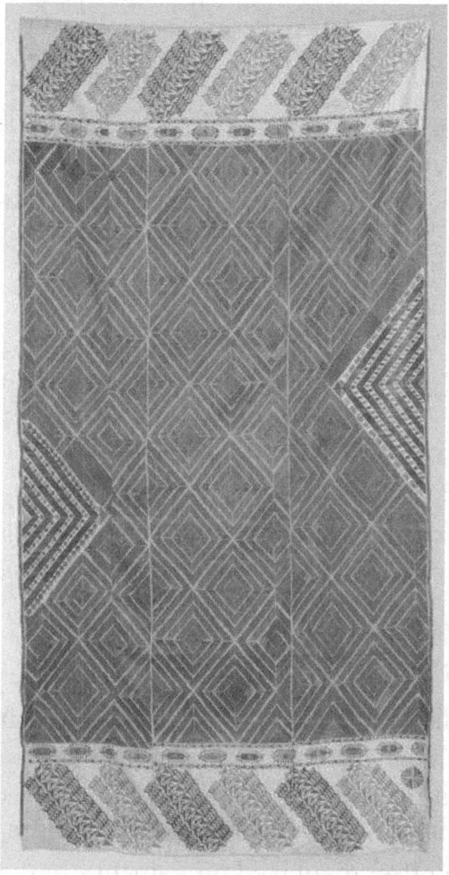

Darshan Dwar

Darshan Dwar, that can be translated as "the gate through which God can be seen", unlike other phulkari was not made for a person but for a temple as an offering to thank the gods after a wish had been fulfilled.

For this reason, while a dowry could contain dozens of phulkari, darshan dwar has never been made in big quantities.

Like other figurative pieces this particular kind of phulkari was made in east Punjab, a mostly non-Islamic area which allowed the development of a broad variety of human and animal representations.

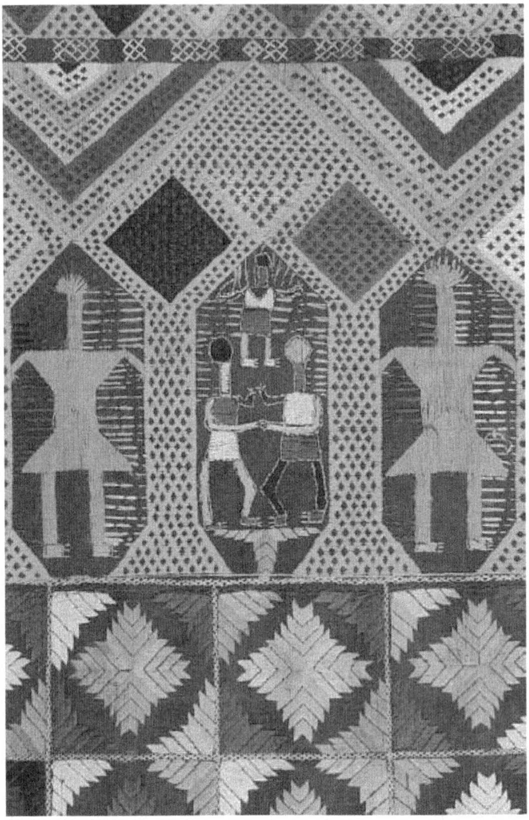

Sainchi Phulkari

Sainchi phulkari are figurative pieces narrating the life in the villages of south east Punjab.

Local animals (goats, cows, elephants, big cats, scorpions, peacocks) are represented moving among wrestlers, farmers, weavers, etc.

Train is also often displayed on sainchi phulkari, this means of transportation, brought by the British in the second half of the19th century, having had a big impact on local populations' life.

Beyond their aesthetic value, sainchi phulkari can be compared to our nowadays media as they depict the ways of life, interests and environment of the old time rural people of Punjab.

In addition, they were produced in a relatively small area (Firozpur and Bhatinda districts) and required high embroidery skills. These are all the reasons why they became so appreciated by collectors and occupy a very unique position among the different varieties of phulkari.

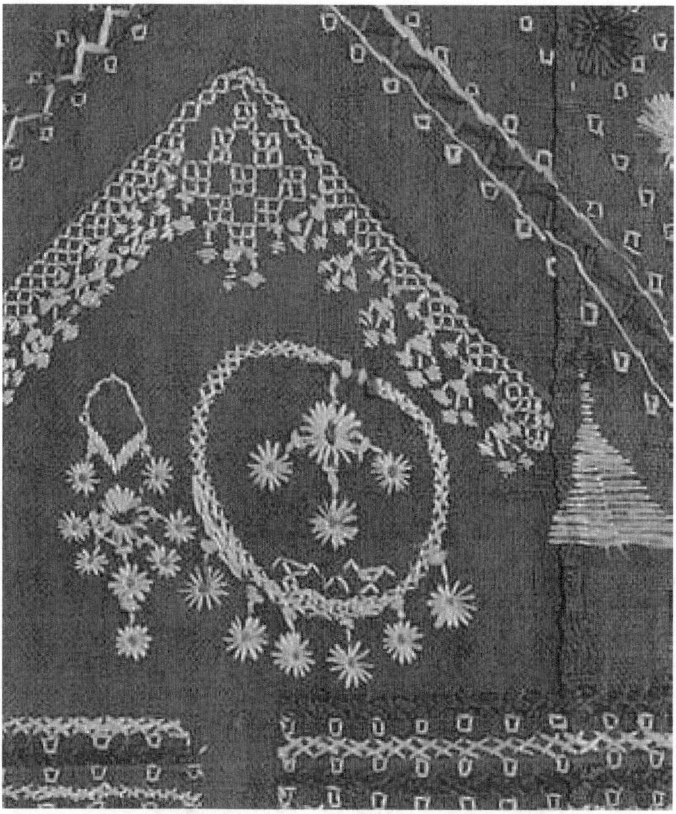

Vari-da-bagh

("Vari": gift offered to the bride by her in-laws)

This bagh was gifted to the bride by her in-laws when she was entering their house, her new home, on the wedding day.

It is an exceptional fact as all the other phulkari were part of her dowry and, thus, were provided by her own family.

Vari-da-bagh is always made on an orange-reddish khaddar and, except for its border and sometimes a small decoration, it is always embroidered on its whole surface with a single golden or orange coloured pat.

This bagh's main pattern is a group of three or four small concentric lozenges of growing size included in each other. Despite the fact that only one colour of pat is used, these lozenges are easily revealed by the reflections of light. The outer one symbolizes the Earth, the next one the city and the third one the familial house. It happens that this last lozenge is split into four smaller ones probably symbolizing the parents of the groom and the newly married couple.

The bride was wrapped in this bagh by her mother in law when she was receiving the keys of her new house, thereby meaning that the bride was becoming responsible for the maintenance of the house.

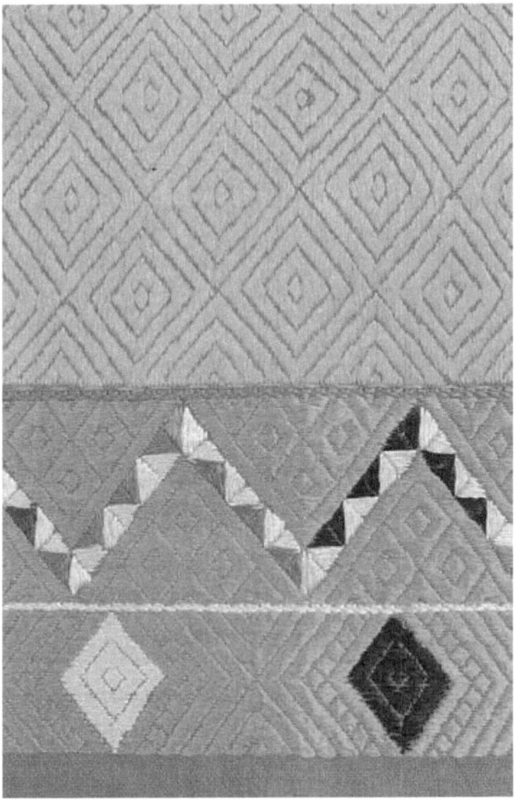

Bawan Bagh (or Bawan Phulkari)

"Bawan" means " fifty-two " in Punjabi and refers to the mosaic of fifty-two different patterns which decorate this piece (the number of patterns can be at times more or less than 52).

Bawan bagh (or phulkari) was in fact a display of samples used by professional embroiderers to show their skills and the patterns they could provide to their clients.

This explains why bawan bagh (or phulkari) is the rarest of all the bagh and phulkari.

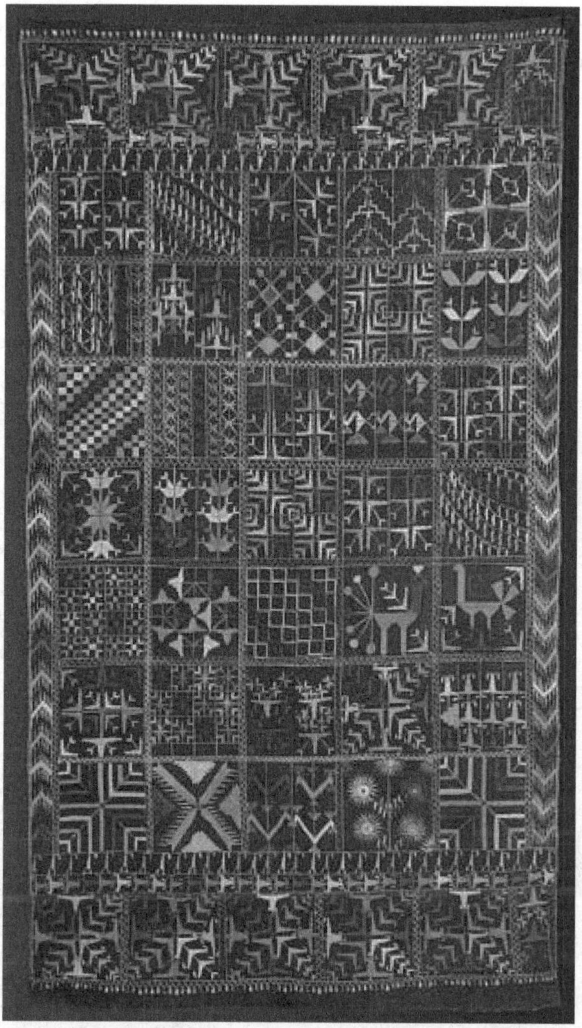

Chope

The bride's maternal grandmother (Nani) was starting chope's embroidery as soon as her granddaughter was born. Instead of the common darning stitch, she was using the Holbein stitch which has the specificity of creating the same design on both the sides of the khaddar. This can be interpreted as the grandmother's wish to make her granddaughter equally happy in her life and after her death, on the two sides of her existence.

Chope was made to wrap and dry the bride after the ritual bath she was having before her wedding, for this practical reason chope is bigger than other phulkari.

Its khaddar was invariably dyed in red or orange colour, symbol of passion and happiness. It is worth noticing that chope was never bordered so that this happiness could be unlimited...

Pat was always chosen in golden tones to express desire and wealth. The Patterns were big triangles symmetrically distributed on the two sides of the chope's longitudinal axis. They were maybe symbolizing male and female principles separated by a distance expressing the fact that the wedding's night had not taken place yet and, thus, that the bride and groom had not had physical intimacy. On another hand these triangles could also represent stylized peacocks.

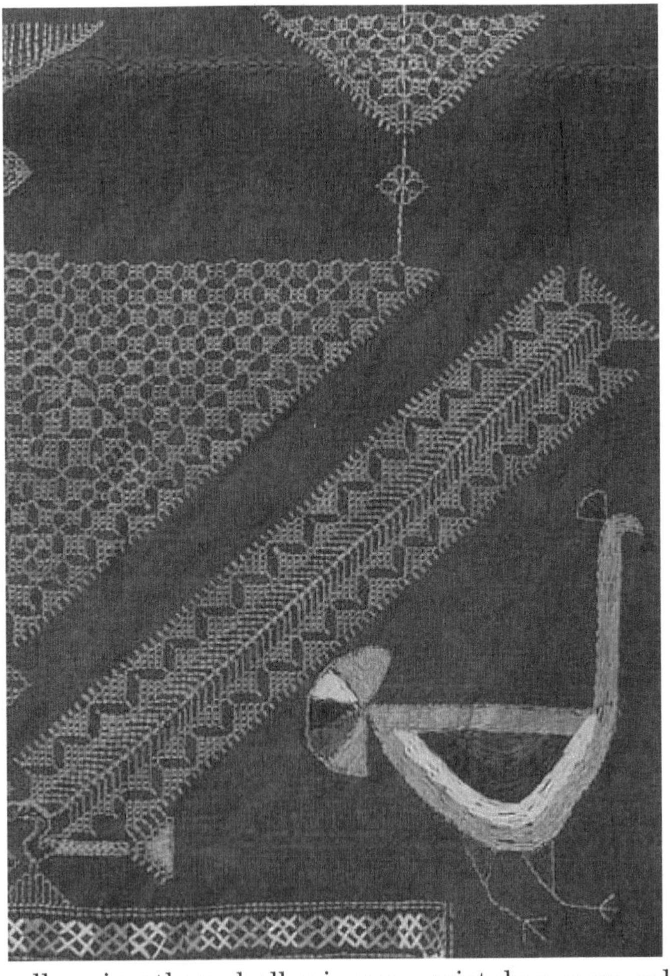

As well as in other phulkari, some mistakes were voluntarily introduced into the embroidery work in order to protect the bride from the evil eye ("nazar"). Indeed a perfect piece could have attracted others' jealousy. This principle of keeping others' envy away showing imperfections is found in many oriental traditions. In India, for instance, some black round spots are often drawn on babies faces for this purpose. Sometimes, chope was also used to cover and hide the bride's dowry, making it invisible to jealous minds and thus keeping the nazar away.

Surajmukhi

Surajmujkhi, the sunflower, refers to the main pattern of this phulkari. From a technical point of view this type of phulkari is unique as it is the only one that mixes in comparable proportions Holbein stitch (used to make chope phulkari) and the regular darning stitch.

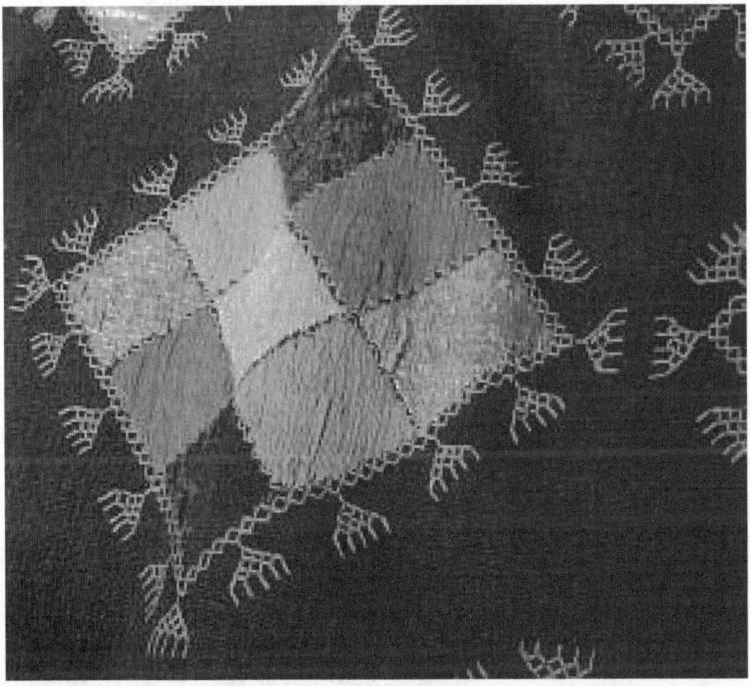

Kaudi Bagh

Among their patterns, these bagh include chains of small white squares representing stylized cowries. Used as currency in the old times these shells have now lost all of their value and using them as ornaments has thus become a sign of humility. From another point of view, the shape of these shells can remind of female genitals and make them become symbols of fertility. Kaudi phulkari were often worn by women wanting to increase their chance to become pregnant.

Panchranga Bagh

Meaning "Five colours", this bagh is decorated with chevrons of five different colours. In The same way, similar pieces like satranga ("Seven colours") bagh are also available.

Meenakari Bagh (or "Ikka Bagh")

This bagh, often made of gold and white coloured pat, is decorated with small multicoloured lozenges referring to enamel work (meenakari) or to "diamond" playing cards' suit.

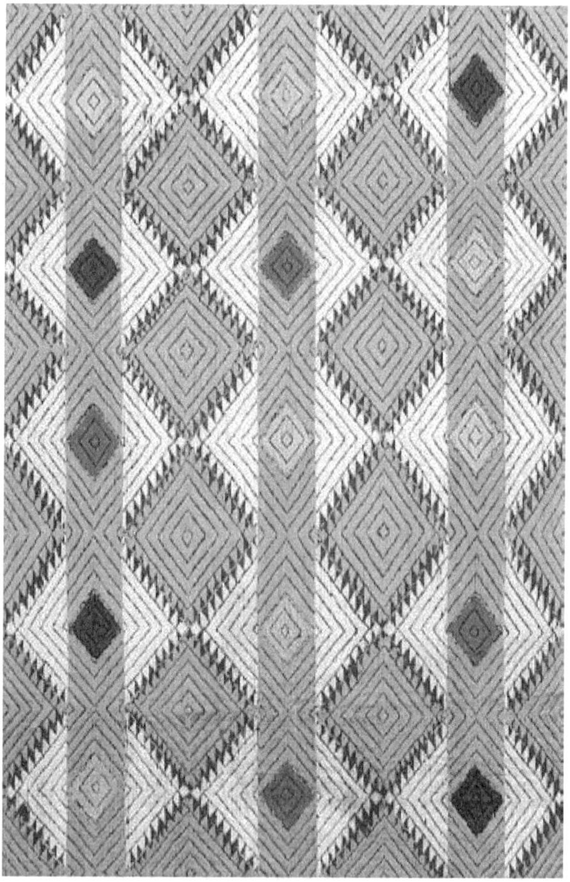

Phulkari Today

Phulkari and bagh displayed in collections are mostly 50 to 150 years old. They had been bought for a few rupees or exchanged against kitchen utensils in villages of Punjab, years back, by local intermediaries and then sold to dealers in big cities like Delhi or Peshawar.

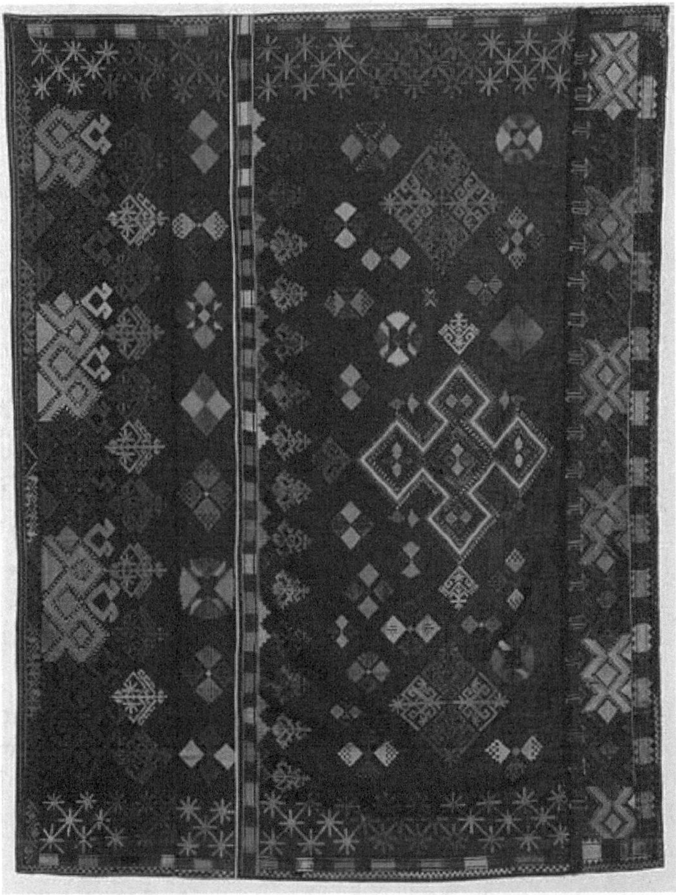

Some associations have been trying hard to keep this art alive but nowadays phulkari are almost exclusively industrially made. They are available in cloth markets of Punjab's big cities (Patiala, Amritsar...) along with embroidered kurtas and cushions.

The fact that this tradition in its original form is now almost over, that Punjab's villages have been washed out of their best pieces and that the information on phulkari's value in the occidental market is now easily available all over the World through the Internet, has increased the prices of fine phulkari and bagh in very big proportions.

These pieces have now almost totally moved from villages to collectors and museums like Quai Branly or V&A.

Kantha Embroidery

Kantha is a type of embroidery popular in West Bengal. The use of kantha is popular in "Kantha saris" traditionally worn by women in Bengal. Kantha stitching is also used to make simple quilts, commonly known as Nakshi Kantha. Women in Bengal typically use old saris and cloth and layer them with kantha stitch to make a light blanket, throw or bedspread, especially for children. Kantha is very popular with tourists visiting Bengal and is a specialty of Bolpur

Weave

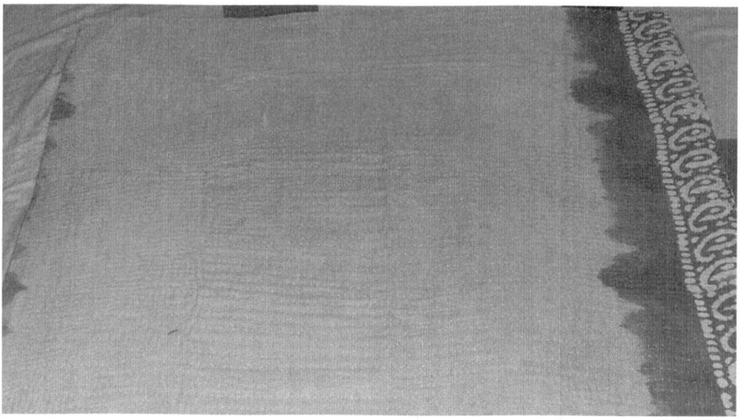

Figure: *Kantha used as bed for a baby*

Kantha is still the most popular form of embroidery practised by rural women. The traditional form of Kantha embroidery was done with soft dhotis and saris, with a simple running stitch along the edges. Depending on the use of the finished product they were known as *Lepkantha* or *Sujni Kantha.*

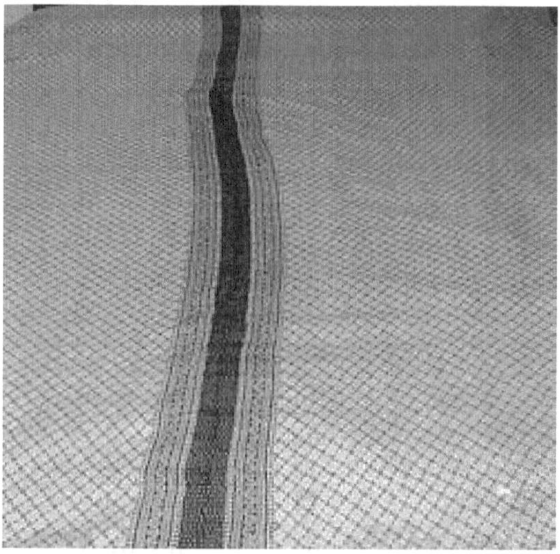

Figure: *kantha used as bed*

The embroidered cloth has many uses including women's shawls and covers for mirrors, boxes, and pillows. In the best examples, the entire cloth is covered with running stitches, employing beautiful motifs of flowers, animals birds and geometrical shapes, as well as themes from everyday activities. The stitching on the cloth gives it a slight wrinkled, wavy effect. Contemporary Kantha is applied to a wider range of garments such as sarees, dupatta, shirts for men and women, bedding and other furnishing fabrics, mostly using cotton and silk.

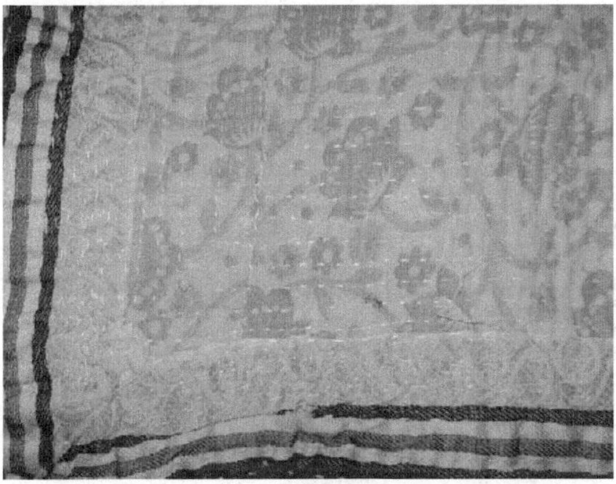

Figure: *Closeup of a kantha. In the left and bottom* Paar *is shown, also the running stitches (white) are seen*

Nakshi Kantha

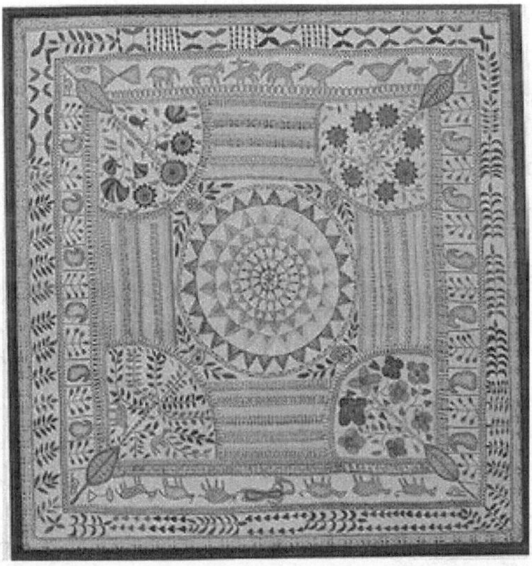

Figure: *Traditional nakshi kantha*

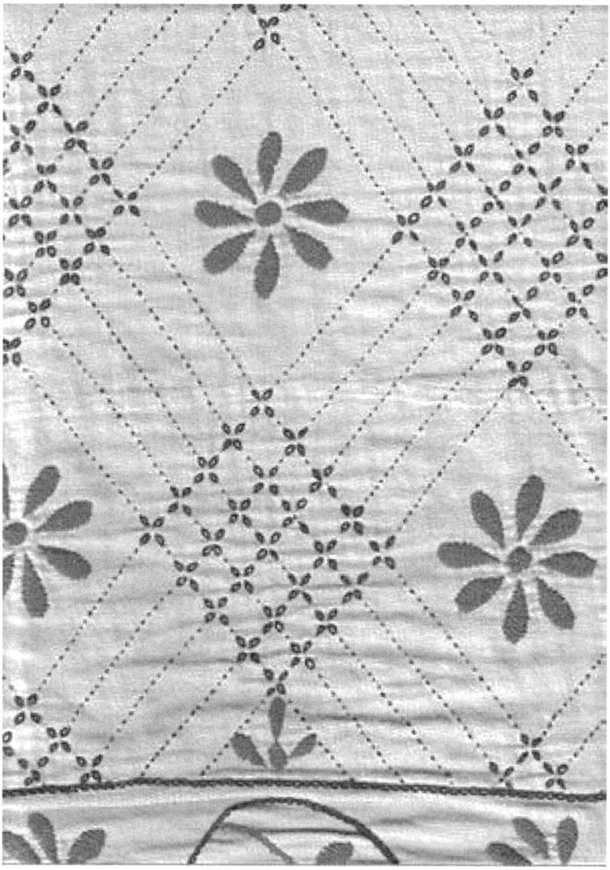

Figure: *Close view of a contemporary Nakshi kantha with flower motif*

Nakshi kantha, a type of embroidered quilt, is a type of folk art of Bangladesh and West Bengal, India. The art has been practiced in rural Bengal for centuries. The basic material used is thread and old cloth. Kanthas are made throughout Bangladesh, but the greater Mymensingh, Rajshahi, Faridpur and Jessore areas are most famous for this craft.

The colourful patterns and designs that are embroidered resulted in the name "Nakshi Kantha", which was derived from the Bengali word "naksha", which refers to artistic patterns. The early kanthas had a white background accented with red, blue and black embroidery; later yellow, green, pink and other colours were also included. The running stitch called "kantha stitch" is the main stitch used for the purpose. Traditionally, kantha was produced for the use of the family. Today, after the revival of the nakshi kantha, they are produced commercially.

Making

Traditionally old sarees, lungis and dhotis were used to make kanthas. Kantha making was not a full-time job.

Women in almost every household were expert in the art. Rural women worked at leisure time or during the lazy days of the rainy season, so taking months or even years to finish a kantha was normal. At least five to seven sarees were needed to make a standard-size kantha. Today the old materials are replaced by new cotton cloths. Traditionally the thread was collected from the old sarees. That is rarely done today.

When a kantha is being made, first the sarees are joined together to attain the required size, and then layers are spread out on the ground. The cloths are then smoothed, and no folds or creases are left in between. During the process, the cloth is kept flat on the ground with weights on the edges. Then the four edges are stitched and two or three rows of large running stitches are done to keep the kantha together. At this stage, the kantha can be folded and stitched at leisure time.

Originally, designs and motifs were not drawn on the cloth. The design was first outlined with needle and thread, followed by focal points, and then the filling motifs were done. In a kantha with a predominant central motif the centre was done first, followed by corner designs and the other details. In some types of kanthas (carpet, lik and sujni, etc.) wooden blocks were used to print the outline. The blocks are replaced today by patterns drawn in tracing papers.

Types

The following is how kanthas are categorized, according to the stitch type:

Running Stitch

The Running stitch kantha is truly the indigenous kantha. They are subdivided into Nakshi (figured) and par tola (patterned). Nakshi (figured) kanthas are further divided into motif or scenic kanthas.

Lohori Kantha

The name was derived from Persian word 'lehr', which means wave. This type of kantha is particularly popular in Rajshahi. These kanthas are further divided into soja (straight or simple), Kautar khupi (pigeon coop or triangle), borfi or diamond (charchala, atchala or barachala).

Lik or Anarasi

The Lik or Anarasi (pine apple) type of kantha is found in the Chapainawabgonj and Jessore areas. The variations are lik tan, lik tile, lik jhumka, and lik lohori.

Cross Stitch or Carpet

This type of kantha was introduced by the English during the British Rule in India. The stitch employed in these kanthas is the cross stitch.

Sujni Kantha

This type of kantha is found only in Rajshahi area. The popular motif used is the undulating floral and vine motif.

Influence of Religion and Folk Belief

Stitches: The earliest and most basic stitch found in kanthas is the *running stitch*. The predominant form of this stitch is called the *phor* or kantha stitch. The other forms of stitches used are the Chatai or *pattern darning*, Kaitya or *bending stitch*, *weave running stitch darning stitch*, *Jessore stitch* (a variation of darning stitch), *threaded running stitch*, Lik phor or anarasi or ghar hasia *(Holbein) stitches*. The stitches used in modern day kantha are the *Kasmiri stitch* and the *arrow head stitch*. Stitches like the *herring bone stitch*, *satin stitch*, *back stitch* and *cross stitch* are occasionally used.

Types

Kanthas generally denote quilts used as wrappers; however, all articles made by quilting old cloth may also be referred to by the same generic name. However, depending on the size and purpose, kanthas may be divided into various articles, each with its specific names. The various types of kantha are as follows:

Quilt (lep in Bengali): A light quilted covering made from the old sarees/dhotis/lungis and sometimes from sheet cloths.

Large Spread (Naksi Kantha in Bengali): An embellished quilt embroidered in traditional motifs and innovative style

Puja Floor Spread (Ason in Bengali): Cloth spread for sitting at a place of worship or for an honoured guest.

Cosmetic Wrapper (Arshilota in Bengali): A narrow embroidered wrapper to roll and store away a woman's comb, mirror, eye kohl, vermilion, sandal paste, oil bottle, etc. Often, a tying string is used to bind the wrap, as in later day satches.

Wallet (Batwa Thoiley in Bengali): Small envelop shaped bag for keeping money, betel leaves, etc.

Cover for Quran (Ghilaf in Arabic and Bengali): Envelope shaped bag to cover the Quran.

Prayer Mats (Jainamaz in Bengali): Mats used by Muslims to say prayers.

Floor Spread (Galicha in Bengali): Floor coverings.

Cloths wrapper (Bostani, Guthri in Bengali): A square wrapper for books and other valuables.

Cover (Dhakni in Bengali): Covering cloths of various shapes and sizes.

Ceremonial Meal Spread (Daster Khan in Bengali): A spread for eating place, used at meal time.

Pillow Cover (Balisher Chapa or Oshar in Bengali): A flat single piece pillow cover.

Handkerchief (Rumal): Small and square in shape.

Today newer uses are found for nakshi kanthas, such as bedspreads, wall hangins, cushion covers, ladies' purses, place mats, jewellery boxes, dress fronts, skirts border, shawls and sharees.

Motifs

Motifs of the nakshi kantha are deeply influenced by religious belief and culture. Even though no specific strict symmetry is followed, a finely embroidered naksi kantha will always have a focal point. Most kanthas will have a lotus as focal point, and around the lotus there are often undulating vines or floral motifs, or a shari border motif. The motifs may include images of flower and leaves, birds and fish, animals, kithen forms even toilet articles.

While most kantas have some initial pattern, no two naksi kantas are same. While traditional motifs are repeated, the individual touch is used in the variety of stitches, colours and shapes. The notable motifs found in naksi kantha are as follows:

Lotus Motif

The lotus motif is the most common motif found in kanthas. This motif is associated with Hindu iconography and thus is also very popular in the kantha. The lotus is the divine seat. It is also symbolic of cosmic harmony and essential womanhood. The lotus is also the symbol of eternal order and of the union of earth, water and, sky. It represents the life-giving power of water, and is also associated with the sun for the opening and closing of the petals. It is also the symbol of the recreating power of life.

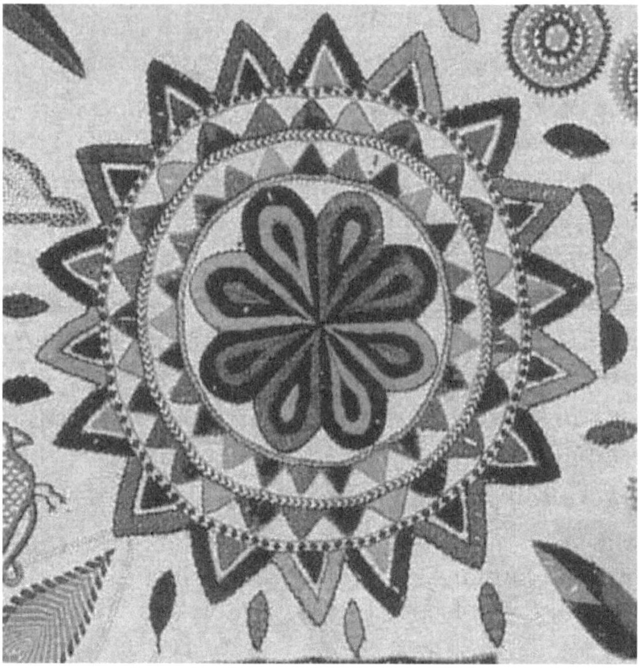

Figure: *Lotus motif*

With the drying up of water, the lotus dies and with the rain it springs to life again. The lotus is associated with purity and the goddess Laksmi, the goddess of good fortune and abundance. There are various forms of lotus motifs, from the eight-petaled *astadal padma* to the hundred petaled *satadal*. In the older kanthas, the central motif is almost always a fully bloomed lotus seen from above.

Solar Motif

The solar motif is closely associated with the lotus motif. Often, the lotus and the solar motifs are found together at in the centre of a nakshi kantha. The solar motif symbolizes the life giving power of the sun. The sun is associated with the fire which plays a significant part in Hindu rites, both religious and matrimonial.

Moon Motif

The moon motif has a religious influence, and is popular amongst the Muslims. Mostly it is in the form of a crescent moon accompanied by a star. This motif is particularly found in *jainamaz* kanthas.

Wheel Motif

The wheel is a common symbol in Indian art, both Hindu and Buddhist. It is the symbol of order. The wheel also represents the world. The wheel is a popular motif in kanthas even when the maker has forgotten the significance of the symbol. The motif is relatively easy to make with *chatai phor.*

Swastika Motif

Su asti in Sanskrit means it is well. As a motif in Indian art, it dates back to the Indus Valley civilization. It is symbol of good fortune. It is also known as *muchri* or *golok dhanda.* With the passage of time, the design is more curvilinear than the four armed swastika of the Mohenjodaro seal. The symbolic design has significant influence in Hinduism, Buddhism, and Jainism.

Tree of Life Motif

The influence of this motif in Indian Art and Culture (as with kantha) may be traced back to the Indus Valley civilization. *It is likely that the Indus people conceived the pipal as the Tree of Life...with the devata inside embodying the power of fecundity.* During the Buddhist times, the cult of the tree continued. Pipal is sacred to the Buddha because he received enlightenment under its shade. It reflects the fecundity of nature and is very popular in Bengal. Vines and creepers play an important role in kanthas and they contain the same symbolisation as that of tree of life. A popular motif in Rajshahi lohori is thr betel leaf.

Kalka Motif

This is a latter day motif, dating from Mughal times. The kalka or paisley motif originated in Persia and Kashmir and has become an integral image of the subcontinental decorative motif. It can be compared with a stylized leaf,mango or flame. The kalka is an attractive motif and number of varieties are experimented. Similar motifs can be found in traditional kashmiri Shawls.

Other Motifs

- The Water Motif:
- The Mountain Motif:
- The Fish Motif:
- The Boat Motif:
- The Footprint Motif:
- The Rath Motif:

- The Mosque Motif:
- The Panja or Open Palm Motif:
- Agricultural Implements:
- Animal Motifs:
- Toilet Articles:
- Kithen Implements:
- The Kantha Motif:
- The Palanquin Motif:

Borders

Most nakshi kanthas have some kind of border. Either a sari border is stitched on or a border pattern is embroidered around the kantha. The common border found in kanthas are as follows:

- The Paddy stalk or date branch (dhaner shish or khejur chari)
- The Scorpion border(Biche par in Bengali)
- The Wavy or bent Border (Beki in Bengali)
- The Diamond border (Barfi)
- The Eye border (chok par in Bengali)
- The Amulet border (Taabiz par in Bengali)
- The Necklace border (mala par in Bengali)
- The Ladder Border (Moi taga)
- The Gut taga
- The Chick taga
- The nolok taga
- The Fish border (Maach par in Bengali)
- The panch taga
- The Bisa taga
- The Anaj taga
- The shamuk taga
- The wrench border
- The anchor (grafi par in Bengali)
- The pen border (kalam par in Bengali)

Chikankari

Chikankari is fine art of embroidery made with white untwisted yarn with the help of a needle on a fine plain cloth. The cloth is generally plain white, pink, maroon, shades of green etc. so that the embroidery work is visible. Earlier chikankari was done on fine white cotton fabric called muslin or mulmul, but with decline of availability of material, gradually the work was started being done on other fabrics like Organdie, Cotton and Silk, Voil, Chiffon, Lenin, Rubia, Khadi, Handloom cloth, Terry Cotton, Polyester, Georgette, Terry voil.

During 17th-18th century, this fine embroidery 'Chikan' was produced in Dhaka, which was later, brought to Lucknow from East Bengal by the Nawabs of Awadh. Chikankari flourished and got its due recognition under the patronage of the rulers of Awadh. Some historians opine, that Chikan is a Persian craft. The word 'Chikan' is probably a derivative from the Persian word 'Chikin' or 'Chikeen' which means a kind of embroidered fabric. Possible linguistic connection could be chiq/chic which is Persian word for 'purdah'.

This is a home based industrial activity which is mainly performed by women artisans and workers. Firstly, designs are printed on the cloth with washable colours and different stitches or embroidery work is done on cloth. Due to the variety of stitching-styles involved in Chikankari, it is claimed to be one of its kind hand embroidery that is impossible to imitate. Chikan embroiders claim of about thirty-two different types and patterns of stitching work. They have given interesting names to these stitches.

During British rule this art form suffered heavily. The import of super fine low priced mill textile from England caused the decline of the trade. Many Artists remained confined to the homes of artisans and those who were fond of the craft only carried out this art form. This also resulted into exploitation of helpless chikan workers. However after Independence efforts to revive this industry were launched.

Gota Work

Gota work is a type of Indian embroidery that originated in Rajasthan, India. Gota embroidery uses the applique technique. Small pieces of zari ribbon are applied onto the fabric with the edges sewn down to create elaborate patterns. Gota embroidery is used extensively in South Asian wedding and formal clothes.

Overview

Gota is a strip of gold or silver or various other coloured ribbons of varying width, woven in a satin or twill weave. It is used along with kinari work. The dresses with gota work are used for special occasions or religious occasions. Gota is crafted using appliqué technique with a strip of gold or silver or various other coloured ribbons of different widths woven in a satin or twill weave. It involves placing woven gold cloth onto fabrics such as georgette or bandhini to create different surface textures.

Originally real gold and silver metals were used to embroider but were eventually replaced by copper coated with silver as the genuine way of making it was very expensive. Nowadays there are even more inexpensive options available. The copper has been replaced by polyester film which is further metalized and coated to suit requirements. This is known as Plastic Gota and is highly durable as it has a good resistance to moisture and does not tarnish as opposed to metal based Gota.

The process is lengthy and time consuming. The first step is to trace the design on the fabric. This is done by placing a tracing paper with the design on it on the fabric and spreading a paste of chalk powder over it. This traces the design on the fabric. Depending on the design, the Gota is cut and folded into various shapes. It is then appliquéd by hemming or back stitching it on the fabric.

Attractive patterns which are specific to the region and each motif has its own distinguishing name. The motifs usually inspired by nature and comprise of flowers, leaves and birds or animals such as peacocks, parrots and elephants. Gota creates a rich and heavy look but is yet light to wear.

In Rajasthan, outfits with Gota work are worn at auspicious functions. It is generally done on dupattas, turban edges and ghagras.

Zardozi

Zardozi or Zar-douzi work is a type of embroidery in Iran, India and Pakistan.

Iran

Zardozi is one of the most important elements of Persian cultural signs and Handicrafts. It is named around the country by names such Zar-douzi, Kam-douzi, Gol-douzi and Kaman-douzi. Today it is more popular in Hormozgan, especially in Bandar-e Lenge and Bandar-e Abbas and Minab that known as the centre of that. Persian Zardozi's are three kinds:

- Some are completely sewing the basic fabric with Bakhie in order to make a new sight of pattern and colours, such as

Baloch's Souzan-douzi, Rasht's Qollab-douzi and Kerman's Pate-douzi.

- Some are in different way sewing with less density of work on original fabric. In this way they cross the strings throughout the woof of the original fabric and sew this string to each other to made a lattice and colourful pattern. Such as Sekke-douzi and Qollab-douzi in Isfahan.
- Another way is sewing a variety of patterns on original fabric with golden and silver strings. Such as Dah-Yek-Douzi (1 of 10 sewing which today is demode), Naqade-douzi, Tafte-douzi, Kous-douzi Zari-douzi or Golabatoun-douzi.

India

It prospered during the Mugal Emperor, Akbar, but later a loss of royal patronage and industrialization led to its decline. Today, it is popular in the Indian cities of Lucknow, Farrukhabad and Chennai. In 2013 the Geographical Indication Registry (GIR) accorded the Geographical Indication (GI) registration to the *Lucknow Zardozi* – the world renowned textile embroidery from Lucknow. The Zardozi products manufactured in areas in Lucknow and six surrounding districts of Barabanki, Unnao, Sitapur, Rae Bareli, Hardoi and Amethi became a brand and can carry a registered logo to confirm their authenticity.

5

Textile Arts by Region

Textile arts of Indonesia

Balinese Textiles: Balinese textiles are reflective of the historical traditions of Bali. Bali has been historically linked to the major courts of Java before the 10th century; and following the defeat of the Majapahit kingdom, many of the Javanese aristocracy fled to Bali and the traditions were continued. Bali therefore may be seen as a repository not only of its own arts but those of Java in the pre-Islamic 15th century. Any attempt to definitively describe Balinese textiles and their use is doomed to be incomplete. The use of textile is a living tradition and so is in constant change. It will also vary from one district to another. For the most part old cloth (excepting the especially sacred) are not venerated for their age. New is much better. In the tropics cloth rapidly deteriorates and so virtue is generated by replacing them.

Endek

The patterning technique of *endek* is ikat of the weft. Once solely the prerogative of high caste Balinese families, *endek* was woven as individual pieces on a back strap loom but now is produced in large quantities by the yard in workshops in Gianyar, Denpasar, Tabanan and other places on ATBM looms (*alat tenun bukan mesin* or unmechanized looms).

Traditional cloth: The earliest extant *endek* date from the late 19th century and come from the North Balinese Kingdom of Buleleng and are predominantly of geometric design. The colour of these early cloths are red.These usually had *songket* ends. Only later do yellows and green appear and the *songket* was omitted.

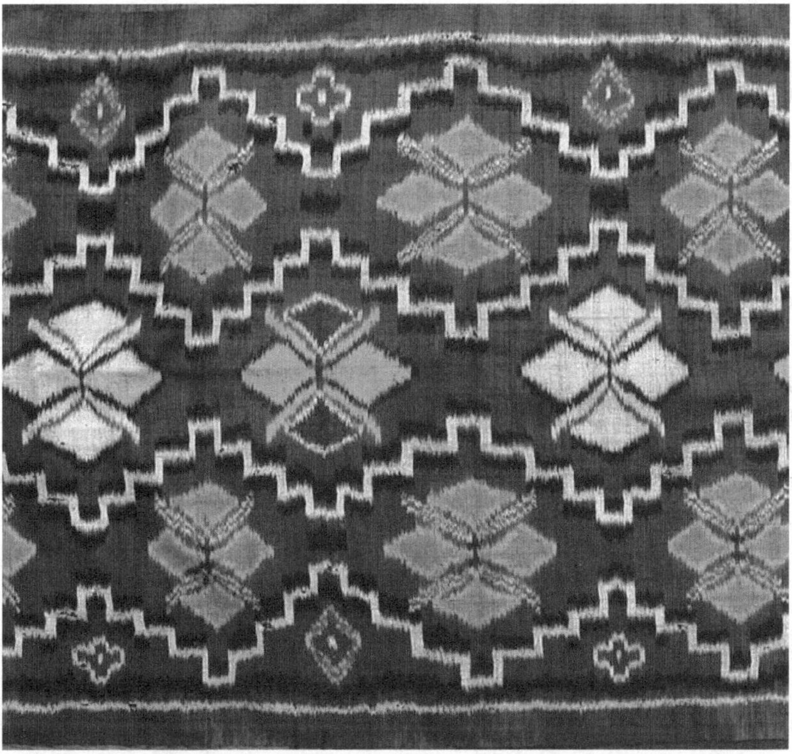

***Figure:** Old silk Endek from Singaraja, early 20th century* tumpak bela design

Keling

Keling are cloths traditionally woven in stripes of red, yellow, dark blue or black from hand spun cotton dyed with natural dyes obtained from the roots of the *sunti* for the reds, and the fruit of the *kunti* for the yellows. In earlier times most of the women of Nusa Penida wore keling underskirts described by Claire Holt in the 1930s. She described multicoloured striped cloth worn under the dark blue upper *kain* in such a way that only a small part showed.

The name is thought by some to be derived from the Balinese word *keling* which refers to *Indian merchant*. The roots may be related to an older legend concerning the primal ancestors of the village Tenganan, the king Kaung and his wife Keling. This is supported by the observation that the cloths are traditionally worn by women.

Ritual uses of keling include in the *otonin* 6 month ceremony for a child, in ceremonies to keep away evil spirits and in other rites of passage.

Bebali

Bebali is the name usually ascribed to a small group of textiles that appear to have been completely sacred in function. The weave is broadly spaced giving the textile a delicate gauze like quality. According to Gittinger in 1970, What is known about them comes entirely from records in the Museum fur Volkskunde Basel, however *bebali* textiles can be bought today in the Kumba Sari market in Denpasar. Hauser-Schaubilin states that there are at least nine differently pattered *bebali* cloths, each with its own name.

There is, for example, cloth with a white warp and weft broken by green, yellow and red stripes known as *cenana kawi* whose function is in the 3 month ritual and also are laid out in the central shrine of an ancestral temple. *Bias membah* (running sand) has a white warp and weft in which grey and white stripes alternate. *Enkakan taluh*(smashed egg) has a vivid red-and white checked pattern. It is bought to the temple as an apparel for Brahma, the god residing in the south. Two examples of bebali cloth are firstly flat cloth, for example, *Kain cepuk, Kain Songket, Kain Sekordi.* Secondly round cloth, where the cloth is removed from the loom and the threads not cut leaving a seamless cloth sheet., In the north and south of Bali known as *Kain Wangsu*l meaning to 'go round' or to 'return'.

In the east of Bali especially Klungkung and Karangasem they are called *Gedogan* or 'circle', the circle represents zero. Ida Ayu Ngurah Puniari (Ibu Dayu) writes that the Gedogan or Wangsul is not symmetrical, this represents purusa and predana, (male and female) where the left and right hand sides will not line up, when warping on the loom a few extra threads are added so one side is uneven.These bebali cloths are now being made with natural dyes and manufactured cottons in the traditional manner with a quality that is comparable with the earlier collected pieces of the1920's.

Cepuk

Kamben cepuk is an ikat of the weft from the island of [Nusa Penida]. These textiles were used as special ceremonial clothing in the past but now more commonly serve as temple decoration.

Geringsing

Geringsing is the name of the double ikat cloth that is woven in the village of Tenganan Pegringsinga. About 20 patterns of *geringsing* are known and the dimensions of the cloths range fron 20 cm to 60 cm wide and can be over 2 metre long. The palette of *geringsing* is typically red, neutral, and black. *Geringsing* are regarded as sacred cloths, "ascribed supernatural properties, especially to assist in forms of healing, including exorcism." It is mentioned in the poem *Rangga Lawe* which tells of the first Majapahit king, Raden Wijaya giving his warriors gerinsing sashes to protect the in Battle. The The first European to describe geringseng was W.O.J Nieuwenkamp, he discovered where they came from and made a journey to Tenganan.

The weaving technique is the dying of the thread is complex and ritualized, as described in the page on geringsing. Once dyed, the warp is laid out on the loom and the cloth is woven in a loose balanced weave. The pattern is carried by both the warp and the weft. Great precision is needed at all stages of the production. Using a pick the weaver adjust the weft with each pass of the shuttle to make sure the alignment of the pattern is precise.

Ider-ider

Ider-ider are a length of cloth onto which a story, often from the Ramayana or Mahabharata has been embroidered. These are used as a valance for a temple or a *balé*. All forms of textile techniques can be used including chain stitching, applique, sequins.

Lamak

Lamak are long banners that are hung from *penjor* at the festival of *galungan* and in front of temples and shrines at other important festivals. The design of lamak generally has a stylized figure at the top, represented by a triangular skirt, followed by a long pattered fiels, ending in a row of *tumpa* In most cases they are made from cross cut and applied palm leaf and therefore are quite perishable. Only occasionally are they made from cotton woven in a supplementary weave.

Prada

In Bali *prada* also sometimes called *perada* is the name given to the technique of decorating a cloth with gold dust or gold leaf. *Prada* is not exclusively a Balinese textile. Old javanese sources suggest that it was popular in the aristocratic circles of the East Javanese kingdom of Majapahit

Technique Batik from Java was once commonly the base material but now a brightly coloured commercial cloth is usually used. In the past a whitish glue (*ancur*) obtained from fish bones, or a darker glue made from water buffalo skin was applied and the gold then applied. Real gold *prada* is almost never seen today. It has been replaces by cloth printed with a gold paint or a plastic foil. Uses *Prada* is now seen in almost every ceremonial function. It is used to decorate ceremonial umbrellas for processions, it wraps temples, decorates the penjor ceremonial flags, is used in dancer's costumes and almost anywhere that some glitter is required.

Songket

Songket is the technique in which a supplementary weft is used to create the pattern. The early *songkèt* were entirely of silk with a supplementary weft of gold thread. Today mixed cloths are seen with cotton, gimp golden and silver threads, viscose and artificial silk. Originally the preserve of the highest castes, with the democratization of Balinese society anyone who can afford to buy them is now able to do so.

Thus *songket* has become an integral part of the ceremonial wardrobe of well-to-do Balinese. Both men and women wear full-body songket wraps for some of life's most important moments. At a Balinese wedding, the bride and groom wear a pair of matching songket. The Balinese also wear songket when their teeth are filed in a ceremony called metatah.

Textile Arts of Ukraine

Ukrainian embroidery occupies an important place among the various branches of Ukrainian decorative arts. Embroidery has a rich history in Ukraine, and has long appeared in Ukrainian folk dress as well as played a part in traditional Ukrainian weddings and other celebrations. Appearing all across the country, Ukrainian embroidery varies depending on the region of origin. From Poltava, Kiev, and Chernihiv in the east, to Volyn and Polissia in the northwest, to Bukovyna, and the Hutsul area in the southwest, the designs have a long history which defines its ornamental motifs and compositions, as well as its favourite choice of colours and types of stitches.

Variations

Ukrainian embroidery has many variations from region to region, or even village to village. However, most embroidery is generally similar overall for most Ukrainians. Even with these variation, the styles of needlework found throughout Ukraine, when taken together, represent a definite Ukrainian national style of embroidery. Red and black were the most common colours of Ukrainian embroidery. Ukrainian folk embroidery is notable for great variety of its techniques.

Central and Eastern Ukraine

In the Central and Eastern parts of Ukraine, embroidery usually consists of geometric forms and plant ornaments. The colour range of the motifs is very delicate and very diverse as to individual details. In the Poltava Region, the colours usually include pale blue, white, light ochre, pale green and gray tones. Poltava products are especially famed for their "white-on-white" and openwork embroidery. The red, red-blue (or red-black) colour scheme plays an important role in Central- and Eastern-Ukrainian embroidery, as it did throughout almost the whole of Ukraine.

Western Ukraine

In Western Ukraine, especially the Hutsul region, embroidery uses geometric ornament and a sharply contrasting palette. Besides the now widely used cross-stitch, there is still the ornamental needle-weaving stitch called "nyzynka", which is executed predominantly on the reverse of the fabric and gives a sort of "tweed" effect. This is one of the most archaic of traditional Ukrainian stitches that, in combination with the predetermined areas of white background material that peek through the densely laid threads, emphasizes the clear-cut silhouette of the main patterns.

In the Lemko region, the oldest embroideries were executed in red and red-blue linear motifs. Over time, other colours, such as blue, green and yellow, were added.

In the Boiko region, embroideries varied from simple red-blue geometric motifs in the western reaches of their territory, to wide, densely worked geometric and/or floral patterns in the eastern and southern reaches. Boikos were also well known for their finely embroidered pleated smocking work called "bryzhky", which were found mainly around the collars and sleeve cuffs of women's and men's shirts, but also along the top hems of women's aprons.

The embroideries of Bukovyna are among the richest in all of Ukraine, often combining as many as nine or more colours, including silver and gold metallic thread as well as coloured glass beads. It also uses a number of stitches.

The needlework of Pokuttya was also rich and intricately executed, and also quite varied. Red was the predominant colour in many of the styles of embroidery in this region, usually being worked in thick home-processed wool threads, sometimes with accents of yellow, green and blue added. Although cross-stitch was not uncommon, the older and more traditional technique was that of the so-called “curly stitch” (quite popular, in fact, throughout many areas of Southwestern Ukraine). In some parts of Pokuttya and neighbouring Podillya, wide motifs of intricately worked white-on-white embroidery combined with open work were popular. The embroideries of Podillya were similar in many respects to that of both Bukovyna and Pokuttya, with discreet yet recognizable differences in colour scheme, motifs and placement that nonetheless set them apart.

In Halychyna, there is a variety of embroidery styles that were specific for individual localities, such that when one sees a piece of embroidery there is no mistaking its origin.

Northern Ukraine

In the northwest and north of Ukraine (including the Ukrainian ethno-historic territory of Poland) needlework traditions have been preserved relatively intact from the oldest of times. Red, as well as red-blue and red-black were the predominant colour schemes in the archaic geometric embroideries of these northern regions of Ukraine, executed primarily in dense rows of a horizontal needle-weaving stitch (called “zavolikannia”) that created horizontal bands of patterns reminiscent of weaving. Floral motifs are also popular in the North, using red, red-blue or red-black palette as the needle-woven bands, but in the much more recent technique of cross-stitch.

Textile Arts of Denmark

Faroese shawl

A Faroese shawl is a traditional piece of clothing from the Faroe Islands. The most distinguishing characteristic of Faroese shawls is the centre back gusset shaping. Each shawl consists of two triangular side panels, a trapezoid-shaped back gusset, an edge treatment, and usually shoulder shaping. The shoulder shaping allows these shawls to drape over the shoulders and remain in place as the wearer moves, even if the shawl is not pinned in place.

Instead of a more familiar triangular, rectangular or circular shape, Faroese shawls are shaped like butterfly wings. Some have very long ends so they can be tied around the wearer’s waist for extra warmth. The shawls often feature elaborate lace work. Lace knitting is a traditional handcraft of peoples of the Faroe Islands.

These shawls are traditionally knit from domestic wool of native sheep grown primarily for meat. Natural colours of brown, black, grey and creamy white are most often used. Some shawls may have colour features in place of lace, or combinations of colour panels or stripes and lace panels.

The notation used for recording patterns for these shawls is unique. Patterns are drawn out showing the back gusset and one side panel with numerical shaping instructions noted on the diagram. Lace patterns are drawn showing where the eyelets go, but without specifying where the accompanying decreases should go.

Most shawls are begun at the neck, but Faroese shawls are begun from the bottom by casting on hundreds of stitches. As the work progresses, structural decreases between the side panels and back gusset reduce the number of stitches until very few remain at the neck. Since garter stitch is used, the shawls are reversible, except where colour panels are used.

Tønder Lace

Tønder lace is a point-ground type of handmade bobbin lace identified with the Tønder region of Denmark since about 1850, although lace of many types has been made there since as early as 1650. The term is also used more broadly, to refer to any bobbin lace made in Denmark.

Tønder lace was traditionally made in fine linen thread, imported from the Netherlands. Since the disappearance of the very fine linen threads, it has commonly been made in cotton. It is characterized by honeycomb fillings in motifs, square tallies in the ground, and the use of a gimp, a heavy thread outlining the cloth-stitch motifs. It often had large holes in the motif, called "Copenhagen holes", which were an attempt on the part of the lacemakers to speed up production of the lace, as they strove to compete with the cheaper machine-made lace. The designs used were similar to Mechlin lace, with lots of flowers.

History

Tønder lace was mainly made during the late 18th and early 19th centuries. Production started in 1647 when a merchant brought lacemakers from Westphalia to Tønder to teach lacemaking to the general population. Christian IV protected the manufacture of local lace, and didn't wear any foreign lace. In 1712 several lacemakers from Brabant accompanied the troops of King Frederick IV on their return from the Netherlands, bringing new techniques. Tønder lace was a major industry, and most of the region's girls were employed in making it. Little boys, before they were strong enough to work in the fields, were also taught to make lace. In 1801 20,000 people in Tønder and the immediately surrounding area were employed making lace. When machine-made lace was introduced in the late 1800s, the handmade lace industry gradually ceased to be economically important to the region. It never died out entirely though, and is still made today, mostly by hobbyists.

Textile Arts of England

Art Needlework

Art needlework was a type of surface embroidery popular in the later nineteenth century under the influence of the Pre-Raphaelites and the Arts and Crafts Movement.

Artist and designer William Morris is credited with the resurrection of the techniques of freehand surface embroidery based on English embroidery styles of the Middle Ages through the eighteenth century, developing the retro-style which would be termed *art needlework*. Art needlework emphasized delicate shading in satin stitch with silk thread accompanied by a number of novelty stitches, in sharp contrast with the counted-thread technique of the brightly coloured Berlin wool work needlepoint craze of the mid-nineteenth century.

In embroidery as in other crafts, Morris was anxious to encourage self-expression via handcrafts. His shop Morris & Co. sold both finished custom embroideries and kits in the new style, along with vegetable dyed silks in which to work them. Art needlework was considered an appropriate style for decorating artistic dress.

The Royal School of Art Needlework (now Royal School of Needlework) was founded as a charity in 1872 under the patronage of Princess Helena to provide apprenticeships in the new/old style. Morris's daughter May, an accomplished needlewoman and designer in her own right, was active in the School from its inception.

Art needlework was introduced to America at the 1876 Centennial Exposition in Philadelphia.

English Embroidery

English embroidery includes embroidery worked in England or by English people abroad from Anglo-Saxon times to the present day. The oldest surviving English embroideries include items from the early 10th century preserved in Durham Cathedral and the 11th century Bayeux Tapestry, if it was worked in England. The professional workshops of Medieval England created rich embroidery in metal thread and silk for ecclesiastical and secular uses. This style was called *Opus Anglicanum* or "English work", and was famous throughout Europe.

With the Protestant Reformation of the 16th century, the focus of English embroidery increasingly turned to clothing and household furnishings, leading to another great flowering of English domestic embroidery in the Elizabethan and Jacobean eras. The end of this period saw the rise of the formal sampler as a record of the amateur stitcher's skills. Curious fashions of the mid-17th century were raised work or stumpwork, a pictorial style featuring detached and padded elements, and crewel work, featuring exotic leaf motifs worked in wool yarn.

Canvaswork, in which thread is stitched through a foundation fabric, and surface embroidery, in which the majority of the thread sits on top of the fabric, exist side-by-side in the English tradition, coming in and out of fashion over the years.

In the 19th century, the craze for Berlin wool work, a canvaswork style using brightly coloured wool, contrasts with art needlework, associated with the Arts and Crafts Movement, which attempted to resurrect the artistic and expressive styles of medieval surface embroidery under the influence of the Gothic Revival and the Pre-Raphaelites.

Although continental fashions in needlework were adopted in England, a number of popular styles were purely English in origin, including the embroidered linen jackets of the turn of the 17th century, stumpwork, and art needlework.

Medieval Period

Anglo-Saxon

Little physical evidence survives to reconstruct the early development of English embroidery before the Norman Conquest of 1066. Stitches reinforcing the seams of a garment in the Sutton Hoo ship burial may have been intended as decoration, and so be classed as embroidery, and fragments of a scrolling border worked in stem stitch were recovered from a grave in Kempston, Bedfordshire. Some embroidered pieces of about 850 preserved in Maaseik, Belgium, are generally assumed to be Anglo-Saxon work based on their similarity to contemporary manuscript illustrations and sculptures of animals and interlace.

The documentary evidence is rather richer than the physical remains. Part of the reason for both these facts is the taste among the late Anglo-Saxon elite for embroidering using lavish amounts of precious metal thread, especially gold, which both gave items a magnificence and expense worth recording, and meant that they were well worth burning to recover the bullion. Three old vestments, almost certainly Anglo-Saxon, recycled in this way at Canterbury Cathedral in the 1370s, produced over £250 of gold – a huge amount. Richly embroidered hangings were used in both churches and the houses of the rich, but vestments were the most richly embellished of all, of a "particularly English" richness. Most of these were sent back to Normandy or burnt for their metal after the Norman conquest. An image of part of a huge gold acanthus flower on the back of a gold-bordered chasuble, almost certainly depicting a specific real vestment, can be seen in the Benedictional of St. Æthelwold (fol. 118v).

Scholars agree that three embroidered items from the coffin of St Cuthbert in Durham are Anglo-Saxon work, based on an inscription describing their commission by Queen Ælfflæd between 909 and 916. These include a stole and maniple ornamented with figures of prophets outlined in stem stitch and filled with split stitch, with halos in gold thread worked with underside couching. The quality of this silk embroidery on a gold background is "unparalleled in Europe at this time."

Scholarly consensus favours an Anglo-Saxon, probably Kentish origin for the Bayeux tapestry. This famous narrative of the Conquest is not a true woven tapestry but an embroidered hanging worked in wool yarn on a tabby-woven linen ground using outline or stem stitch for lettering and the outlines of figures, and couching or laid work for filling in figures.

Opus Anglicanum

The Anglo-Saxon embroidery style combining split stitch and couching with silk and goldwork in gold or silver-gilt thread of the Durham examples flowered from the 12th to the 14th centuries into a style known to contemporaries as *Opus Anglicanum* or "English work". Opus Anglicanum was made for both ecclesiastical and secular use on clothing, hangings, and other textiles. It was usually worked on linen or dark silks, or later, worked as individual motifs on linen and applied to velvet.

Throughout this period, the designs of embroidery paralleled fashions in manuscript illumination and architecture. Work of this period often featured continuous light scrolls and spirals with or without foliations, in addition to figures of kings and saints in geometrical frames or Gothic arches.

Opus Anglicanum was famous throughout Europe. A "Gregory of London" was working in Rome as a gold-embroiderer to Pope Alexander IV in 1263, and the Vatican inventory in Rome of 1295 records well over 100 pieces of English work. Notable surviving examples of Opus Anglicanum include Syon Cope and the Butler-Bowden Cope of 1330–50 in the Victoria and Albert Museum, embroidered with silver and silver-gilt thread and coloured silks on silk velvet, which was disassembled and later reassembled into a cope in the 19th century.

Professional Embroiderers

By the 13th century, most English goldwork was made in London workshops, which produced ecclesiastical work, clothing and furnishings for royalty and the nobility, heraldic banners and horse-trappings, and the ceremonial regalia for the great Livery Companies of the City of London and for the court.

The founding of the embroiderer's guild in London is attributed to the 14th century or earlier, but its early documents were lost in the Great Fire of London in the 17th century. An indenture of 23 March 1515 records the establishment of Broderers' Hall in Cutter Lane in that year, and the guild was officially incorporated (or reincorporated) by Royal Charter under Elizabeth I in 1561 as the Worshipful Company of Broderers. Professional embroiderers were also attached to the great households of England, but it is unlikely that those working far from London were members of the Company.

From the middle of the 14th century, money that had previously been spent on luxury goods like lavish embroidery was redirected to military expenditure, and imported Italian figured silks competed with native embroidery traditions. Varieties of design in textiles succeeded each other very rapidly, and they were more readily available than the more leisurely produced needlework. The work produced by the London workshops was simplified to meet the demands of this deteriorating market. The new techniques required less work and smaller quantities of expensive materials. Surface couching replaced underside couching, and allover embroidery was replaced by individual motifs worked on linen and then applied to figured silks or silk velvets. Increasingly, designs for embroidery were derived directly from woven patterns, "thus losing not only their former individuality and richness, but also their former ... story-telling interest."

Renaissance to Restoration

The second great flowering of English embroidery, after Opus Anglicanum, took place in the reign of Elizabeth I. Although the majority of surviving English embroidery from the medieval period was intended for church use, this demand decreased radically with the Protestant Reformation. In contrast, the bulk of the surviving embroidery of the Tudor, Elizabethan, and Jacobean eras is for domestic use, whether for clothing or household decoration. The stable society that existed between the accession of Elizabeth in 1558 and the English Civil War encouraged the building and furnishing of new houses, in which rich textiles played a part. Some embroidery was imported in this period, including the canvas work bed valances once thought to be English but now attributed to France, but the majority of work was made in England—and increasingly, by skilled amateurs, mostly women, working domestically, to designs by professional men and women, and later to published pattern books.

Tudor and Jacobean Styles

A general taste for abundant surface ornamentation is reflected in both household furnishings and in fashionable court clothing from the mid-16th century through the reign of James I. A 1547 account of the wardrobe of Henry VIII shows that just over half of the 224 items were ornamented with embroidery of some kind, and embroidered shirts and accessories were popular New Year's gift to the Tudor monarchs. Fine linen shirts, chemises, ruffs, collars, coifs and caps were embroidered in monochrome silks and edged in lace. The monochrome works are classified as blackwork embroidery even when worked in other colours; red, crimson, blue, green, and pink were also popular.

Outer clothing and furnishings of woven silk brocades and velvets were ornamented with gold and silver embroidery in linear or scrolling patterns, applied bobbin lace and passementerie, and small jewels.

Appliqué work was popular in the Tudor era, especially for large-scale works such as wall hangings. In Medieval England, rich clothing had been bequeathed to the church to be remade into vestments; following the dissolution of the monasteries at the Reformation, the rich silks and velvets of the great monastic houses were cut up and repurposed to make hangings and cushions for private homes. Shapes cut from opulent fabrics and small motifs or slips worked on fine linen canvas were applied a background fabric of figured silk, velvet, or plain wool and embellished with embroidery, in a style deriving from the later, simpler forms of Medieval work. Canvaswork in which the linen ground was covered entirely by tent, gobelin, or cross stitches in wool or silk thread was often used for cushion covers and small bags. Notable examples like the Bradford carpet, a pictorial table cover, were likely the work of professionals in the Broderers' Company.

Polychrome (multicoloured) silk embroidery became fashionable in the reign of Elizabeth, and from c. 1590 to 1620 a uniquely English fashion arose for embroidered linen jackets worn informally or as part of masquing costume. These jackets usually featured scrolling floral patterns worked in a multiplicity of stitches. Similar patterns worked in 2-ply worsted wool called crewel on heavy linen for furnishings are characteristic of Jacobean embroidery.

Pattern Sources

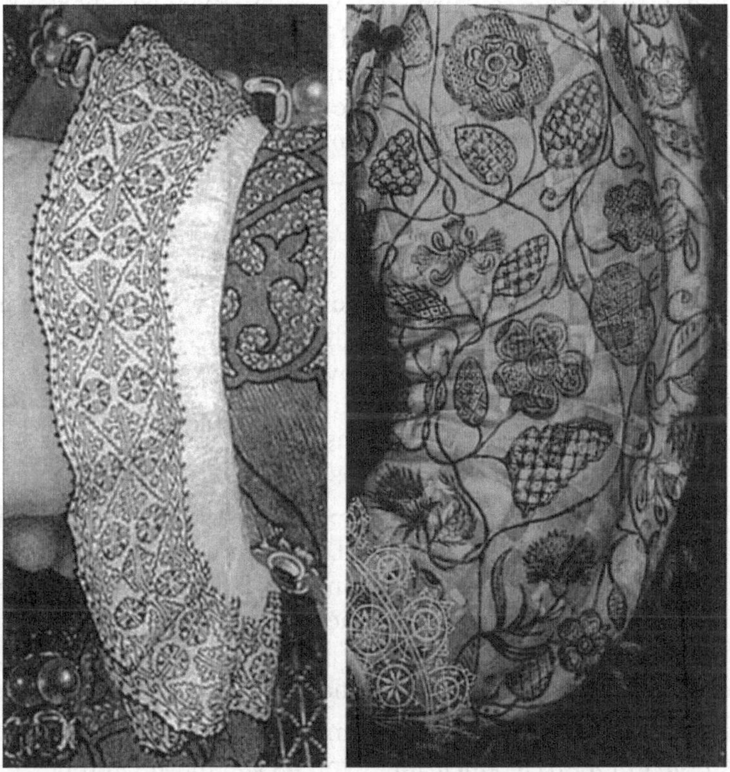

Figure: *Blackwork embroidery of the 1530s (left) and 1590s (right).*

Pattern books for geometric embroidery and needlelace were published in Germany as early as the 1520s. These featured the stepped, angular patterns characteristic of early blackwork, ultimately deriving from medieval Islamic Egypt. These patterns, seen in the portraits of Hans Holbein the Younger, were worked over counted threads in a double running stitch (later called *Holbein stitch* by English embroiderers).

The first pattern book for embroidery published in England was *Moryssche & Damaschin renewed & encreased very popular for Goldsmiths & Embroiderers* by Thomas Geminus (1545). *Moryssche* or Moresque refers to Moorish or arabesque designs of spirals, scrolls, and zigzags, an important part of the reportoire of Renaissance ornament in many media. Scrolling patterns of flowers and leaves filled with geometric *filling stitches* are characteristic of blackwork from the 1540s through 1590s, and similar patterns worked in coloured silks appear from the 1560s, outlined in backstitch and filled with detached buttonhole stitch. Additional pattern books for embroiderers appeared late in the century, followed by Richard Shorleyker's *A Schole-house for the Needle* published in London in 1624. Other sources for embroidery designs were the popular herbals and emblem books. Both domestic and professional embroiderers probably relied on skilled draughtsmen or *pattern-drawers* to interpret these design sources and draw them out on linen ready to be stitched.

Early Samplers

Printed pattern books were not easily obtainable, and a sampler or embroidered record of stitches and patterns was the most common form of reference. 16th-century English samplers were stitched on a narrow band of fabric and totally covered with stitches. These *band samplers* were highly valued, often being mentioned in wills and passed down through the generations. These samplers were stitched using a variety of needlework styles, threads, and ornament.

The earliest dated surviving sampler, housed in the Victoria and Albert Museum, was made by Jane Bostocke who included her name and the date 1598 in the inscription, but the earliest documentary reference to sampler making goes back another hundred years, to the 1502 household expense accounts of Elizabeth of York, which record the purchase of an ell of linen to make a sampler for the queen.

From the early 17th century, samplers became a more formal and stylized part of a girl's education, even as the motifs and patterns on the samplers faded from fashion.

Pictorial Embroidery and Stumpwork

Following the death of James I and the accession of Charles I, elaborately embroidered clothing faded from popularity under the dual influences of rising Puritanism and the new court's taste for French fashion with its lighter silks in solid colours accessorised with masses of linen and lace. In this new climate, needlework was praised by moralists as an appropriate occupation for girls and women in the home, and domestic embroidery for household use flourished. Embroidered pictures, mirror frames, workboxes, and other domestic objects of this era often depicted Biblical stories featuring characters dressed in the fashion of Charles and his queen Henrietta Maria, or after the Restoration, Charles II and Catherine of Braganza.

These stories were executed in canvaswork or in coloured silks in a uniquely English style called *raised work*, usually known by its modern name *stumpwork*. Raised work arose from the detached buttonhole stitch fillings and braided scrolls of late Elizabethan embroidery. Areas of the embroidery were worked on white or ivory silk grounds in a variety of stitches and prominent features were padded with horsehair or lambswool, or worked around wooden shapes or wire frames. Ribbons, spangles, beads, small pieces of lace, canvaswork slips, and other objects were added to increase the dimensionality of the finished work.

Crewel

Sets of bed hangings embroidered in crewel wools were another characteristic product of the Stuart era. These were worked on a new fabric, a natural twill weave from Bruges with a linen warp and cotton weft. Crewel wools of the 17th century were firmly twisted unlike the soft wools sold under that name today, and were dyed in deep rich shades of green, blue, red, yellow, and brown. Motifs of flowers and trees, with birds, insects, and animals, were worked at large scale in a variety of stitches. The origins of this work are in the polychrome embroidery on scrolling stems of the Elizabethan era, later blended with the Tree of Life and other motifs of Indian palampores, introduced by the trade of the East India Company.

After the Restoration, the patterns became ever more fanciful and exuberant. "It is an almost impossible task to describe the large leaves, since they bear no resemblance to anything natural, they are, however, rarely angular in outline, rejoicing rather in sweeping curves, and drooping points, curled over to display the under side of the leaf, a device that gave opening for much ingenuity in the arrangement of the stitches."

Although usually called "Jacobean embroidery" by modern stitchers, crewel has its origins in the reign of James I but remained popular through the reign of Queen Anne and into the early 18th century, when a return to the simpler forms of the earliest work became fashionable.

Glorious Revolution to the Great War

Later Stuart

The accession of William III and Mary II following the Glorious Revolution of 1688 triggered another change in needlework fashions. Associations of stumpwork with the reign of the deposed Stuarts combined with Mary's Dutch taste ushered in new styles influenced by Indian chintzes. From the 1690s, household furnishings such as chair covers and firescreens were the focus of embroidery in the home.

Georgian

In the Georgian era, canvaswork was popular for chair coverings, footstools, screens and card tables. Embroidered pictures and upholstery both reflected the popular pastoral theme of men and women in the sheep-cropped English countryside. Other recurring themes include exotic Tree of Life patterns influenced by earlier crewelwork and chinoiserie with its fanciful imagery of an imaginary China, asymmetry in format and whimsical contrasts of scale. In contrast, *needlepainting* in silks and wools produced naturalistic portraits and domestic scenes. Embroidery was once again an important element of fashion in the early 18th century. Aprons, stomachers, hanging pockets, shoes, gowns, and men's coats and waistcoats were all decorated with embroidery.

Later Samplers

By the 18th century, sampler making had become an important part of girls' education in boarding and institutional schools. A commonplace component was now an alphabet with numerals, possibly accompanied by various crowns and coronets, all used in marking household linens. Traditional embroidered motifs were now rearranged into decorative borders framing lengthy inscriptions or verses of an "improving" nature and small pictorial scenes. These new samplers were more useful as a record of accomplishment to be hung on the wall than as a practical stitch guide.

Tambourwork

Tambourwork was a new chainstitch embroidery fad of the 1780s influenced by Indian embroidered muslins. Stitched originally with a needle and later with a small hook, tambour takes its name from the round embroidery frame in which it was worked. Tambour was suited to the light, flowing ornament appropriate to the new muslin dresses of this period, and patterns were readily available in periodicals like the *Lady's Magazine* which debuted in 1770.

Tambourwork was copied by machine early in the Industrial Revolution. As early as 1810, a "worked muslin cap ... done in tambour stitch by a steam-engine" was on the market, and machine-made netting was in general use as a background by the 1820s.

Smocking

The linen smock-frocks worn by rural workers, especially shepherds and waggoners, in parts of England and Wales from the early eighteenth century featured fullness across the back, breast, and sleeves folded into "tubes" (narrow unpressed pleats) held in place and decorated by smocking, a type of surface embroidery in a honeycomb pattern across the pleats that controls the fullness while allowing a degree of stretch.

Embroidery styles for smock-frocks varied by region, and a number of motifs became traditional for various occupations: wheel-shapes for carters and wagoners, sheep and crooks for shepherds, and so on. Most of this embroidery was done in heavy linen thread, often in the same colour as the smock.

By the mid-nineteenth century, wearing of traditional smock-frocks by country laborers was dying out, and a romantic nostalgia for England's rural past led to a fashion for women's and children's clothing loosely styled after smock-frocks. These garments are generally of very fine linen or cotton and feature delicate smocking embroidery done in cotton floss in contrasting colours; smocked garments with pastel-coloured embroidery remain popular for babies.

Berlin Work

In the early 19th century, canvaswork in tent or *petit point* stitch again became popular. The new fashion, using printed patterns and coloured tapestry wools imported from Berlin, was called Berlin wool work. Patterns and wool for Berlin work appeared in London in 1831. Berlin work was stitched to hand-coloured or charted patterns, leaving little room for individual expression, and was so popular that "Berlin work" became synonymous with "canvaswork". Its chief characteristic was intricate three-dimensional looks created by careful shading. By mid-century, Berlin work was executed in bright colours made possible by the new synthetic dyes. Berlin work was very durable and was made into furniture covers, cushions, bags, and slippers as well as for embroidered "copies" of popular paintings. The craze for Berlin work peaked around 1850 and died out in the 1870s, under the influence of a competing aesthetic that would become known as *art needlework.*

Art Needlework

In 1848, the influential Gothic Revival architect G. E. Street co-wrote a book called *Ecclesiastical Embroidery.* He was a staunch advocate of abandoning faddish Berlin work in favour of more expressive embroidery techniques based on Opus Anglicanum. Street's one-time apprentice, the Pre-Raphaelite poet, artist, and textile designer William Morris, embraced this aesthetic, resurrecting the techniques of freehand surface embroidery which had been popular from the Middle Ages to the 18th century. The new style, called art needlework, emphasized flat patterns with delicate shading in satin stitch accompanied by a number of novelty stitches. It was worked in silk or wool thread dyed with natural dyes on wool, silk, or linen grounds.

By the 1870s, Morris's decorative arts firm Morris & Co. was offering both designs for embroideries and finished works in the art needlework style. Morris became active in the growing movement to return originality and mastery of technique to embroidery. Morris and his daughter May were early supporters of the Royal School of Art Needlework, founded in 1872, whose aim was to "restore Ornamental Needlework for secular purposes to the high place it once held among decorative arts." Textiles worked in art needlework styles were featured at the various Arts and Crafts exhibitions from the 1890s to the Great War.

Textile Arts of France

Alençon lace or point d'Alençon is a needle lace that originated in Alençon, France. It is sometimes called the "Queen of lace." Lace making began in Alençon during the 16th century and the local industry was rapidly expanded during the reign of Louis XIV by Jean-Baptiste Colbert, who established a Royal Workshop in the town to produce lace in the Venetian style in 1665. The purpose of establishing this workshop was to reduce the French court's dependence on expensive foreign imports. The local lacemakers soon modified the Venetian technique and Alençon emerged as a unique style around 1675.

Though the demand for lace went into sharp decline following the French Revolution, it recovered some of its popularity during the

Second French Empire before entering terminal decline at the end of the 19th century with changes in fashion and the development of cheaper, machine-made lace.

Lace making survived on a small scale and the technique was preserved by Carmelite nuns in Alençon. In 1976 a National Lace Workshop was established in the town to ensure that this lace-making technique survives. There is a permanent exhibition of lace and a display showing how it is made in the Musée des Beaux Arts et de la Dentelle, located in the town centre and adjoining the Workshop. The workshops themselves are open to the public only on certain days of the year.

Blonde Lace

Blonde lace is a continuous bobbin lace from France that is made of silk. The term *blonde* refers to the natural colour of the silk thread. Originally this lace was made with the natural-coloured silk, and later in black. Most blonde lace was also made in black. It was made in the 18th and 19th centuries. The pattern, which is generally of flowers, is made with a soft silk thread, thicker than the thread used for the ground. This causes a big contrast between the flowers and the ground. It uses the same stitiches as Chantilly lace and Lille lace, and is similarly made in strips 5 inches wide and invisibly joined. Blonde lace is not as good as Chantilly lace though, as the ground isn't as firm, nor is the pattern as regular.

Blonde lace became very popular, and replaced Mechlin lace. It is very soft, and thus was well suited to the gathered trimmings fashionable during the nineteenth century. Blonde lace was used by royalty, and was worn in the portraits of the daughter of George IV, Princess Charlotte in 1817, and of Queen Adelaide in 1830. In 1805 blonde lace was popular in Paris.

Blonde lace was made in Caen from 1744, in parts of Flanders, in Barcelona, and, in small quantities, in the east Midlands of England from about 1806. It didn't suffer when other lacemakers were reduced to the brink of ruin in 1821 to 1832 by the introduction of machine-made bobbin net. In fact, the demand for blonde actually increased, and Caen exported great quantities, by smuggling, to England. It was one of the earliest laces to be copied by machine- in 1833 the traverse warp machine (invented in 1811) made it for a full season, and it was sold without saying it was machine-made, at handmade prices, with no one the wiser. By 1840 blonde lace was out of favour.

Spanish Blonde Lace

There was a lot of blonde lace made in Spain, mostly in the Catalonia region, and especially in Barcelona. It had all the same qualities as blonde lace made elsewhere, with very large flowers. It was used mainly for mantillas and scarfs and became part of the archetypical image of a Spanish lady.

Chantilly Lace

Chantilly lace is a handmade bobbin lace named after the city of Chantilly, France, in a tradition dating from the 17th century, though the most famous are silk laces introduced in the 18th century. Though called *Chantilly lace*, most of the lace bearing this name was actually made in Bayeux in France and Geraardsbergen, now in Belgium.

Chantilly lace is known for its fine ground, outlined pattern, and abundant detail. The pattern is outlined in *cordonnet*, a flat untwisted strand. The best Chantilly laces were made of silk, and were generally black, which made them suitable for mourning wear. White Chantilly lace was also made, both in linen and silk, though most Chantilly laces were made of silk. The black silk Chantilly lace became especially popular, and there was a large market for it in Spain and the Americas. Chantilly and the Spanish laces (such as Blonde lace) were the most popular black laces. Little white Chantilly was ever {?}made. Another notable thing about Chantilly lace is the use of a half-and-whole stitch as a fill to achieve the effect of light and shadow in the pattern, which was generally of flowers. The background, or *réseau*, was in the form of a six pointed star, and was made of the same thread as the pattern, unlike the otherwise similar Blonde lace. The lace was produced in strips approximately four inches wide, and then joined with a stitch that left no visible seam. Chantilly lace remained popular in the 19th century, when every fashionable lady had a black or white Chantilly shawl, made in Brussels or Ghent.

6

Textile Arts of Greece

Byzantine Silk

Byzantine silk is silk woven in the Byzantine Empire (Byzantium) from about the fourth century until the Fall of Constantinople in 1453.

The Byzantine capital of Constantinople was the first significant silk-weaving centre in Europe. Silk was one of the most important commodities in the Byzantine economy, used by the state both as a means of payment and of diplomacy. Raw silk was bought from China and made up into fine fabrics that commanded high prices throughout the world. Later, silkworms were smuggled into the Empire and the overland silk trade gradually became less important. After the reign of Justinian I, the manufacture and sale of silk became an imperial monopoly, only processed in imperial factories, and sold to authorized buyers.

Byzantine silks are significant for their brilliant colours, use of gold thread, and intricate designs that approach the pictorial complexity of embroidery in loom-woven fabric. Byzantium dominated silk production in Europe throughout the Early Middle Ages, until the establishment of the Italian silk-weaving industry in the 12th century and the conquest and break-up of the Byzantine Empire in the Fourth Crusade (1204).

Development

In the time of the Roman Empire, silk textiles reached the West overland via the Silk Road across Asia from China, passing through the Parthian Empire and later Sassanid Empire to trading centres in Syria. Imports of raw silk, silk yarn, and finished fabrics are all recorded, but the techniques of producing these textiles from the silkworm *bombyx mori* remained a closely guarded secret of the Chinese until the Emperor of the East Justinian (483–565) arranged to have silkworm eggs smuggled out of Central Asia in 553-54, setting the stage for the flowering of the Byzantine silk-weaving industry.

New types of looms and weaving techniques also played a part. Plain-woven or tabby silks had circulated in the Roman world, and patterned damask silks in increasingly complex geometric designs appear from the mid-3rd century. Weft-faced compound twills were developed not later than 600, and polychrome (multicoloured) compound twills became the standard weave for Byzantine silks for the next several centuries. Monochrome lampas weaves became fashionable around 1000 in both Byzantine and Islamic weaving centres; these fabrics rely on contrasting textures rather than colour to render patterns. A small number of tapestry-woven Byzantine silks also survive. Regulations governing the use of expensive Tyrian purple dyestuffs varied over the years, but cloth dyed in these colours was generally restricted to specific classes and was used in diplomatic gifts. Other dyes used in Byzantine silk workshops were madder, kermes, indigo, weld, and brazilwood. Gold thread was made with silver-gilt strips wrapped around a silk core.

Figured (patterned) Byzantine silks of the 6th (and possibly 5th) centuries show overall designs of small motifs such as hearts, swastikas, palmettes and leaves worked in two weft colours. Later, recognizable plant motifs (such as lotus leaves and flowers) and human figures appear. Surviving textiles document a rich exchange of techniques and iconographic themes between Constantinople and the newly-Islamic textile centres of the Mediterranean and Central Asia in the years after the Muslim conquests of the 7th century. Designs of the 8th and 9th centuries show rows of roundels or medallions populated with pairs of human or animal figures reversed in mirror-image on a vertical axis. Many motifs echo Sassanian designs including the tree of life, winged horses, lions, and imaginary beasts, and there are numbers of surviving pieces where specialists cannot agree between a Byzantine or Islamic origin. Fashionable patterns evoked the activities and interests of the royal court, such as hunting scenes or the quadriga (four-horse chariot).

Woven Textiles

Of the five basic weaves used in Byzantium and the Islamic weaving centres of the Mediterranean – tabby, twill, damask, lampas and tapestry – the most important product was the weft-faced compound twill called samite. The word is derived from Old French *samit*, from medieval Latin *samitum, examitum* deriving from the Byzantine Greek îÜìéôïí *hexamiton* "six threads", usually interpreted as indicating the use of six yarns in the warp. In samite, the main warp threads are hidden on both sides of the fabric by the ground and patterning wefts, with only the binding warps that hold the wefts in place visible.

These rich silks – literally worth their weight in gold – were powerful political weapons of the Byzantine Empire between the 4th and 12th centuries. Diplomatic gifts of Byzantine silks cemented alliances with the Franks. Byzantium granted silk-trading concessions to the sea powers of Venice, Pisa, Genoa and Amalfi to secure naval and military aid for Byzantine territories.

The influence exerted by Byzantine silk weaving was profound. Byzantine silk court ritual and ecclesiastical practices were adopted by the Franks, just as Byzantine court furnishing styles and dress codes were echoed across the Islamic world. Byzantium developed elaborate silk court attire and set the style for use of silk in civil and military uniforms and for rich religious vestments.... These silks served as a form of portable wealth that could be profitably disposed of in times of need.

Silks survive in Western Europe from the graves of important figures, used in book bindings, and also reliquaries. But it is clear they had a number of uses as hangings and drapes in churches and the houses of the wealthy, as well as for clothing and vestments. The sources rarely mention the specific origin of silks, but sometimes describe the designs in enough detail to allow an identification as Byzantine.

Anglo-Saxon England had silks from at least the late 7th century, brought back from Rome by Benedict Biscop and others. They were an essential, and easily carried, purchase for well-off pilgrims to Rome or the Holy Land (where Syrian or Egyptian silk might also be bought), and were available in England from English traders who certainly had bases in Rome and Pavia, and probably also bought from Scandinavian traders using the Baltic route. A unique special arrangement had to be made whereby the English crown paid directly a sum to Pavia in lieu of the customs duty on silk, which the Pavians found too difficult or dangerous to collect from English merchants. Diplomatic gifts also cascaded down from the Imperial court in Constantinople, with the rulers who received them passing many on to other rulers, and churches both in and outside their territory. Charlemagne gave not only King Offa of Mercia silks, but also the dioceses of Mercia and Northumbria.

Tapestry and Embroidery

In addition to woven dress and furnishing fabrics, Byzantine workshops were also known for woven tapestries and richly embroidered textiles with decoration that often included figurative scenes. The most impressive example to survive is the 10th century "*Bamberger Gunthertuch*", a woven tapestry piece over two metres square, with a mounted emperor between two female personifications. Nearly a century after it was made it was acquired by the Bishop of Bamberg in Germany, on a pilgrimage to Constantinople. He died during the journey and it was used for his shroud. Embroidered religious scenes were also used for vestments and hangings, and the famous English *Opus Anglicanum* seems to have been heavily influenced by Byzantine embroidery. This continued Late Antique trends, which among other evidence are known from finds in Egyptian cemetreies, and the complaint by Saint Asterius of Amasia in around 410 about his flock in northeastern Turkey, where he says the laity decorated their clothes with religious images:

> ... they artfully produce, both for themselves and for their wives and children, clothing beflowered and wrought with ten thousand objects....When, therefore, they dress themselves and appear in public, they look like pictured walls in the eyes of those that meet them. And perhaps even the children surround them, smiling to one another and pointing out with the finger the picture on the garment; and walk along after them, following them for a long time. On these garments are lions and leopards; bears and bulls and dogs; woods and rocks and hunters ... You may see the wedding of Galilee, and the water-pots; the paralytic carrying his bed on his shoulders; the blind man being healed with the clay; the woman with the bloody issue, taking hold of the border of the garment; the sinful woman falling at the feet of Jesus; Lazarus returning to life from the grave.

In doing this they consider that they are acting piously and are clad in garments pleasing to God. But if they take my advice let them sell those clothes and honour the living image of God. Do not picture Christ on your garments. It is enough that he once suffered the humiliation of dwelling in a human body which of his own accord he assumed for our sakes. So, not upon your robes but upon your soul carry about his image.

The Egyptian cemetrey examples are usually in less fine textiles than silk, and are typically roundels or other simple shapes with a border and a scene inside. This style of design seems not dissimilar to mentions and the few survivals of religious embroidery from the West many centuries later. Some Western embroidery was imported, other pieces no doubt done locally on imported silk, though other materials were used. The only survival of such work on the largest scale, the enormous Bayeux Tapestry (incomplete at 0.5 by 68.38 metres or 1.6 by 224.3 ft) is wool embroidered on a plain linen background, and not technically a tapestry at all. However smaller scale figurative hangings and clothes in silk are mentioned.

Decline

In 1147, during the Second Crusade, Roger II of Sicily (1095–1154) attacked Corinth and Thebes, two important centres of Byzantine silk production, capturing the weavers and their equipment and establishing his own silkworks in Palermo and Calabria. After the capture of Constantinople in 1204 by the forces of the Fourth Crusade (1202–1204) and the establishment of the Latin Empire (1204–1261) and other "Latin" states in the Byzantine territories, the Byzantine silk industry contracted, supplying only the domestic luxury market, and leadership in European silk-weaving and design passed to Sicily and the emerging Italian centres of Lucca and Venice.

Textile Arts of Hawaii

Aloha Shirt

The Aloha shirt, commonly referred to as a Hawaiian shirt, is a style of dress shirt originating in Hawaii. It is currently the premier textile export of the Hawaii manufacturing industry. The dress shirts are printed, mostly short-sleeved, and collared. They usually have buttons, sometimes for the entire length of the dress shirt, and sometimes just down to the chest (pullover). Aloha dress shirts usually have a left chest pocket sewn in, often with attention to ensure the printed pattern remains continuous. Aloha shirts may be worn by men or women; women's aloha shirts usually have a lower-cut, v-neck style. The lower hem is straight, as the shirts are not meant to be tucked in.

Aloha shirts exported to the mainland United States and elsewhere are called Hawaiian shirts and often brilliantly coloured with floral patterns or generic Polynesian motifs and are worn as casual, informal wear.

Traditional men's aloha shirts manufactured for local Hawaiian residents are usually adorned with traditional Hawaiian quilt designs, tapa designs, and simple floral patterns in more muted colours. Contemporary aloha shirts may have prints that do not feature any traditional Hawaiian quilt or floral designs and instead may have such elements as automobiles, drinks, sports team logos, or other elements arranged in the same pattern as a traditional aloha shirt.

Aloha shirts manufactured for local wear are considered formal wear in business and government, and thus are regarded as equivalent to a shirt, coat, and tie (generally impractical in the warmer climate of Hawaii) in all but the most formal of settings. Malahini (newcomers) and tourists (visitors) often wear designs of many bright colours while Kama»aina (or those who have been living in the islands for a long time) seem to prefer less busy patterns. These shirts often are printed on the interior, resulting in the muted colour on the exterior, and are called "reverse print". For those not familiar, it may appear to be a defect in manufacturing as the shirt appears to be sewn together inside-out.

The related concept of "Aloha Attire" stems from the Aloha shirt. Semi-formal functions such as weddings, birthday parties, and dinners are often designated as "Aloha Attire", meaning that men wear Aloha shirts and women wear muumuu or other tropical prints. Because Hawaii tends to be more casual, it is rarely appropriate to attend such functions in full evening wear like on the mainland; instead, Aloha Attire is seen as the happy medium between excessive formality and casual wear (i.e. business casual). "Aloha Friday," a now-common tradition of celebrating the end of the workweek by wearing more casual attire on Fridays, initially grew out of an effort to promote aloha shirts. Although not uncommon to see professional women participating in Aloha Friday, it is more common to see men dressing this way.

The modern Aloha shirt was devised in the early 1930s by Chinese merchant Ellery Chun of King-Smith Clothiers and Dry Goods, a store in Waikiki. Chun began sewing brightly coloured shirts for tourists out of old kimono fabrics he had leftover in stock. The Honolulu Advertiser newspaper was quick to coin the term Aloha shirt to describe Chun's fashionable creation. Chun trademarked the name. The first advertisement in the Honolulu Advertiser for Chun's Aloha shirt was published on June 28, 1935. Local residents, especially surfers, and tourists descended on Chun's store and bought every shirt he had. Within years, major designer labels sprung up all over

Hawaii and began manufacturing and selling Aloha shirts en masse. Retail chains in Hawaii, including mainland based ones, may mass-produce a single aloha shirt design for employee uniforms.

After World War II, many servicemen and servicewomen returned to the United States from Asia and the Pacific islands with aloha shirts made in Hawaii since the 1930s. Tourists began flocking to Hawaii in the 1950s as faster airplanes allowed for easier travel and the former U.S. territory became a state in 1959. Alfred Shaheen, a textile manufacturer, revolutionized the garment industry in postwar Hawaii by designing, printing and producing aloha shirts and other ready-to-wear items under one roof. The tropical-print shirts for men and sundresses for women became standard and sometimes tacky souvenirs for travelers, but Shaheen raised the garments to the level of high fashion with artistic prints, high-grade materials and quality construction. Tori Richard was a prominent designer of these shirts, establishing a business in Honolulu in 1956. Elvis Presley wore a Shaheen-designed red aloha shirt featured on the album cover for the *Blue Hawaii* soundtrack in 1961.

The aloha shirt has at times been associated with the gay community, as made clear in the season 8 episode of The Simpsons Homer's Phobia. The association may stem from the tendency of Magnum, P.I. main character Thomas Magnum, portrayed by Tom Selleck, to regularly wear aloha shirts on the show, as it was set on the island of Oahu, Hawaii. Selleck was rumored to be gay, though he has since denied those rumors. Any association with the court case Baehr v. Miike, a lawsuit in which three same-sex couples argued that Hawaii's prohibition of same-sex marriage violated the state constitution which later provided an impetus for the enactment of the federal Defense of Marriage Act (DOMA) in 1996, is likely secondary at best, as the case wasn't initiated until 1991, roughly three years after the end of the television show's broadcast.

Aloha Week

In 1946, the Honolulu Chamber of Commerce funded a study of aloha shirts and designs for comfortable business clothing worn during the hot Hawaiian summers. The City and County of Honolulu passed a resolution allowing their employees to wear sport shirts from June–October. City employees were not allowed to wear aloha shirts for business until the creation of the Aloha Week festival in 1947. The Aloha Week festival was motivated by both cultural and economic concerns: First held at Ala Moana Park in October, the festival revived interest in ancient Hawaiian music, dancing, sports, and traditions. There was a holoku ball, a floral parade, and a makahiki festival attended by 8,000 people. Economically, the week-long event first attracted visitors during October - traditionally a slow month for tourism - which benefited the Hawaiian fashion industry as they supplied the mu»umu»u and aloha shirts worn for the celebration. Aloha Week expanded in 1974 to six islands, and was lengthened to a month. In 1991, Aloha Week was renamed to Aloha Festivals.

In the end, Aloha Week had a direct influence on the resulting demand for alohawear, and was responsible for supporting local clothing manufacturing: locals needed the clothing for the festivals, and soon people in Hawaii began wearing the clothing in greater numbers on more of a daily basis. Hawaii's fashion industry was relieved, as they were initially worried that popular clothing from the mainland United States would eventually replace aloha attire.

Aloha Friday

In 1962, a professional manufacturing association known as the Hawaiian Fashion Guild began to promote aloha shirts and clothing for use in the workplace, particularly as business attire. In a campaign called "Operation Liberation", the Guild distributed two aloha shirts to every member of the Hawaii House of Representatives and the Hawaii Senate. Subsequently, a resolution passed in the Senate recommending aloha attire be worn throughout the summer, beginning on Lei Day. The wording of the resolution spoke of letting "...the male populace return to 'aloha attire' during the summer months for the sake of comfort and in support of the 50th state's garment industry."

In 1965, Bill Foster, Sr., president of the Hawaii Fashion Guild, led the organization in a campaign lobbying for "Aloha Friday", a day employers would allow men to wear aloha shirts on the last business day of the week a few months out of the year. Aloha Friday officially began in 1966, and young adults of the 1960s embraced the style, replacing the formal business wear favoured by previous generations. By 1970, aloha wear had gained acceptance in Hawaii as business attire for any day of the week.

Hawaii's custom of Aloha Friday slowly spread east to California, continuing around the globe until the 1990s, when it became known as Casual Friday. Today in Hawaii, alohawear is worn as business attire for any day of the week, and "Aloha Friday" is generally used to refer to the last day of the work week. Now considered Hawaii's term for "Thank God It's Friday" (TGIF), the phrase was used by Kimo

Kahoano and Paul Natto in their 1982 song, "It's Aloha Friday, No Work 'til Monday", heard every Friday on Hawaii radio stations across the state.

Feather Cloak

Featherwork cloaks have been used by several cultures.

Hawaii

Elaborate feather cloaks called *»ahu»ula* were created by early Hawaiians for the *ali»i* (royalty). Feathers were also used in women's skirts called *pa»u.* The *»i»iwi* (Vestiaria coccinea) and *»apapane* (*Himatione sanguinea*), which provided red feathers, were killed and skinned due to their abundance. Yellow feathers were obtained from the mostly black and rarer *»ô»ô* (*Moho nobilis*) and *mamo* (*Drepanis pacifica*) using a catch and release philosophy to ensure future availability.

Maori

In Maori culture feathers are a sign of chiefly rank, and the kakahu (feather cloak), is still used as sign of rank or respect.

Irish

The elite class of poets known as the filid wore a feathered cloak, the tuigen.

Famous Works

- Nahi»ena»ena's Pa»u, feather skirt of Princess Nahi»ena»ena and funeral garment of Hawaiian royals
- Kamehameha's Cloak, feather cloak of Kamehameha I made entirely of the golden-yellow feather of the mamo, used by the Kings of Hawaii
- Kiwalao's Cloak, feather cloak of Kîwala»ô captured by Kamehameha I in 1782, used by the Queens of Hawaii
- Liloa's Ka»ei, sash of King Liloa of the island of Hawaii

Kapa

Kapa is a fabric that was made by Native Hawaiians from the bast fibres of certain species of trees and shrubs in the orders Rosales and Malvales. It is similar to tapa found elsewhere in Polynesia but differs in the methods used in its creation. Kapa was based primarily on the creative combination of linear elements that cross and converge to form squares, triangles, chevrons and diagonal forms, giving a feeling of boldness and directness. (The Hawaiian /k/ phoneme corresponds to Polynesian /t/.)

Kapa was used primarily for clothing like the *malo* worn by men as a loincloth and the *pa»u* worn by women as a wraparound. Kapa was also used for *kîhei* used over the shoulders. Other uses for kapa depended on caste and a person's place in ancient Hawaiian society.

Kapa moe (bed covers) were reserved for the *ali»i* or chiefly caste while kapa robes were used by *kahuna* or priestly caste. Kapa was also used as banners where leis were hung from it and images of their gods were printed on it.

Cultural anthropologists over the course of the twentieth century identified techniques in the creation of kapa that was unique to the Hawaiian Islands. *Wauke* (*Broussonetia papyrifera*) was the preferred source of bast fibres for kapa, but it was also made from *»ulu* (*Artocarpus altilis*), *ôpuhe* (*Urera* spp.), *ma»aloa* (*Neraudia melastomifolia*), *mamaki* (*Pipturus albidus*), *»akala* (*Rubus hawaiensis*), *»akalakala* (*R. macraei*), and *hau* (*Hibiscus tiliaceus*). In the 18th century, pieces of kapa were often made of grooving or ribing. It is done by pushing the dampened cloth into the grooves of a special board. The *wauke* tree was cut and soaked in water.

It was then laid on a *kua kuku* (polished stone tablet) and beaten with a *hôhoa* (rounded beater). After the first phase of beating, the kapa was transferred to a sacred house to be beaten a second time but in a religious manner.

Each kapa manufacturer used a beater called an *kuku*, a beater with four flat sides that were each carved differently. Another way to carve the kapa is by starting on the four-sided affairs, with the coarsest grooves on one side used first in breaking down the bast, or wet bark.

Then, the beating continued using two sides with finer grooves. Lastly, finishing touches were accomplished with the remaining smooth side of the beater. The carvings left an impression in the cloth that was hers alone. After the European discovery of the Hawaiian Islands, Western traders travelled to Hawai especially for kapa.

The process of making kapa was done primarily by women. Young girls would learn by helping their mothers, over time doing the majority of the work, and when older she could make kapa by herself.

Tapa Cloth

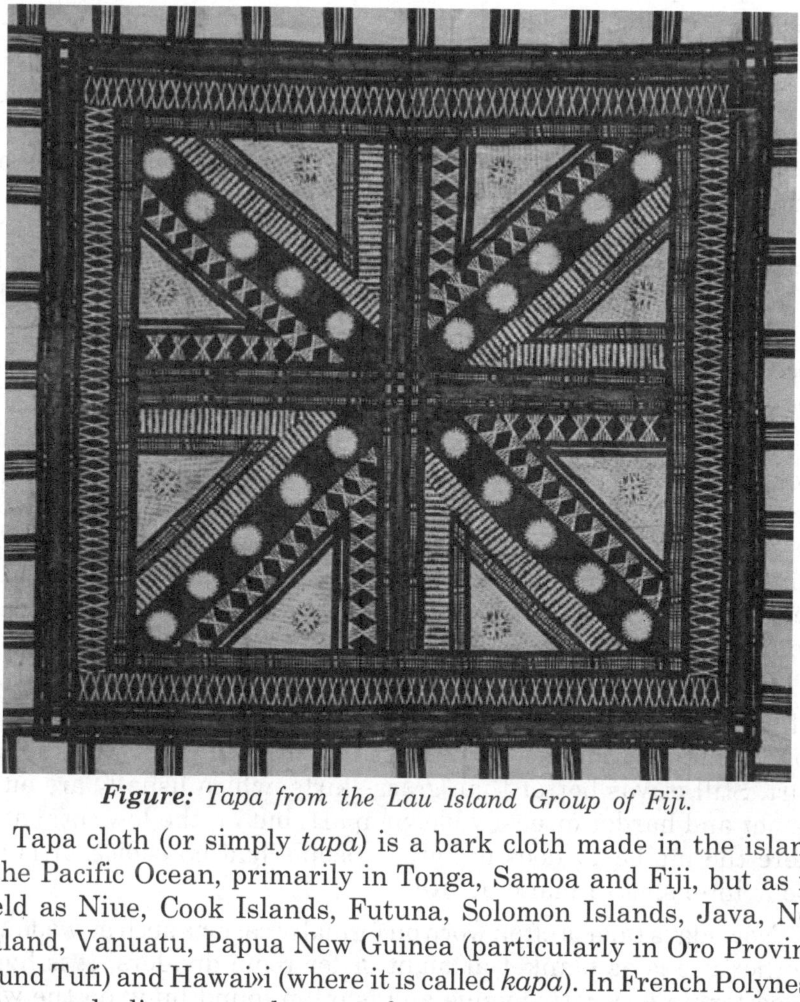

Figure: *Tapa from the Lau Island Group of Fiji.*

Tapa cloth (or simply *tapa*) is a bark cloth made in the islands of the Pacific Ocean, primarily in Tonga, Samoa and Fiji, but as far afield as Niue, Cook Islands, Futuna, Solomon Islands, Java, New Zealand, Vanuatu, Papua New Guinea (particularly in Oro Province around Tufi) and Hawai»i (where it is called *kapa*). In French Polynesia it has nearly disappeared, except for some villages in the Marquesas.

General

The cloth is known by a number of local names although the term tapa is international and understood throughout the islands that use the cloth. The word tapa is from Tahiti and the Cook Islands, where Captain Cook was the first European to collect it and introduce it to the rest of the world. In Tonga, tapa is known as ngatu, and here it is of great social importance to the islanders, often being given as gifts. In Samoa, the same cloth is called siapo, and in Niue it is hiapo. In Hawai»i, it is known as kapa. In Rotuma, a Polynesian island in the Fiji group, it is called 'uha and in other Fiji islands it is called masi. In the Pitcairn islands it was called ahu. It is also known as tapia.

All these words give some clue to the origin. *Masi* could mean the (bark of the) dye-fig *(Ficus tinctoria)*, endemic to Oceania, and probably the one originally used to make tapa. Somewhere in history, during the voyages of migration the *hiapo* or *siapo* was introduced from Southeast Asia, the paper mulberry tree (*Broussonetia papyrifera*). The bark of this tree is much better to use, and put the use of the dye-fig into oblivion. Only its name remained in Fiji. *Tapa* finally, has the meaning of border or strip. It seems likely that before the glueing process became common to make large sheets only narrow strips were produced.

Tapa can be painted, decorated by rubbing, stamping, stencilling, smoking (Fiji: "masi Kuvui") or dyeing. The patterns of Tongan, Samoan, and Fijian tapa usually form a grid of squares, each of which contains geometrical patterns with repeated motifs such as fish and plants, for example four stylised leaves forming a diagonal cross. Traditional dyes are usually black and rust-brown, although other colours are known.

In former times the cloth was primarily used for clothing, but now cotton and other textiles have replaced it. The major problem with tapa clothing is that the tissue loses its strength when wet and falls apart. Still it was better than grass-skirts, which usually are either heavier and harder or easily blown apart, but on the low coral atolls where the mulberry does not grow, people had no choice. It is also labour intensive to manufacture.

Nowadays tapa is often worn on formal occasions such as weddings. Another use is as blanket at night or for room dividers. It is highly prized for its decorative value and is often found hung on the walls as decoration. In Tonga a family is considered poor, no matter how much money they have, if they do not have any tapa in stock at home to donate at life crises like marriages, funerals and so forth. If the tapa was donated to them by a chief or even the royal family, it is more valuable. It has been used in ceremonial masks in Papua New Guinea and the Cook Islands (Mangian masks). It was used to wrap sacred objects, e.g., "God staffs" in the Cook Islands.

Fabrication

As Tonga is the country where tapa is still a part of daily life, the following description is given for that country. Although on other islands the overall process is about the same, there might be smaller or larger differences.

In Tonga *hiapo* is the name given to the paper mulberry tree. People have bunches of them growing in a corner of their plantations. They are cut and brought home where the first task is to strip the bark from the trees. The strips are about hand wide and person long. The wood left over is named *mokofute*. The bark consists of two layers. In the next step the outer bark is to be scraped or split off from the inner bark. This work is called *ha»alo*. The outerbark is discarded; the innerbark, named *tutu* or *loututu*, is left over. It is dried in the sun before being soaked.

After this, the bark is beaten on a wooden *tutua* anvil using wooden mallets called *ike*. In the beating the bark is made thinner and spread out to a width of about 25 cm. This phase of the work is called *tutu* (or *tutua*). The mallets are flat on one side and have coarse and fine grooves on the other sides. First the coarse sides are used and, towards the end of the work, the flat side (*ta-tu»a*). The continuous "thonk" beats of the tapa mallet is a normal sound in Tongan villages. If several women work together they can make a concert out of it. In that case there might be one who *tukipotu*, beats the end of the *tutua* to set the rhythm.

When the strips are thin enough, several are taken and beaten together into a large sheet. Some starch from the *kumala*, or *manioke* may be rubbed on places which are unwilling to stick. This part of the work is called *»opo»opo*, the glue is called *tou* and the resulting sheet of tapa is called *feta»aki*. It then consists of two layers of strips in perpendicular direction, the upper one called *lau»olunga* and the lower one *laulalo*. A knife or sharp shell named *mutu* is used to trim the edges, and the pieces fallen off in this process are called *papanaki*. When the white feta»aki is smoked brown, it is called *sala*.

Often the women of a whole village work together on a huge sheet of tapa. A donation is made to the church or their chief at an important occasion. Such sheets are about 3 m wide and 15, or 30, or sometimes even 60 m long. The 15 metre pieces are called *launima* (meaning five-sheet, because the sheet is five squares), and the 30 m pieces are called *lautefuhi*.

Friedrich Ratzel in *The History of Mankind* described, in 1896, the fabrication of tapa as follows:

"A circular cut is made with a shell in the bark above the root of the tree; the tree is broken off, and in a few days, when the stem is half-dry, the bark and bast are separated from it. The bast is then cleaned and macerated in water, after which it is beaten with the ribbed club on a wooden block. This beating enlivens a village in Tonga as threshing does in Europe. In half an hour the piece will have changed in shape from a strip almost to a square. The edges are snipped with shells, and a large number of the pieces are drawn separately over a semi-cylindrical wooden stamp, on which the pattern, worked in coco-fibre, is stretched and smeared with a fluid at once adhesive and colouring. On each a second and third layer is placed; and the piece, three layers thick, is coloured more strongly in the parts which are thrown into relief by the inequalities of the bed. Others are annexed to it both at the side and the end, until pieces a yard wide, and 20 to 25 yards long, are produced.

Painting

The *feta»aki* is almost always painted. It then becomes *ngatu*, the Tongan word for the final product. The painting is done over the whole length, but only the central 2.5 metre in the width direction. On both sides there is an unpainted border of about 20 cm wide, which is called the *tapa* (in Tonga). To paint it, the sheets are put over a huge wooden drum covered with stencils or *kupesi* (*upeti* in Samoa). These stencils are made from coconut front midribs (or any other sticks of a few millimetre thick) and made in the pattern which will be used. There are a handful of standard *kupesi* designs, like the 'pine road' (the road from the palace to the royal cemetrey), or the 'shield of Tonga', or the 'lion' (the king), or the 'dove' (the king as ruler), and more abstract figures like the 'Manulua' (two birds).

The tapa sheet is put over the drum and the women rub with force a dabber with some brown paint (made from the *koka* tree *(Bischofia javanica))* over the sheet. This work is called *tata»i*. Where they rub over a rib of the *kupesi* more paint will stick to that position while very little will stick elsewhere. In this way the basic pattern is put on the sheet.

Once a part is done, they lift up the sheet and proceed to the next strip and so forth. Only when the whole sheet has been preprocessed, it will be spread out on the ground and with a brush (made from *Pandanus* seeds). The women will accentuate the faintly visible marks with some more generous paint, this time made from the *tongo*, the mangrove *(Rhizophora mangle)*. Both *koka* and *tongo* paint are always brown, but the latter is much darker. Black is not used in Tonga, although it is characteristic for Fiji.

It is customary that during the paint process lines are drawn on the *ngatu* along the width every 45 cm or more. The *kupesi* too are made to the size that they will fit in the divisions thus made. Such a division is known as *langanga* and they are numbered (on the blank *tapa*) from one to as many as needed for the whole length. When a smaller piece of ngatu is needed, the sheet is cut along a *langanga* division. A 4 to 6 *langanga* piece is called *fola»osi*. An 8-piece is *fatuua*, while a 10 *langanga* piece of *ngatu* is known as *toka hongofulu*. Less common are the double *fatuua*, named *fatufa* or double of that again, the *fatuvalu*.

These are the traditional *ngatu*, as evidenced by the extensive vocabulary used (still many more terms exist). Nowadays for the tourist trade other sizes and designs can be made as well.

Lauhala

Lauhala, *lau* meaning "leaf" in the Hawaiian language, refers to the leaves of the hala tree *(Pandanus tectorius)*.

The hala tree is of great cultural, health and economic importance in many Pacific Islands. The fruit of the tree is used as a food source in many Pacific Islands. The fruits are often consumed fresh or as a preserved food while the trunks of *P. tectorius* can be used as building material, and leaves for thatching. Though many parts of the hala tree are utilized, in Hawaii the most common use of Hala is the leaves.

Hawaiians distinguish five kinds of the hala tree according to the colour and size of the fruits:

- *hala »ula* (orange red)
- *hala lihilihi »ula* (red tip, becoming yellow to the centre)
- *hala »îkoi* (bright orange only at the tip)
- *hala melemele* (yellow)
- *hala pia* (not quite white, small fruit)

Weaving

Many Pacific cultures weave, plait, or braid the leaves of the *P. tectorius* to create useful items such as baskets, mats and hats. Though it is a long and arduous process to prepare the leaves for weaving, the final products are works of art with a pleasing earthy feel.

Remains of *lauhala* from burial caves in Hawai»i show almost the same patterns as more recent woven objects, therefore the tradition of this craft seems to be very old. The district of Puna on the Island of Hawai»i was known for the abundance of *hala*.

Types of Lauhala

The favoured lauhala for weaving was called "lauhala kilipaki". The leaves of this *Pandanus sp.* were exceptionally soft and durable. They were highly prized for their beauty in colour and the ease with which they could be plaited. Special sleeping mats were created out of the "Hinano", male flower, of the hala tree.

The light coloured bracts were very soft and pliable and made very finely woven mats reserved for the chiefs. They were especially prized because of their scarcity. Male plants are much less common in the wild than female, and they only make a few flowers per season. The bracts are also very short, about 25 centimetres (9.8 in) long and 15 centimetres (5.9 in) wide, with only about two thirds of the bract actually usable for weaving.

Hienaena's Pau

Nahi»ena»ena's Pa»u is the largest known Hawaiian feather cloak. It is a feather skirt (pa»u) made for Princess Nahi»ena»ena.

Story

The pa»u, or feather skirt, was made about 1824 for the Princess Nahi»ena»ena, the daughter of King Kamehameha I and Keôpuolani, a highborn chiefess considered the most "sacred" of Kamehameha's wives. Descended from ali»i on Maui and the ruling chiefs of Hawaii island, Keôpuolani had a better family background than Kamehameha himself. Nahi»ena»ena and her brothers were of the highest rank and were seen as "the strength and purity of the Hawaiian people."

This special ceremonial garment symbolizes that rank. The pa»u was only worn once by the princess, apparently reluctantly. She was about 9 years old when the only engraving of her was drawn. The bodies of King Kamehameha II and Queen Kamamalu had been brought back from Great Britain on the HMS *Blonde*, and the first Christian memorial service was held for a Hawaiian King. She was conflicted with her religious beliefs; Keôpuolani and Queen Ka»ahumanu had converted to Christianity after the death of Kamehameha I and rejected the old Hawaiian religion, which the pa»u represented. She would run away and hide when ceremonial occasions demanded she wear the pa»u.

Description

The garment was 20 × 2.5 ft (6.1 × 0.76 m), which Nahi»ena»ena wore by wrapping around her. It was cut in half and resewn after

Nahi»ena»ena's death in 1836, and currently measures 10 × 5 ft (3.0 × 1.5 m). The pa»u is made mostly of yellow feathers from the now-extinct »ô»ô and mamo birds. Both birds were mostly black but had patches of yellow under their wings and tail.

A geometric pattern of alternating triangles of black ô»ô feathers and red-orange feathers of the now-endangered »i»iwi bird lines the edge of the pa»u. While these birds were widely collected by the Native Hawaiians for their feathers, it is more likely that their ultimate extinction was due to habitat loss and disease.

The triangles are thought to represent shark teeth or mountains, which are both symbols of power, but it still remains a mystery. Small bundles of a half-dozen or fewer feathers, about an inch long, are tied into the eye using netting made from olona vegetable fibres. There are an estimated 1 million feathers on the skirt, meaning that 200,000 birds were probably involved.

Aftermath

After the death of Nahi»ena»ena, the pa»u remained in the royal family and was kept at »Iolani Palace. It was reconfigured and worn by dead Hawaiian royalty while lying in state. There is a single reference that it was used at the funeral of Kamehameha III in 1854, and photos show it covering the coffin of King Kalakaua in 1891. The Bernice P. Bishop Museum stored it for more than 100 years in a secure temperature- and humidity-controlled room. Bishop Museum collections manager Betty Kam called it "a one-of-a-kind treasure".

The pau was displayed for one day at the Bishop Museum's Polynesian Hall on June 11, 2003 which was Kamehameha Day, as a tribute to the princess and her father. The rare artifact was guarded by practitioners the Hawaiian martial art of lua in traditional garb. This was the first public showing of the pa»u in 10 years, though it was displayed at a Bishop Museum fund-raiser in May 2003. It was also displayed in a 2006 exhibit.

Hawaiian Quilt

A Hawaiian quilt is a distinctive quilting style of the Hawaiian Islands that uses large radially symmetric applique patterns. Motifs often work stylized botanical designs in bold colours on a white background.

Hawaiian quilt applique is made from a single cut on folded fabric. Quilting stitches normally follow the contours of the applique design.

Figure: *A Hawaiian quilt.*

History

Hawaiian quilting derives from the kapa moe, an indigenous bed cover textile. Kapa was constructed from the inner bark of local trees. Traditional kapa was beaten and felted, then dyed in geometric patterns.

Quilting may have begun in the Hawaiian islands with the arrival of missionaries and Western fabrics in the 1820s. The climate of Hawaii is unsuitable for cotton cultivation and kapa is unsuitable for quilting so all Hawaiian quilts are constructed from imported material. The earliest written reference comes from Isabella Bird who visited Hawaii in 1870 and wrote a travelogue *Six Months in the Sandwich Islands*.

Flag Quilts

Another Hawaiian quilt style incorporates multiple copies of the Hawaiian flag and commemorate the state's former independence as a sovereign kingdom. Many of these flag quilts date back to the overthrow of the monarchy, when displaying the Hawaiian flag was considered treason. Quilts bearing symbols of the monarchy were a form of silent resistance.

Other Styles

Hawaiian quilters also made other styles of quilts including embroidering quilts and crazy quilting. The most famous Hawaiian crazy quilt is the one made by Queen Liliuokalani during her internment after the overthrow of the monarchy.

Value

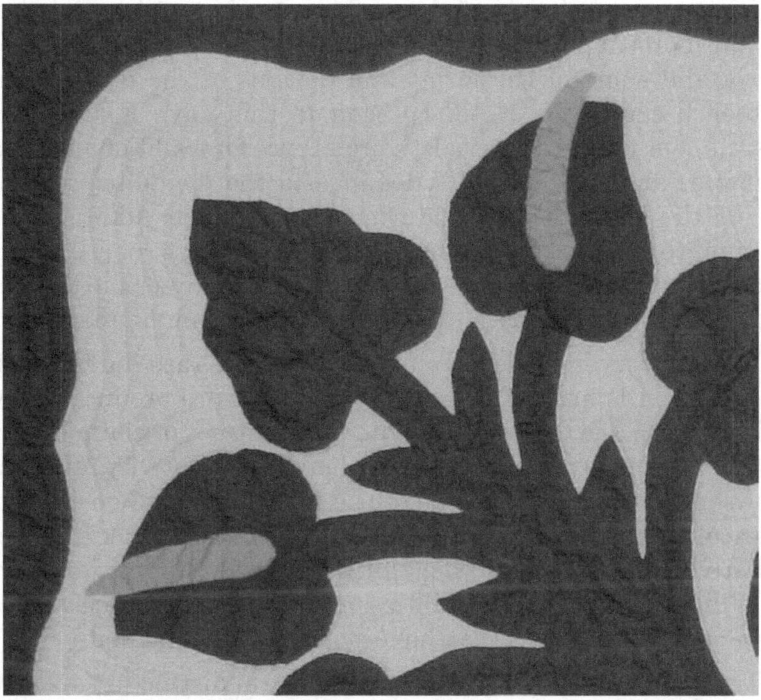

Figure: *Detail.*

Antique flag quilts fetch higher prices than applique quilts: high quality flag quilts may be valued at $40,000 - $60,000 while applique quilts sell for $9000 – $15,000. Factors that affect price include the quality of the original construction, preservation of the item's colour and physical integrity, and provenance.

Textile Arts of Japan

Textiles provide an interesting and revealing vantage point to look at any society. This is particularly the case with Japanese textiles. Beginning in the early modern era when Japan increased its urbanization, textiles became a badge of social status. Because of their closeness to the human body in clothes and other uses, textiles show by their motif, colour and garment shape much about Japan and its culture. In addition, they send messages as to an individuals age, rank, gender, social, political and religious affiliation. In Japan they also often denoted an individuals occupation, special function and association with special groups.

This is the case throughout Japanese history but is perhaps even more apt during the Edo period when economic, commercial and social conditions created levels of change that made textiles and clothing an even more important form of social identification. Many of the criteria and some of the forms and designs of the eighteenth and nineteenth century can still be seen to this day. For example, a preference for natural materials, a preference for traditional decorating techniques and as if a subtle defiance to the dwindling interest in wearing the kimono – the enduring status of the yukata. Textiles continue to this day to demonstrate their commercial uses of demonstrating a shops main activities. This can be seen in the present usage of noren (doorway curtain) and advertising banners.

Many observers believe Tsujigahana textiles are the zenith of the Japanese textile arts. These textiles which were produced between the fourteenth and the early seventeenth century for clothes, banners and other items are examples of the height of creativity and beauty. In one sense Tsujigahana textile can be seen as a reflection of Japanese historical changes. Many of the best pieces of tsujigahana reflect the decorative extravagance of the later Edo period. This comminglinging of very different artistic sensibilities produced many miracles of artistic and technical brilliance that have not yet been equaled.

Textiles reached a high degree of cultural distinction and artistic appreciation in the Edo and succeeding Meiji periods (1868 – 1912). The social and commercial importance of their role in turn instilled vigor and a greater range of artistic expression. With ties to religion, peasant life and in part as a reaction to a growingly complex urban culture, Japans' textile traditions evolved from commoner textile traditions that had been utilized for centuries. Away from the palace workshops, weavers, dyers and neeedleworkers added to local traditions by adapting foreign techniques, revitalizing patterns by absorbing exotic motifs and creating innovative design.

During the Edo and Meiji periods, elite classes commissioned complicated and diverse fabrics in rich silk brocades and filmy gauze weaves. The lower classes, working within the strictly regulated feudal guidelines for clothing material, patterns and colours were not stagnant during this period. They often created new forms with bold images that were intricate in their subtle nuances. Dyeing emerged as an art form in its own right during this period. Although the use of vibrant colours was often prescribed by the Shogun or economically cost prohibitive, the use of brighter colours increased during this period

Through the centuries, Japanese textiles have often followed two diverse genuses – the textiles produced for and worn by commoners and those of the higher social classes. Although it might at first be thought that the one could never rival the other, in artistic form and creativity, both branches of the textile art are deeply moving embellishments of the country's folk culture.

- Bunka shishu

F

- Fukusa
- Furoshiki

I

- Ise-katagami

K

- Kariyushi shirt

Kasuri

K cont.

- Katazome
- Kichô
- Kijôka-bashôfu
- Kumejima-tsumugi

N

- Nishijin

Noren

S

- Saga Nishiki
- Shibori

T

- Tsutsugaki

Y

- Yuki-tsumugi

Textile Arts of Korea

Korean fabric arts are craft of making fabric and textiles produced by the people on the Korean Peninsula. They have a long history, which includes fabrics such as guksa, nobang, sha, jangmidan, Korean-made jacquard, brocade and satin. Or crafts such as the Korean quilts known as bojagi, Korean embroidery, Korean knots, Korean clothing and the rarer arts of Korean blinds weaving and Korean paper clothing.

Hanbok

Hanbok (South Korea) or ChosOn-ot (North Korea) is the traditional Korean dress. It is often characterized by vibrant colours and simple lines without pockets. Although the term literally means "Korean clothing", *hanbok* today often refers specifically to hanbok of ChosOn Dynasty and is worn as semi-formal or formal wear during traditional festivals and celebrations.

Throughout history, Korea had a dual clothing tradition, in which rulers and aristocrats adopted different kinds of mixed foreign-influenced indigenous styles, while the commoners continued to use a distinct style of indigenous clothing that today is known as Hanbok.

Basic Composition and Design

Traditional women's hanbok consists of *jeogori*, a blouse shirt or a jacket and *chima*, a wrap-around skirt, which is usually worn full. The ensemble is often called *chima jeogori*. Men's hanbok consists of *jeogori* and *baji* which means pants in Korea. The *baji* were baggy pants in traditional men's hanbok.

Jeogori

Jeogori is the basic upper garment of the hanbok, which has been worn by both men and women. It covers the arms and upper part of the wearer's body. The basic form of a *jeogori* consists of *gil*, *git*, *dongjeong*, *goreum* and sleeves. *Gil* (8®) is the large section of the garment in both front and back side and *git* (C®) is a band of fabric that trims the collar. *Dongjeong* (Ù³È) is a removable white collar placed over the end of the *git* and is generally squared off. The *goreum* (à¬„¹) are coat-strings that tie the *jeogori*. Women's *jeogori* may have *kkeutdong* (]°Ù³), a different coloured cuff placed at the end of the sleeves. There are two jeogori that may be the earliest surviving archaeological finds. One from a Yangcheon Heo Clan tomb is dated 1400-1450, while the other was discovered inside a statue of Buddha at Sangwonsa Temple (presumably left as an offering) that has been dated to the 1460s.

The form of *Jeogori* has changed over time. While men's *jeogori* remained relatively unchanged, women's *jeogori* dramatically shortened during ChosOn dynasty, reaching its shortest length at the late 19th century. However, due to reformation efforts and practical reasons, modern *jeogori* for women is longer than its earlier counterpart. Nonetheless the length is still above the waist line. Traditionally, *goreum* were short and narrow, however modern *goreum* are rather long and wide. There are several types of *jeogori* according to fabric, sewing technique, and shape.

Chima

Chima refers to "skirt" which is also called *sang* (ó^) or *gun* (Ù^) in hanja. The underskirt, or petticoat layer is called *sokchima*. According to remaining murals of Goguryeo, and an earthen toy excavated from the neighbourhood of Hwangnam-dong, Gyeongju, Goguryo women wore a *chima* first, and then *jeogori* over *the chima*, covering its belt.

Although striped, patchwork skirts, and gored skirts are known from the Goguryeo period, from the ChosOn dynasty (redirected from Joseon)at least skirts were made from rectangular cloth that was pleated or gathered into a skirt band. This waistband extended past the skirt fabric itself, and formed ties so that the skirt could be fastened around the trunk of the body.

Sokchima was largely made in a similar way to the overskirts until the early 20th century when straps were added, later developing into a sleeveless bodice or 'reformed' petticoat. By the mid 20th century, some outer *chima* had also gained a sleeveless bodice, that was then covered by the *Jeogori*.

Baji

Baji refers to the bottom part of the men's hanbok. It is the formal term for 'pants' in Korean. Compared to western style pants, it does not fit tightly. The roomy nature of the cloth is due to a design aimed at making the cloth ideal for sitting on the floor. It performs similar role today for modern trousers, but Baji is commonly used in Korea for any kinds of pants. There are two in front of baji, and a person can tighten up whenever needed.

Baji are classified as unlined trousers, leather trousers, silk pants, cotton pants according to dress, sewing way, embroidery and so on.

Po

Po is a generic term referring to an outer robe or overcoat, which was worn mostly by men since the Goryeo period until the Chos On period. *Durumagi* is a variety of *po* that was worn to protect the cold.

It had been widely worn as an outer robe over *jeogori and* baji. It is also called jumagui, juchaui, *or* juui.

"Po" is also called "Jeogori", written as in hangul. Jeogori inherited the Chinese Ming ao skirt's white collar and Jin. As buttoned blouse, skirt in front of the two on each seam have Jin, female's Jeogori has a long belt hung in front of the dress, also have an effect of adornment. Jeogori below the cuff is refers to the jacket sleeves, characterized by a traditional Korean house in the eaves of natural feminine curves. There are differences between the men and women's Jeogori. Men's Jeogori coarse to with line and flat; Women's Jeogoris have beautifully decorated curves which are short and beautiful.

Jokki and Magoja

Jokki is a type of vest while *magoja* is an outer jacket. Although *jokki* and *magoja* were created at the end of the ChosOn Dynasty in which the Western culture began to affect Korea, the garments have been considered parts of traditional clothing. Each is additionally worn over *jeogori* for warmth and style. *Magoja* was an originally Manchu style clothing, but was introduced to Korea after Heungseon Daewongun, the father of King Gojong returned from his political exile in Manchuria in 1887. Magoja derived from *magwae* that he wore at that time to protect cold weather of the region. It was good to keep warmth and easy to wear, so that magoja became popular in Korea. It is also called *"deot jeogori"* (literally "an outer jeogori") or *magwae*.

Magoja does not have *git*, band of fabric that trims the collar, *goreum* (tying strings) unlike *jeogori* and *durumagi* (overcoat). *Magoja* was originally a male garment, but later became a unisex clothing. The magoja for men has *seop* (6Á, overlapped column on the front) and its length is longer than women's magoja, so that its both sides of the bottom are open. A magoja is made of a silk and is adorned with one or two buttons which are usually made from amber. In a male magoja, buttons are attached to the right side on contrary to women's magoja.

At first, women wore the magoja for style rather than as a daily outfit and especially Kaeseong people used to wear it a lot. It is made of a silk and the colour for women tends to be a neutral colour to harmonize with other garments such as *jeogori* and *chima* which are worn together. In spring and autumn, a pastel tone is used for the women's magoja, so that wearers could wear it over a jeogori for style. As for men's magoja worn during spring and summer, jade, green, gray, dark grey were used.

Children's Hanbok

In old days, *Kkachi durumagi* (literally "a magpie's overcoat") were worn as *seolbim*, new clothing and shoes worn on Seollal, New Year's Day in the Korean calendar, while at present, it is worn as a ceremonial garment for *doljanchi*, celebration for a baby's first birthday. It is a children's colourful overcoat. It was worn mostly by young boys. The clothes is also called *obangjang durumagi* which means "an overcoat of five directions". It was worn over *jeogori* (a jacket) and *jokki* (a vest) while the wearer could put *jeonbok* (a long vest) over it. *Kkachi durumagi* was also worn along with headgear such as *bokgeon* (a peaked cloth hat), *hogeon* (peaked cloth hat with a tiger pattern) for young boys or *gulle* (decorative headgear) for young girls.

Modern hanbok for children consists of only two or three pieces and can be put on easily. They are usually made of less expensive fabrics since they are only worn once or twice a year during bigger holidays like Chuseok and Seolnal. Children are also dressed up in hanbok on their first birthday, *dol*.

Occasions

Hanbok is classified according to its purposes: everyday dress, ceremonial dress and special dress. Ceremonial dresses are worn on formal occasions, including a child's first birthday, a wedding or a funeral. Special dresses are made for shamans and officials.

History

Antiquity: The hanbok can trace its origin to nomadic clothing in the Scytho-Siberian cultural sphere of northern Asia, widespread in ancient times. The earliest evidence of this common style of northern Asia can be found in the Xiongnu burial site of Noin Ula in northern Mongolia, and earliest evidence of hanbok's basic design features can be traced to ancient wall murals of Goguryeo before the 3rd century BCE.

Reflecting its nomadic origins in northern Asia, hanbok was designed to facilitate ease of movement and also incorporated many shamanistic motifs. From this time, the basic structure of hanbok, namely the *jeogori* jacket, *baji* pants, and the *chima* skirt, was established. Short, tight trousers and tight, waist-length jackets were worn by both men and women during the early years of the Three Kingdoms of Korea period. The basic structure and these basic design features of hanbok remains relatively unchanged to this day.

Towards the end of the Three Kingdoms period, noblewomen began to wear full-length skirts and hip-length jackets belted at the waist and noblemen began to wear roomy trousers bound in at the ankles and a narrow, tunic-style jacket cuffed at the wrists and belted at the waist.

Although most foreign influence on Hanbok didn't last or was superficial, Mongolian clothing is an exception as the only foreign influence that made significant visible changes to Hanbok. After Goryeo Dynasty (918–1392) signed peace treaty with the Mongol Empire in the 13th century, Mongolian princesses who married into Korean royal house brought with them Mongolian fashion which began to prevail in both formal and private life. As a result of this influence, the *chima* skirt was shortened, and *jeogori* was hiked up above the waist and tied at the chest with a long, wide ribbon, the *goruem* (instead of being belted) and the sleeves were curved slightly. Cultural exchange was not one way however. Goryeo had significant cultural influence on the Mongols court of Yuan Dynasty, the most visible of which was adoption of women's hanbok by the aristocrats, queens and concubines of the Mongol court.

Chos On Dynasty

The early ChosOn dynasty appeared to continue the women's fashion for baggy, loose clothing, such as those seen on the mural from the tomb of Bak Ik (1332–1398). However, by the 16th century, the jeogori had shortened to the waist, and appears to have become closer fitting, although not to the extremes of the bell-shaped silhouette of the 18th and 19th centuries.

Today's hanbok is the direct descendant of hanbok as worn in the ChosOn dynasty period, specifically the late 19th century. Hanbok had gone through various changes and "fashion fads" during the five hundred years under the reigns of ChosOn kings and eventually evolved to what we now mostly relate to as a typical hanbok.

Everyday Wear

During the ChosOn Dynasty, the chima or skirt adopted fuller volume while the jeogori or blouse took more tightened and shortened form, which are features quite distinct from the hanbok of previous centuries, when *chima* was rather slim and *jeogori* baggy and long, reaching well below the waist level. After the Imjin War economic hardship on the peninsula may have influenced the closer-fitting styles that would use less fabric. However, this explanation doesn't take into account the ever expanding voluminous size of the dress which must have increased the use of fabric despite the disastrous effects of the war.

In the eighteenth century, the short length of *jeogori* reached extremity as to scarcely cover the breasts. Therefore women of respectable social backgrounds began to wear a piece of long cloth called *heoritti* around the breast. *Heoritti* was originally worn as an undergarment beneath the *jeogori*, but was now worn as an outwear. The common and lowborn classes, however, often eschewed the *heoritti* altogether, as a way of indicating that they had given birth to a son. This also may have assisted with breastfeeding.

During the seventeenth and eighteenth centuries the fullness of the skirt was concentratrated around the hips, thus forming a silhouette similar to Western bustles. The fullness of the skirt reached its extreme around 1800. During the nineteenth century fullness of the skirt was achieved around the knees and ankles thus giving *chima* a triangular or an A-shaped silhouette, which is still the preferred style to this day. Many undergarments such as *darisokgot, soksokgot, dansokgot*, and *gojengi* were worn underneath to achieve desired forms.

A clothes reformation movement, which aimed to lengthen *jeogori,* experienced quite a success in the early twentieth century and has continued to influence the shaping of modern hanbok. Modern *jeogori* are longer, although still halfway between the waistline and the breasts. *Heoritti* are sometimes exposed for aesthetic reasons. At the end of nineteenth century, Daewon-gun introduced *Magoja*, a Manchu-style jacket, to Korea, which is often worn over *jeogori* to this day.

Men's hanbok saw little change compared to women's hanbok. The form and design of *jeogori* and *baji* hardly changed.

However, men's lengthy outwear, equivalent of modern overcoat went through quite a dramatic change. Before the late 19th century, *yangban* men almost always wore *jungchimak* when going abroad. *Jungchimak* had very lengthy sleeves and its lower part had splits on both sides and occasionally on the back so as to create fluttering effect when walking. To some this was considered fashionable, and to some, namely stoic scholars, it was nothing but pure vanity. Daewon-gun successfully banned *jungchimak* as a part of his clothes reformation programme and *jungchimak* eventually disappeared.

Durumagi, which was previously worn underneath *jungchimak* and basically a house dress substituted *jungchimak* as the formal outwear for *yangban* men. *Durumagi* differs from its predecessor in that it has tighter sleeves and does not have splits on either sides and the back. It is also slightly shorter in length. Men's hanbok has remained relatively the same since the adoption of *durumagi*.

Korean Embroidery

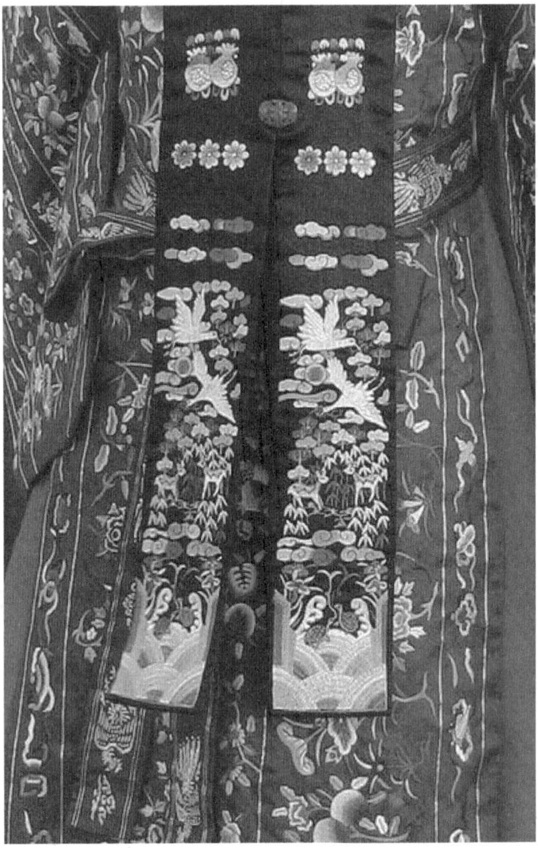

Figure: *Detail of colourful Korean embroidery.*

Korean embroidery techniques and artifacts have a long history, but there is the most evidence from the Joseon Dynasty, after the 14th century in Korea. This article talks about the history, styles, preservation, artists, and examples of screens, costumes, and domestic wares of this exacting and beautiful art form.

People used needles made out of bones of fish or animals to sew and weave animal skins and the bark or leaves of trees.

Chasu, the Korean word for embroidery, was a method of cultivating beauty in every corner of daily life. *Pokshik chasu*, *kiyong chasu*, *kamsang chasu* and Buddhist *chasu* are the four types of Chasu.

- Pokshik chasu is the embroidery on clothes.
- Kiyong chasu is the embroidery decorated on various materials used in the king's palace.
- Kamsang chasu represented a type of artistic piece.
- Buddhist chasu came from Buddhism. Buddhist chasu was used in the statues of Buddha or various temples. Chasu has begun from the prehistoric era when the humans first started to make clothes.

Textile Arts of Mexico

The Textiles of Mexico have a long history. The making of fibres, cloth and other textile goods has existed in the country since at least 1400 BCE. Fibres used during the pre-Hispanic period included those from the yucca, palm and maguey plants as well as the use of cotton in the hot lowlands of the south. After the Spanish conquest of the Aztec Empire, the Spanish introduced new fibres such as silk and wool as well as the European foot treadle loom. Clothing styles also changed radically.

Fabric was produced exclusively in workshops or in the home until the era of Porfirio Díaz (1880s to 1910), when the mechanization of weaving was introduced, mostly by the French. Today, fabric, clothes and other textiles are both made by craftsmen and in factories. Handcrafted goods include pre-Hispanic clothing such as huipils and sarapes, which are often embroidered.

Clothing, rugs and more are made with natural and naturally dyed fibres. Most handcrafts are produced by indigenous people, whose communities are concentrated in the centre and south of the country in states such as Mexico State, Oaxaca and Chiapas. The textile industry remains important to the economy of Mexico although it has suffered setback due to competition by cheaper goods produced in countries such as China, India and Vietnam.

Pre-Hispanic Period

The oldest known fabric fragments in Mexico have been found in the arid north of the country in states such as Coahuila, Chihuahua and Durango and date to approximately between 1800 and 1400 BCE. In pre-Hispanic times, the most common woven fibres in dry areas were from the yucca and palm trees, with cotton grown in the hot humid areas near the coast. It was unknown to the Aztecs until they conquered cotton growing areas and began demanding it as tribute. Then, only the upper classes were permitted to wear it. Given the important status cotton cloth had, it is often used as money. For some ceremonial garments, amate or bark paper was used.

Each of the sedentary Mesoamerican cultures had a god of weaving. Women were often buried with woven items they had made. Cortés mentions the Aztecs' skill in weaving in one of this letters to the king of Spain, in very favourable terms.

Colonial Era

After the Spanish conquest of the Aztec Empire, the production of cloth and the wearing of clothes in Mesoamerica changed drastically. Most pre-Hispanic forms of dress and body adornment were banned by the Spanish as "uncivilized." Indigenous, European and Asian fabrics influenced Mexican cloth production by the mid colonial period. The Spanish did not favour the native cotton, nor did they find the material produced on traditional backstrap looms wide enough.

New techniques and materials were introduced. Spanish modes of dress, itself a mixture of European, Asia Minor and Egyptian influences, were introduced as well. At first wool and silk fabric was imported, then sheep and silkworms as well as European foot pedal looms all by the late 1530s.

By 1580, Mexico had become one of the most productive areas for wool and silk cloth. Most of the production was concentrated in the present day states of Oaxaca, Tlaxcala and Puebla. At first Spanish weavers dominated production, but they were soon replaced by native weavers who were making material cheaper.

Instead of prohibiting Indian made fabric, European weavers decided instead to hire them, creating workshops. While the indigenous weavers were not paid much, the Spanish owners did make money. These workshops eventually produced enough fabric for both internal consumption and for export to Spain, the Philippines, Central America and Peru. Silk cloth production was particularly dominant from 1540 to 1580; However, the end of this period, the yearly Manila Galleon was regularly bringing cheaper silk from Asia.

While cotton cloth was not favoured by the Europeans, it was still made and offered as tribute to Spanish overlords. Commercializing the fibre was difficult as the plant grows in the lowlands near the oceans and not near the manufacturing areas in the highlands, and transportation costs were high. Large cotton weaving workshops were not founded until the second half of the 17th century.

Eventually, the production of this fabric as well as wool fabric filled the gap left by the disappearance of Mexican silk fabric production. Wool fabric remained important because it was favoured by the upper tiers of colonial society, and because sheep could be raised near major weaving areas, such as Puebla, Querétaro, Valladolid, Acámbaro, and San Miguel de Allende.

19th Century to Present

In times past, fabric and clothing were made to last for decades, but today fabric is much cheaper and much of what clothing is bought is soon thrown away. This is mostly due to the mechanization of weaving, which has made fabric inexpensive.

In Mexico, as in other parts of the world, the introduction of modern transportation and communications brought about major changes in the production and distribution of goods and in firms' management and structure. In the 19th century, industrialization affected textile production with the introduction of steam-powered machines and the efforts of French immigrants from Barcelonnette, who began to arrive in Mexico in the early 19th century.

The mass production of textiles, especially cotton textiles, developed earlier than in other countries outside of Western Europe and the United States, nearing the same level as in England in the mid-18th century despite social unrest at that time. Mechanization of cloth production began in the 1830s; however, high internal taxes among states kept production facilities small and unconsolidated.

While Mexican production lagged behind that of Europe, certain regions of the country such as La Laguna, in the modern states of Durango and Coahuila, became important producers of cotton fabric. The most widely produced fabric was called "manta," a natural cotton favoured by many indigenous groups.

The development of steamship lines and railroad networks allowed Mexico-produced fabrics to be exported. The consolidation of power by Porfirio Díaz in the 1880s opened up business opportunities and made foreign investment possible. By the end of the 19th century, textile production and distribution was the country's largest manufacturing sector, mostly controlled by French immigrants. The immigrants worked together, forming the "Barcelonnette network."

They started off with small textile mills and dry goods stores, which eventually grew into large factories and department stores, including Palacio de Hierro, which still exists. These French immigrants consolidated textile operations by the end of the 19th century, and by the start of the Mexican Revolution changed their power source from steam to electricity. They also changed textile mills from mostly family-owned organizations to more modern enterprises with professional managers and stock sold on exchanges.

The sewing machine appeared in the early 20th century and became widely used to join fabric and for embroidery . This led to another level of textile production: finished clothing.

Craft and Indigenous Textiles Today

Indigenous Tradition

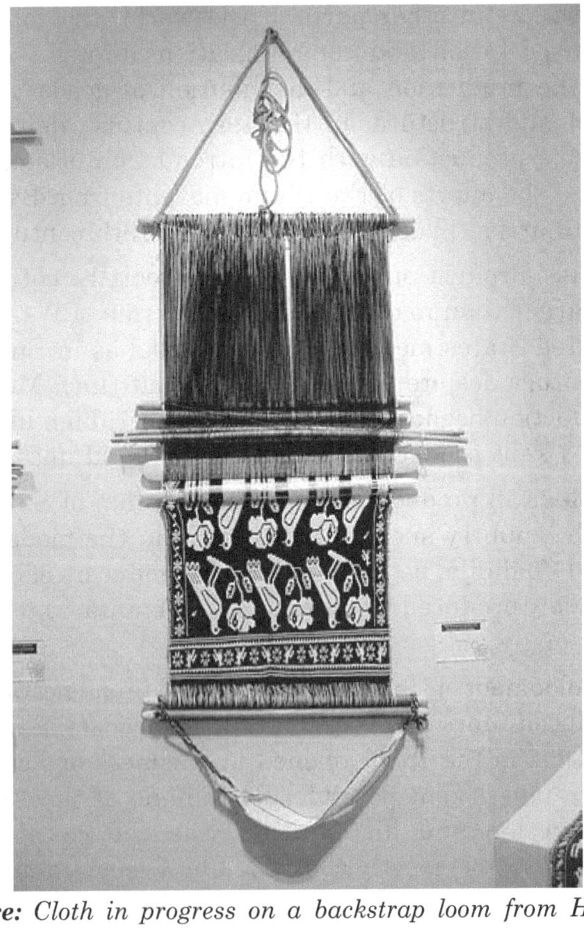

Figure: *Cloth in progress on a backstrap loom from Hidalgo.*

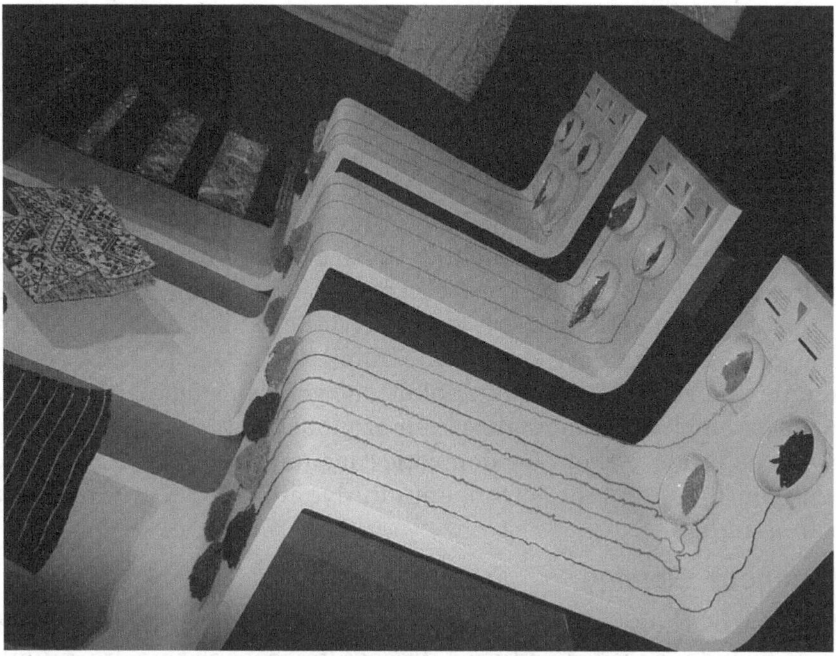

Figure: *Exhibition of colouring with natural dyes at the "Bioartesanías" event at the Museo de Arte Popular.*

Textiles is one of Mexico's more important crafts as it represents the continuation of tradition as well as its fusion with modern designs and techniques. Both pre-Hispanic and colonial era style textiles are still made in Mexico. In addition, many of the textile factories use machines based on old foot pedal looms from the colonial period. There are basically four types of fibres used for fabric production:

- Vegetable products such as cotton
- Animal products such as wool and silk
- Minerals such as gold and silver thread
- Synthetics.

Raw materials for textiles fall into two groups: smooth fibres such as silk, cotton, and wool, introduced to the American continent by the conquistadors; and hard fibres native to Mexico such as ixtle, lechuguilla, reeds, palm, twigs, and willow. In indigenous regions of Mexico, women are responsible for clothing the community, a process which often begins with harvesting natural fibres and then spinning, dyeing, and weaving textiles. In various parts of Mexico, both native backstrap looms and pedal-driven looms of European origin are used to weave principally cotton and wool.

Most handcrafted textiles are produced by the sixty or so indigenous ethnic groups in Mexico, who mostly live in rural areas in the centre and south of the country. In these textiles, traditional indigenous designs, and in some cases techniques still survive. One common technique in craft fabric is brocade, which allows for raised designs to be woven into the cloth. Most indigenous textiles are made at home by women and used for clothing, home use, decorative use and ceremonial use. Items include those that are hand woven, hand embroidered, knitted and more. Clothing is one of the ways that these groups distinguish themselves from each other and the world at large. Some of these garments include the huipil, the quechquemitl, tilmas, sandals and rebozos. A number of ethnic groups, such as the Nahua in central Mexico commercialize their original and traditional creations as well as produce them for domestic consumption. People in coastal areas continue to plant cotton, spin it, dye it with natural elements such as indigo.

Indigenous Clothing

Most of the pre-Hispanic clothing that survives is for women. These include "enredos", or wrap dresses, fajas, or cloth belts, huipils, a type of tunic, quechquemitl, which is a kind of rectangular or square short poncho. The last was originally worn directly on the upper body of a woman but today it is worn over a blouse. Loose-fitting sack dresses, called huipils in Oaxaca and guanengos in Michoacán, are often heavily embroidered with straight stitching, cross stitching and tucks with floral and geometric motifs.

A widely used garment in both indigenous and mixed race communities is the rebozo. This is a long rectangular shawl used both as a wrap and as a means to carry children or heavy objects tied onto the body. The rebozo came about during the colonial period, not in the pre-Hispanic era. The rebozo is a synthesis of three historical influences, the pre-Hispanic "mámatl," the Spanish mantilla and the "repacejo," an Oriental garment. This is a long rectangular piece of cloth with long fringes at both ends. Most rebozos are made with multicoloured designs woven into the pieces using threads of different colours. Those of a single colour are usually made of yarn or thread that has been tie-dyed to produce colour variations in the final piece. This latter style is called "jaspe" or jasper and are usually woven on backstrap looms.

The rebozo has been produced mostly in central Mexico since the colonial period, with some of the best known producers in Mexico

State and Michoacan. Tenancingo is one of the best known producers of craft rebozos, usually made of cotton but wool is also used. Traditional rebozos in the Lake Pátzcuaro area are often of white and blue over a black background and may be embroidered in tiny cross stitch.

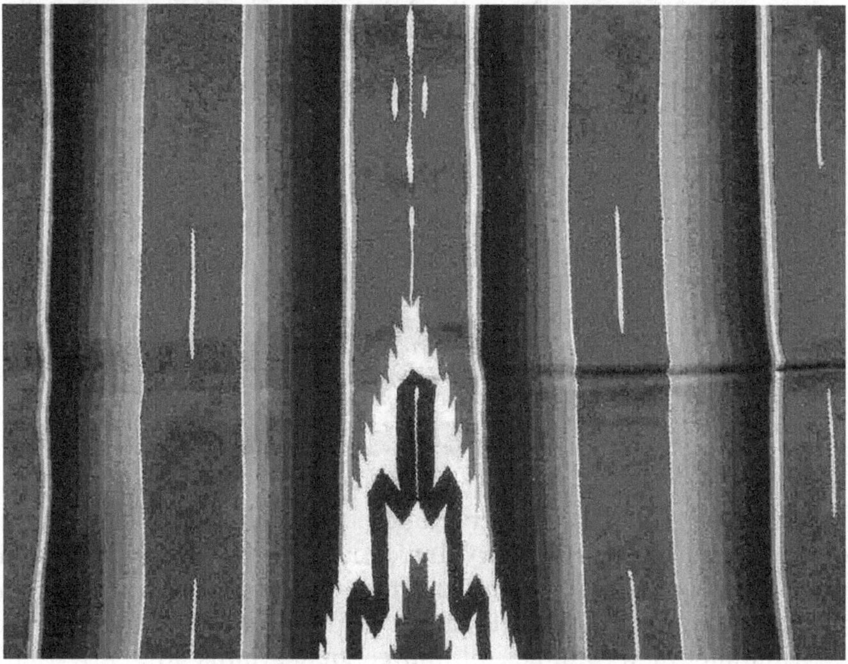

Figure: *Portion of a sarape*

Few pre-Hispanic male clothing pieces survive since many Mesoamerican males went about nude or semi nude, causing Spanish authorities to force them to adopt European shirts and pants early. This early colonial style shirts and pants have changed little in indigenous communities and are now identified with indigenous groups, especially the Tarahumara in Chihuahua, the Tacuates in Oaxaca and the Tzeltals in Chiapas.

Many male garments arc heavily embroidered in multiple colours. Since indigenous pants lack pockets, many men carry decorated bags called morals. The only pre-Hispanic male garment to survive is the sarape, which is used only in certain areas of Mexico.

In addition to clothing, other items are woven such as bedspreads, blankets, hats, cinches and knapsacks. The designs for these are most often woven into the fabric itself, but embroidered stars, border designs, deer, and other can be seen as well. These items may be made with various fibres include those derived from the maguey plant.

Embroidery

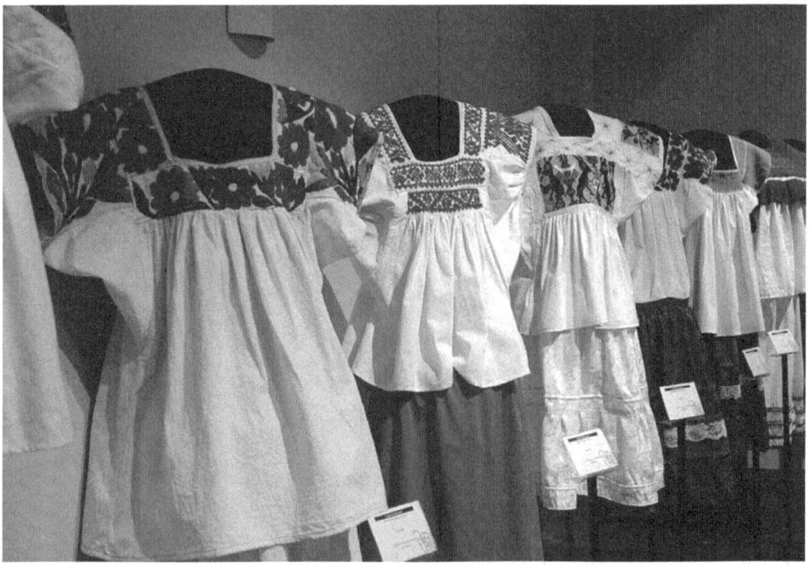

Figure: *Embroidered blouses from the La Huasteca region of Hidalgo.*

One of the most distinctive aspects of indigenous handcrafted textiles is the use of embroidery. Indigenous motifs found on garments range from geometric pattens, zig-zag, spirals, moons, crosses and stepped frets. Thin cloth belts that wrap around the waist (fajillas) are common in a number of indigenous groups and are richly embroidered. The borders are often adorned with zig-zag edging, such as those of the Huichols. The Otomis use a moon pattern on these belts along with their morrals or carrying bags, and the Tarahumara tend to decorate theirs with triangular designs. Many of the embroidery patterns of the huipils in Oaxaca, also show pre-Hispanic influence. Flower designs are popular for embroidering women's clothing among the Otomis, Nahuas, Huastecs, Huichols and others. Spirals and curved designs appear with frequency especially in the centre and south of the country.

In addition to flowers, other themes from nature in woven and embroidered designs include plants, animals such as squirrels, rabbits, deer, armadillos, doves, hummingbirds, pelicans, seagulls and fish. Mazahua embroidered belts are known for their zoomorphic designs and those of Santo Tomás Jalieza tend to have images of large plumed birds. The cloth napkins of San Mateo del Mar have images of aquatic birds such as pelicans and seagulls, with those of the Tacuates of Santiago Zacatepec have borders with many diminutive animals such as centipedes, scorpions, birds, iguanas, cats, foxes and more.

Human figures appear with relative frequency as well. They feature prominently on the embroidered napkins of San Juan Colorado and as Danza de la Pluma dancers on the cloth belts of Santo Tomás Jalieza. Patriotic symbols such as two-headed eagles, the three colours of the Mexican flag and the eagle with serpent crest. These are most prevalent in the central region of the country among the Otomis, Nahuas, Huastecos, Huicholes and others. Christian symbols such as the cross, virgins, saints, angels and other elements were introduced by evangelists in the early colonial period. These appear on small and large pieces such as men's shirts among the Tzotzil in Chiapas, in the fabrics of San Miguel Ameyalco, which feature churches, and the appearance of the Virgin of Guadalupe in many textiles in the Sierra Norte of Puebla.

Popular sayings or phrases also appear especially in the textiles of the Purhepechas around Lake Pátzcuaro and in the state of Puebla.

Looms

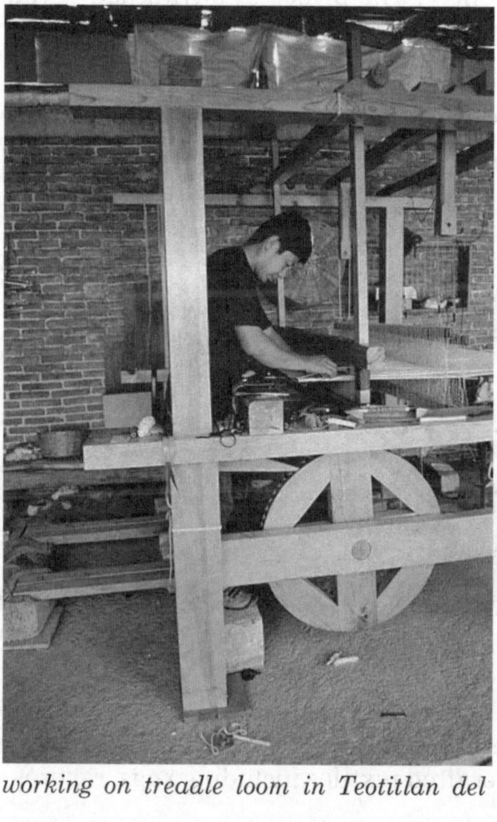

Figure: *Man working on treadle loom in Teotitlan del Valle, Oaxaca*

Two types of looms are employed in the making are handcrafted fabrics, the pre-Hispanic backstrap loom and the introduced European foot pedal loom. Traditionally, weaving, especially on the backstrap loom, was considered to be women's work. Women still produce items such as kitchen cloths, tablecloths, carrying bags and ornamental items with traditional designs. Although considered primitive, the backstrap loom is versatile and allows for different techniques and combinations of techniques, some of which can be very complicated. It allows for the combining of different fibres such as cotton with wool or silk. Designs are woven into the cloth on this loom by changing thread colours and/or by adding items such as shells or other matter into the finished product. The backstrap loom is most prevalent in the south of the country.

The foot pedal loom was brought to Mexico after the Conquest. Unlike pieces done on backstrap looms, pieces done on these machines have traditionally been done by men with wool being the favoured fibre. This type of loom is most extensively used in the centre and north of the country. The principal advantage of this loom is that it allows for pieces of greater width than backstrap looms and has been used to create sarapes, rugs, blankets and more.

Rugs and other items Made in Oaxaca and Mexico State

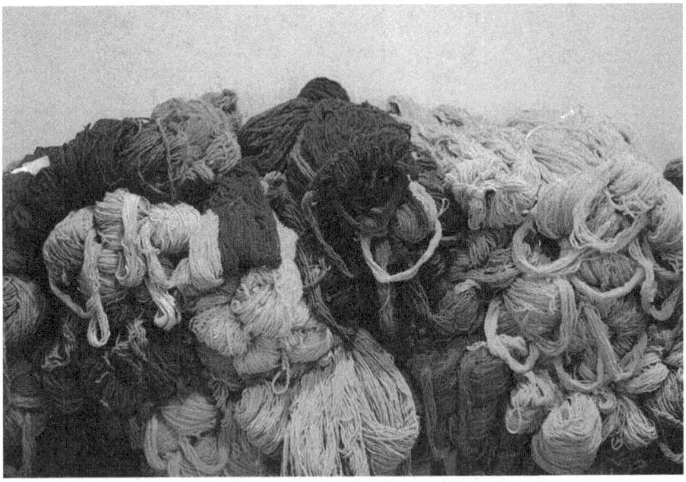

Figure: *Skeins of wool yarn that have been hand dyed with natural dyes.*

Two states that continue to have significant handcrafted textile production are Oaxaca and Mexico State. Oaxaca is known for its variety of handcrafted textiles including rugs, rebozos, tablecloths and traditional clothing such as huipils. These are made backstrap looms or foot pedal looms. In Mexico State craft pieces are mostly produced in Jiquipilco, Tejupilco de Hidalgo, Temascaltepec de González, Temoaya, Valle de Bravo, Zacazonapan, Toluca and Tenancingo producing napkins, tablecloths, sheets, kitchen items, clothing, bathroom items, rebozos and rugs.

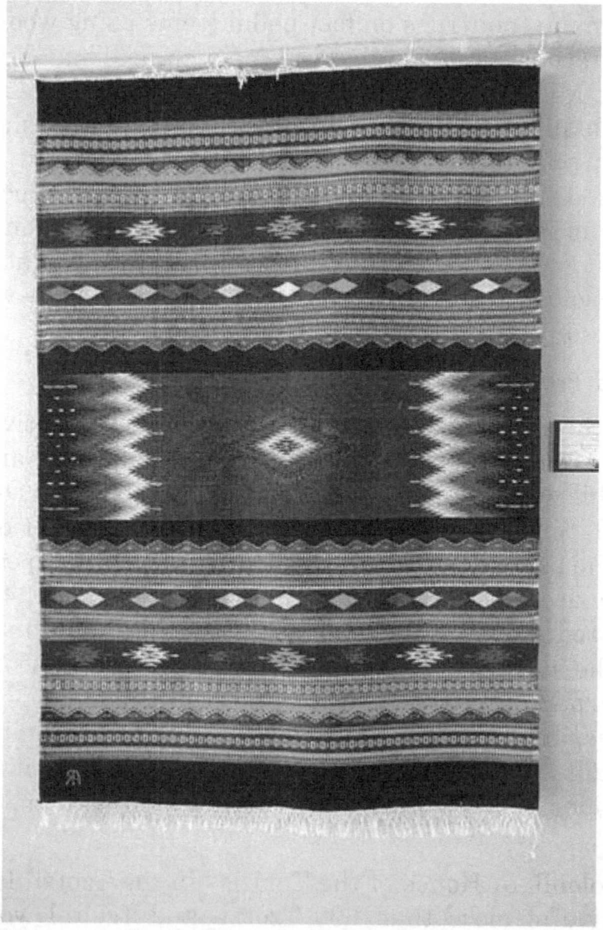

***Figsure:** "Diamante Ojo de Dios" by Antonio Ruiz Gonzalez of Teotitlan del Valle at Museo Estatal de Arte Popular de Oaxaca*

Both states also are significant producers of rugs. The making of knotted rugs by the Otomi in Mexico State is relatively recent. It began in 1969 when Ernesto Fernández Hurtado of the Bank of Mexico decided to promote a pilot centre in Temoaya for the study and manufacture of this type of rug using traditional Otomi designs. Today, these rugs are a distinctive feature in Mexico State crafts. The rugs are made with 100% virgin wool and have an average knot density of 140,000 m2. There are about 21 different designs offered with 250 variations in colours and size. Most are sold in upper-class neighbourhoods of Mexico City, but due to the problem of cheap imitations, some vendors only sell from their workshops.

Teotitlán del Valle in Oaxaca is known for its woven rugs. Most producers make their rugs on foot pedal looms using wool dyed with natural materials such as indigo and the cochineal bug. Rugs are also produced in Mitla, Santa Ana del Valle and Tlacolula de Matamoros along with blankets and a type of sarape. One distinguishing feature of Oaxaca rug production is the use of the cochineal insect. This insect has been used since pre-Hispanic times to dye fibre, producing colours ranging from purple to yellow, varying depending on what the ingredients, such as certain flowers or lime juice, are added. For a time, the use of natural dyes was threatened by cheaper synthetics but the use of natural dyes has made a comeback.

Value and Protection of Handcrafted Textiles

After the Mexican Revolution, references to native Mexican cultures became fashionable, including arts crafts food and regional clothing. This was expressed in the arts by those such as Diego Rivera and Dr. Atl. Since that time, there have been a number of efforts to maintain and expand the textile producing traditions, especially of the south of Mexico. The Textile Museum has a collection of 4,000 pieces and is located in the former monastery of San Pablo in the city of Oaxaca. The museum was opened in 2008 and sponsored by the Alfredo Harp Helú Foundation. The pieces include modern, colonial and pre-Hispanic textiles. Clothing items include huipils, enredos, quechquemilts, skirts, rugs and wall hangings. The collection is in three divisions Textiles of Oaxaca, Textiles of Mexico and Textiles of the World.

Sna' Jolobil, or House of the Textiles in the Tzotzil language, is a cooperative of more than 600 Tzotzil and Tzeltal women in 12 municipalities in Chiapas based in San Cristóbal de las Casas. It was founded to promote and elevate the textile crafts, especially those produced on backstrap looms, with the aim of preserving traditional techniques and designs as well as promoting the economic fortunes of women weavers. The organization has a collection of antique huipils available for study and reproduction as well as workshops in weaving and producing vegetable dyes. The organization has been successful in attracting more young people into the craft. In 1986, it received the Premio Nacional de Ciencias y Artes (National Prize of Sciences and the Artes) and numerous members have earned individual awards for their work.

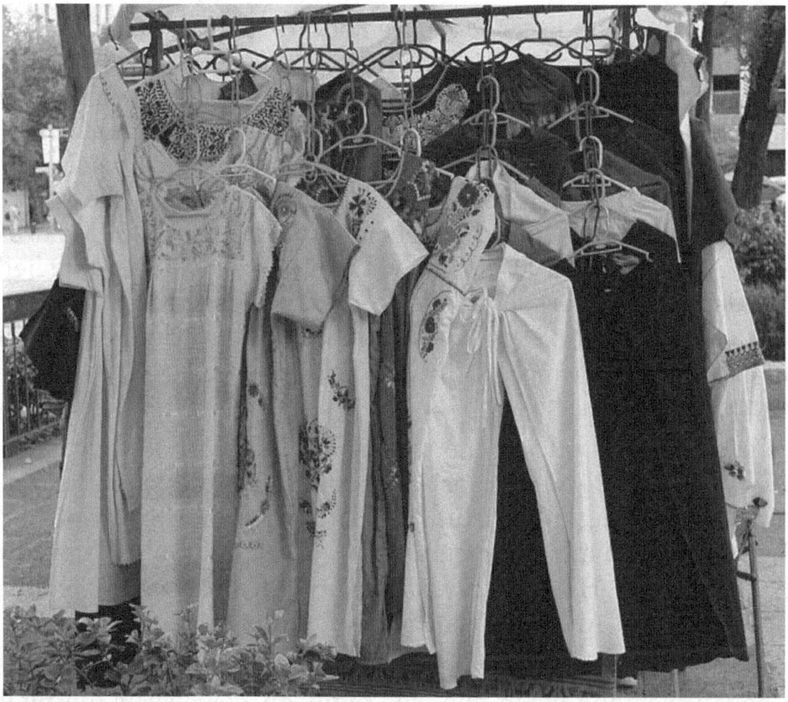

***Figure:** Traditional clothing for sale on a sidewalk in Mexico City*

Federal agencies such as FONART and various state agencies have their own promotional efforts including annual crafts contests and the recognition of masters in various fields, including textiles. Florentina López de Jesús is an Amusgo from Xochistlahuaca, Guerrero. She learned to weave from her mother at six years of age as well as to prepare raw cotton and spin it into yarn. She continued to weave as well as to do other jobs to help out her family.

As an adult she began to make pieces specifically for sale such as tablecloths, placemats, rebozos and huipils, travelling to Ometepec to market. Her work caught the attention of FONART in between 1969 and 1971, which led to her becoming a member of the La Flor de Xochistlahuaca artisans' cooperative. Since then, she has given workshops to people in her region as well as the Curso de Tintes Naturales sobre Algodon (Natural Dyes for Cotton Course) in 1994 and has promoted the use of brown cotton called "coyochi." Her work has won a number of awards including 2nd place Gran Premio de Arte

Popular, FONART in 1987, 1st place Gran Premio de Arte Popular, FONART in 1991 and Premio Nacional de Artesanias de SECOFI in 1993.

Juan Rayón Salinas, whose parents were craftsmen, is from Mexico State. He began working with textiles in 1970, and in 1971 the state government began work to open a Centro de Capacitación de Tapiz y de Bajo Liso to introduce European techniques for making rugs. Traditionally Rayón's hometown of Xonacatlán made wool sarapes, but he entered the centre specializing in throw rugs. He work was recognized and he began to participate in exhibitions in Mexico and abroad. After working for a time with the Centro, he established his own independent workshop. His work can be seen in various cities in Mexico as well as in New York. Also from Xonacatlán, Reyna Rayón Salinas is known for her cloth belts and embroidery, which she has been making since she was 12.

Cosme Flores is from the city of Tlaxcala, son and grandson of weavers who made wool rugs. He began weaving when he was 11 along with working in agriculture. His work has won various prizes such as first place in the Concurso Estatal de Artesanias Tlaxcaltecas in 1993 and 1994. His work is also featured in a permanent exhibition at the Museo de Artes y Tradiciones Populares de Tlaxcala.

Justina Oviedo Rangel is of the Huave ethnic group in Oaxaca. She began weaving when she was eight on her own while playing. When her mother saw her ability, she began to give her formal lessons. She specializes in napkins, placeholders and tablecloths, but also makes huipils. She also makes figures of clay. Her work has won awards such as the Concurso de Tejido de San Mateo del Mar in 1978 and various times since then until 1989.

Evaristo Borboa was born in Tenancingo, Mexico State, where the making of rebozos is a tradition. He began weaving when he was 12, making rebozos using a backstrap loom, rather than the European loom. This means that each of his rebozos are made individually rather 26-30 at a time, which is possible with larger looms. He is also known for his knotted or "ikat" technique as well as the jasper style. Interested in older styles of rebozos, he began in experiment in 1947 with these older designs. In the 1960s, upon visiting the Virgin of Zapopan, he noticed that the image was wrapped only in a simple shawl. He offered to make the image new rebozo, something he has done every year since. Recognition has come late in Borboa's life winning awards from FONART and state agencies starting in the

1990s. Handcrafted textiles have also been promoted as a tourist attraction in its own right. This is especially true in the state of Chiapas. Mexican handcrafted textiles have experienced a resurgence of interest due to the reassessment of them as a luxury item and the rising interest in some consumer sectors in locally crafted wares. Many of these textiles are being incorporated into items sold by globally recognized brands. Louis Vuitton, who has manufacturing facilities in Mexico, sponsored an exhibition called "Historias de Tradición artesanal" (Stories of Artisan Tradition) at the Museo de Arte Popular in Mexico City.

However, handcrafted textiles not only compete with other types of imported textiles, but also countries like China and Guatemala are producing imitations of traditional Mexican indigenous designs. These can be found both inside and outside of Mexico. The Asociacion de Mujeres Empresarias in Chiapas considers the imitations to be a form of pirating and puts native weavers livelihoods at risk. Organizations such as this work to have indigenous designs marked as intangible world heritage to protect it with markers for authenticity—much as is done for tequila or Talavera pottery.

Current Textile Industry

Current Importance of the Sector

Modern textile production in Mexico dates back to the era of Porfirio Díaz from the 1880s to 1910. Today, textile production plays an important role in the gross domestic product of Mexico, since it is exported and generates employment. Textile production includes the making of thread, cloth and decoration, in both natural and synthetic fibres. It accounts for about 1.2% of the total GDP and 7.1% of the manufacturing sector. It is the fourth largest manufacturing activity in the country. From the end of the Mexican Revolution to the mid-2000s, the sector saw steady growth. Much of the growth in the last four decades was spearheaded by "maquiladoras" or manufacturing plants along the northern border, which can import raw materials duty-free to make exportable products.

Another important textile area is the state of Guanajuato, which is Mexico's third largest producer. Some of these products include clothing, thread and sewing fabric, sheets, tablecloths, decorative pillows, rugs, carpets and tarps. Clothing items include jeans, other pants, blouses, tshirts, sweaters, vests, jackets, skirts and others, for national and international brands such as Liverpool, Chipieco, Carhartt,

Echojeans, Polo Ralph Lauren, JCPenney, Old Navy, Timberland and more.

However, in the mid-2000s, the sector began to decline, mostly due to foreign competition. A significant number of jobs have been lost since 2003 as well as a number of factories. Many of these operations and jobs are shifting to Asia.

Exports to the United States

The U.S. is the largest textile importer and almost all textile producing countries compete for a share of this market. Mexico ranks fourth in textile exports to the U.S. according to OTEXA. Mexico's advantages in this market is it proximity and favourable tariffs, especially since the passage of NAFTA. In 2004, all restrictions and quotas on Mexican textiles were lifted in the United States.

However, textile exports to the U.S. fell from more than 11 billion dollars in 2004 to just over 10 billion in 2005, as the U.S. imports more from other countries, who produce more cheaply.

From January through September 2004, U.S. imports of Mexican-made apparel reached $5.069 billion, 4.3% below the total registered for the same period in 2003, according to the CNIV, Mexico's textile industry association. Meanwhile, U.S. imports of Chinese garments grew 21.7% during that period to reach $6.69 billion Yet Mexican-made products began to lose their competitiveness in the U.S. because taxes and tariffs on imports from other countries were also dropping.

Non-U.S. Markets

While the U.S. is by far the major market for Mexican textiles, Mexico has free-trade pacts with 43 countries, one of the largest such networks in the world. Until very recently, this did not include China, which has been seen as an "enemy" rather than as a potential trading partner. There has been changes in this as Mexico seeks to expand business ties with China, especially in attracting capital. In the Americas, Mexico is part of the Central America Tree Trade Agreement, and recently Mexico and Peru struck a deal for the import and export of clothing and other textiles. Mexico's textile exports to Canada increased fivefold by the mid-2000s, raising its market share in that country to five percent. Export growth to Canada has slowed since then but remains fairly strong.

Domestic Clothing Market

Nine major chain stores control 40% of the brick-and-mortar sales, but approximately 58% of the domestic clothing market obtains its goods through illegal channels, either through smuggling, robbery or the evasion of taxes. Much of the illegal Chinese textiles sold in Mexico enter through the United States, where labels are changed to avoid Mexico's 533% tariff on Chinese goods.

Mexico's International Competitors

In addition to those from China, Mexican textile exports face competition from India, Bangladesh, Pakistan, Indonesia, Vietnam, Hong Kong and Central America. In 2000, Mexican textiles held around 12% of the U.S. market while Indian textiles 3.84%. Other Asian countries with presence include Hong Kong (5.7%), Indonesia (5.3), Vietnam and Bangladesh (5% each) .

Much of the reason for this is that labour costs are significantly higher in Mexico than in Asia. Mexico also has regulations that inhibit investment, as well as stricter environmental laws. Mexican fabrics cost 3.45 dollars per square metre while Chinese textiles cost 2.69 dollars. While the cost of Mexican fabric has increased 2%, those from a number of other countries in Asia and Central America have gone down. One major factor behind this is Mexico's relatively expensive labour costs. Another reason Asian products are cheaper is that utilities such electricity, gas and transport is cheaper.

China is Mexico's most important competitor. Not only are products from this country cheaper, the supply chain in China is more organized than in Mexico. For example, most threads used to sew clothing are produced in China; Mexico produces little, creating the need to import such. This can cause production delays. Mexico is also mostly limited to the making of basic items with little added value instead of more fashionable products that sell for more. In addition, Mexico also has protectionist policies designed to inhibit foreign investment and ownership of textile production facilities in the country.

One example of this is the maquiladora industries. Prior to the 2000s, maquiladoras owned by Asian concerns who imported materials from Asia to make products for the U.S. enjoyed the same tax advantages as those who used Mexican suppliers. However, this was changed during the beginning of the 21st century. This caused many Asian maquiladoras to close and move to Asia as the tax advantages no longer compensated for higher labour costs.

Mexico has also complained to the World Trade Organization that China has been engaging in "illegal practices" such as "dumping" (selling abroad at a price lower than local markets) to the detriment of the Mexican industry. Mexico claims that the Chinese government subsidizes textiles sales abroad to gain market share.

Textile Arts of Africa

The earliest surviving sub-Saharan African textiles are cloth fragments and parchment fragments that date to the ninth century BC from sites at Igbo Ukwu of the Igbo people of Nigeria. Some twelfth century cloth fragments date from the Tellem caves in Mali. Surviving thirteenth century samples originate from Benin City in Nigeria.

African textiles are a part of African cultural heritage that came to America along with the slave trade. As many slaves were skilled in the weaving, this skill was used as another form of income for the slave owner.

In most of Africa the weavers were men while the women spun the thread. The weavers in many of the countries were part of a caste-like group and sometimes slaves to noble families. In Yoruba compounds were used where master weavers would teach all the boys weaving and all the girls would learn to spin and dye the yarn. And children did some jobs too, like providing fabric and also weaved at a very young age of 4.

Some examples of African textiles are:

- Aso oke fabric - woven by Yoruba people
- Adire- tie-dye produced by Yoruba people
- Kente cloth - woven by Ashanti and Ewe people
- Barkcloth - produced by the Buganda tribe
- Mudcloth- produced by the Bambara tribe
- Kitenge - produced from Kenya and other regions of East Africa

Cultural Significance

Weaving has many spiritual and mythical meaning behind it. One, is that from the Dogons who believe that each stage of spinning and weaving thread is a symbolic analogy to human reproduction and resurrection. With this, they believe that the processes of spinning and weaving could only be done in daylight hours. To work at night would be to weave silence and darkness into the cloth. The colour of the cloth can also have some spiritual meaning. In one tribe a white cloth used by healing women is thought to be linked to water spirits.

Although there are many meanings to the designs on the cloth very few are directly represented on the cloth itself.

Textiles were also used as a form of identity with each tribe having their own unique patterns which also made it easy to spot outsiders. Many different types of patterns were formed in places that specialized in weaving. Kings would request several types of cloth to show their prestige and importance. Kings would even compare themselves by how many robes they had and what they were made out of.

Weaving and the textiles were and still are very important to the African culture. The textiles included both men and women and the cloth they made was unique to their tribe through the patterns and spiritual meanings behind them. the designs also had aztec designs in Many centuries ago, hair from animals was woven to insulate and protect homes. Hair, along with fibres from various plants and trees, were used to create bedding, blankets, clothing, and wall, window and door hangings. As textiles became more sophisticated, they were also used as currency for trading. Many of the ancient designs and weaving methods are used today and remain an important part of African lifestyles. The main method of decorating cloth throughout Africa is the dyeing of thread or completed cloths. Although there were a small range of locally produced plant dyes that allowed weavers in most areas to produce a few shades of brown, green, yellow, and in some cases red, by far the most important dye in Africa has been indigo. The vast majority of cloth produced on the continent over the centuries was simple designs produced by combining the natural white (and sometimes beige) of the cotton fibres with stripes of various shades of indigo blue. Depending on the relative density of the warp and weft threads, the resulting cloths could have stripes down the strip (warp-faced) or across the strip (weft-faced.)They mostly wore the skin of the animal and some times wove the fur into a piece of clothing.the women wove the fabric and textiles.

Textile Arts of Armenia

The complex history of Armenian weaving and needlework was acted out in the Near East, a vast, ancient and ethnically diverse region. Few are the people who, like the Armenians, can boast of a continuous and consistent record of fine textile production from the first millenium B.C. to the present. Armenians today are blessed by the diversity and richness of a textile heritage passed on by thirty centuries of diligent practice; yet they are burdened by the pressure to keep alive a tradition nearly destroyed in 1915, and subverted by a technology that condemns handmade fabrics to museums and lets machines produce perfect, but lifeless cloth.

Carpets

The oldest existing tufted carpet, dating from the fifth to the third century B.C., was excavated from the frozen Scythian burial mounds at Pasyryk northeast of the Caucasus in the Soviet Union. Called the Pasyryk carpet and preserved in the Hermitage Museum in Leningrad, this extraordinary rug predates other whole examples by more than 1500 years. The rug is in a near perfect state of preservation; it is roughly six feet square and the predominate colour is red-brown. The central design is made of geometric star patterns enclosed in five successive borders, the second of which contains a continuous line of large antlered animals and the fourth from the centre, a procession of men mounted on caparisoned horses. Recent scholarship inclines towards Armenia as the place where it was woven, because of the similarity of motifs in late Urartian and some early Armenian artifacts, and the long history of tufted carpet weaving in Armenia. The Scythians, according to this theory, acquired the rug when passing through the Caucasus.

Whether or not the oldest carpet in the world was made in Armenia, early Greek, Armenian, and Arabic historical sources repeatedly speak about the fine rugs and other textiles woven there. Carpets are mentioned as part of the annual Armenian tribute to the Caliph of Baghdad in the late eighth century. In the later medieval period, Marco Polo praises the rugs woven by Armenians. The characteristic red Armenian dye (vordn karmir) was prized throughout the Mediterranean world. Unfortunately, no rugs have survived from these early centuries. There are a few fragments from the twelfth and thirteenth centuries, uncovered in mosques in Eastern Anatolia, but no convincing origin has been established for any of them, though Armenia has been proposed for several. However, renaissance artists in the west painted rugs imported from the Near East in precise detail allowing scholars to establish some of the basic designs of the fourteenth, fifteenth, and sixteenth centuries.

Until very recently, scholars have dismissed the possible Armenian origin of these carpets. Though there has been much debate during this century on the source of the famous “dragon” carpets, A. Sakisian and others after him propose an Armenian origin for them. The Armenian province of Artsakh (Karabagh) has retained the dragon design into modern times, reinforcing the Armenian origin of seventeenth and eighteenth century examples. A number of these dragon rugs have Armenian inscriptions.

During the dislocation of the first World War, the production of Armenian handloomed rugs nearly ended as did that of so many other crafts. Some survivors, however, continued to weave Armenian rugs until World War II. Furthermore, the wholesale destruction of Armenian life and property in Anatolia and western Armenia from 1915 to 1922 resulted in the loss of heirloom Armenian rugs passed down in families. In the last two decades a new interest in Armenian weaving and rug making has resulted in the re-establishment of the identity of Armenian carpets, which in this century have been, unfortunately, gradually subsumed under the heading of Islamic or Turkish carpets. What has helped in the scientific study of the rugs produced by Armenians has been the habit, already remarked upon in other arts, of weavers leaving a written memorial by way of Armenian inscriptions woven directly into the rugs with names and dates. Hundreds of these inscribed Armenian rugs have now been recorded and several major exhibitions organized around them.

The earliest dated Armenian rug is also one of the largest and most exquisite, the famous Kohar carpet made in the Karabagh (the Armenian district of Artsakh) with an inscription identifying the weaver, Kohar, and the date 1700. Another important carpet woven in 1731 for Catholicos Nersés of Aghuank', probably in Artsakh, is preserved in the monastery of St. James in Jerusalem. The rest of the dated and inscribed Armenian rugs are from the nineteenth and the first quarter of the twentieth centuries.

Armenian rugs, though woven in various regions and in divers styles, are predominantly of the Caucasian type with vivid colours and broad geometric designs; often small figures or animals are placed randomly in the border or field. The most frequently encountered types among the inscribed rugs are Karabagh (Artsakh), Kazak, and Gendje or Ganja. The earlier Karabagh rugs with sunburst or eagle designs seem to have affinities with the famous dragon carpets of an earlier period. Other Karabagh types are popular: Kasim Ushak design, cloudband design, jagged red band design, lempe/lampa design, Lesghi star design, etc. Armenian Kazak rugs are classified by the following types: three medallion design, Lori-Pambak design, Sevan-Kazak design, Karachoph design, etc. Among the most famous Karabagh carpets are a large number produced at the turn of the twentieth century with designs copied from western models [VI/18], which were in great vogue in the Caucasus and Iran. These fall in two large categories, the rose design rugs and the pictorial rugs. There are also a large number of Karabagh, Kazak and village rugs with unique patterns as well as saddle bags or twin bags from Artsakh.

Another type of pictorial rug was also woven by Armenians in the various parts of the world they settled in after 1915. These rugs, usually one of a kind, were woven by individuals to commemorate an event or to honour a person. Many of these have portraits of Soviet leaders — Marx, Lenin, Stalin — or western statesmen or historic symbols. Orphan rugs produced by young Armenian women, parentless survivors of the massacres of 1896 or 1915, under the guidance of American missionaries, are also numerous. To this day, the rug industry remains an important part of the organized crafts in Armenia

Woven and Stamped Textiles: Cloth weaving and textile manufacture is universal. Nearly all cultures engaged in this craft to satisfy need for clothes and coverings. Carbonized fragments of woven textiles have been found in very early excavations in Armenia, but they offer little information about the design and style of early textiles. The fragility of cloth is the major cause for our lack of early examples. The dry desert climate of Egypt or the frozen environment of the Scythian tombs of Pasyryk lacking in Armenia offers the very rare conditions by which early textiles have survived in quantity.

Our knowledge of pre-seventeenth century woven textiles stems mainly from their representation in art, sculptured reliefs such as those of Aght'amar and especially Armenian miniature painting, but also from actual fragments preserved on the insides of the covers of manuscript bindings. These textile fragments are made of various types of cotton, silk, linen and other fabrics and have both woven and stamped patterns. A large number of them are from cloth fashioned outside Armenia: Iran, India, even Byzantium and the west. Because nearly every manuscript up through the seventeenth century used such cloth pieces to hide the unattractive exposed wood on the inside of bindings, there are thousands of these textile samples preserved. Fewer than a hundred have been published. Once available, they will serve as the major resource in reconstructing the history of textiles used in Armenia from the thirteenth to the seventeenth centuries.

From the late seventeenth and especially the eighteenth and nineteenth centuries there is preserved a comparatively large quantity of brocades, embroidery and other textiles almost all used as church decor or priestly vestments. The most important of these in size are the altar curtains, both stamped and embroidered, preserved in the collections of the Catholicossate in Etchmiadzin and the Armenian Patriarchate in Jerusalem. Most of the eighteenth century examples are rich in colour and form and were produced in Madras, India, a major centre of stamped fabrics, where Armenians were well established. These were made by stamping prepared cotton fabrics with carved wooden blocks. This technique was also known in Armenia and used in earlier centuries, but in the later times Madras seemed to control the market. Though these large altar curtains had purely Armenian designs, often the life of St. Gregory or the conversion of Armenian to Christianity, with long Armenian inscriptional bands, they were probably manufactured by Indian workers after designs supplied by Armenian artists.

Among printed or painted altar curtains, other than those produced in Madras, several are of a particular splendor: a stamped curtain from Souchava in Romania dated 1663 with a central motif of the Crucifixion and an upper band devoted to the life of Christ (Etchmiadzin Treasury); two others on dark blue cloth, probably made in Tokat, dated 1756 and the late eighteenth century with the Crucifixion as the most important representation (Etchmiadzin Treasury); others from Karin-Erzerum, Tiflis, Lim at Lake Van (felt appliqué), Constantinople (mostly embroidered), and Europe. The Etchmiadzin collection has been the subject of a recent unpublished thesis in Armenian and the Jerusalem collection of altar curtains will soon be published.

Needlework: Embroidery and Lace: Richly embroidered Armenian textiles have survived in much greater number than plain or printed fabrics. These embroideries are mostly church related: clerical robes and accessories, altar curtains, chalice covers, and miscellany. Among the vestments are miters, crowns, copes, stoles, collars, belts [VI/33], sleeve bands, chasubles, and slippers. Major collections with pieces dating from the seventeenth to the twentieth centuries are kept in the monasteries of Etchmiadzin, Jerusalem, the Mekhitarists in Venice and Vienna, Bzummar in Lebanon and other lesser centres. Rich figural designs on silk, velvet, satins and more modest materials are sewn in vivid colours, the most lavish employ gold and silver thread, pearls and other precious and semi-precious stones. The variety of designs and styles are as astounding as they are beautiful. The perfection of execution, the rendering of figures, garments and faces is as magnificent as the best embroidery work of any period and any nation.

The earliest surviving embroidery is a large thirteenth century fragment from Ani showing asymmetrical lions. The most famous embroidery is the ceremonial banner of 1448, still kept at Etchmiadzin, with full-length portraits of Gregory the Illuminator flanked by King Trdat and St. Hrip'simé, the major figures responsible for the Armenia conversion to Christianity on one side and, on the other, Christ enthroned with the symbols of the four Evangelists.

Among other outstanding embroideries one should note the following; the cope of 1601 in the State Historical Museum, Erevan, showing Christ enthroned with the Evangelists' symbols; a crown of 1651; a stole of 1736 and another on blue ground of 1685; a series of shirt collars in the form of short stoles dated 1734 all of embroidered silver and gold thread on a red ground, the most elaborate of which depicts the Last Supper on the back and John the Baptist, Gregory the Illuminator and St. Hakob on the front; embroidered altar cloths of 1613 from Karin-Erzerum with St. Gregory, of 1619 from Constantinople on a rich emerald coloured ground with silver and gold thread showing the Virgin being presented with the martyred head of St. James (Hakob) with scenes from the Life of Christ in the borders (Jerusalem, Armenian Patriarchate), of 1620 from Constantinople with a monumental scene of the Last Supper bordered by Christological episodes (Jerusalem, Armenian Patriarchate), of 1704-1714 from Constantinople with Christ, the Apostles, St. Gregory and King Trdat, and of 1741 with St. Gregory's vision of Holy Etchmiadzin; the so-called eagle carpet of Catholicos Philippos dated 1651 using silver thread embroidery on silk; and the chalice cloth of 1688 with a central floral motif on a yellow ground with crosses and seraphim in the border. Except where noted, all the examples are in the Treasury at Holy Etchmiadzin.

Embroidery was commonly used to decorate towels, bags, stockings, kerchiefs, table clothes and various textiles. Among the most famous was the work of Marash characterized by polychrome geometric and floral designs on dark or coloured backgrounds. The stitching was done following various grid patterns, designs being built up from star, cross and braided motifs. This embroidery work, whether of the luxurious variety or the more modest type, was done in all Armenian families, often during the isolation of the cold winter months. Many of the richly decorated elements of clerical garb were votive offerings donated by the pious on pilgrimage.

Armenian lace, called janyak or oya, is executed with a single needle and has an extremely ancient history. Its technique was known by all women and passed on from generation to generation. There are different styles and stitches from the various regions of Armenian; among the best known are the Aintab stitch, the Vaspurakan stitch, the Baghesh (Bitlis) stitch and the Kharpert stitch. The delicacy and intricacy of Armenian lace have long been recognized and in recent years specialized studies and exhibits have been devoted to it. Early laces of silk and gold thread or decorated with pearls and jewels were made into chalice covers, and cross and Gospel holders. Lace borders were also often added to embroidered articles. Scarves and kerchiefs were often fringed with a variety of miniature lace flowers.

Few pre-nineteenth century laces have survived. The tradition, however, is very ancient in Armenia. Lace making in Europe was a craft that arrived in the late Middle Ages from Asia Minor. Many scholars believe that the origin of Venetian lace, one of the oldest and most developed lace making centres, should be sought in Armenia. The merchant cities of Italy were in close touch with Armenians during those centuries, so there was ample opportunity to import laces and the technique of making them.

Costumes: The oldest existing Armenian costume is a rather plain thirteenth century child's dress found at Ani, but it is the unique piece we have until the seventeenth century. Liturgical garments are preserved from the seventeenth and eighteenth centuries, but almost no secular examples exist. Nineteenth century garments are, however, plentiful and from them scholars have been able to establish the daily as well as special costumes of Armenian men and women from every region of Armenia. This material has been published in special albums and exhibited in museums in Armenia and the diaspora. Our notion of earlier costumes of the ancient and medieval Armenian periods is based entirely on representations in Armenian art, especially manuscript illustrations.

Textile Arts of Australia

Textiles is one of the most exciting and diverse areas of contemporary practice, embracing new technologies, opportunities and career paths. The Textiles Workshop provides undergraduate and graduate courses, aiming to equip students with a range of practical, critical, and research skills while preparing them for careers as professional artists/designers and work in related fields. The Workshop promotes a creative and innovative approach within a contemporary context through the expertise of its staff, well equipped studio, seminars, excursions, workshops and visits to galleries, design studios and museums. The programme encourages students to connect with their professional field and develop skills for their future careers.

Australian Aboriginal Fibrecraft

Australian Aboriginal fibrecraft refers to the various ways Australian Aborigines created fibres traditionally. Materials used depended on where the people lived in Australia.

Bark

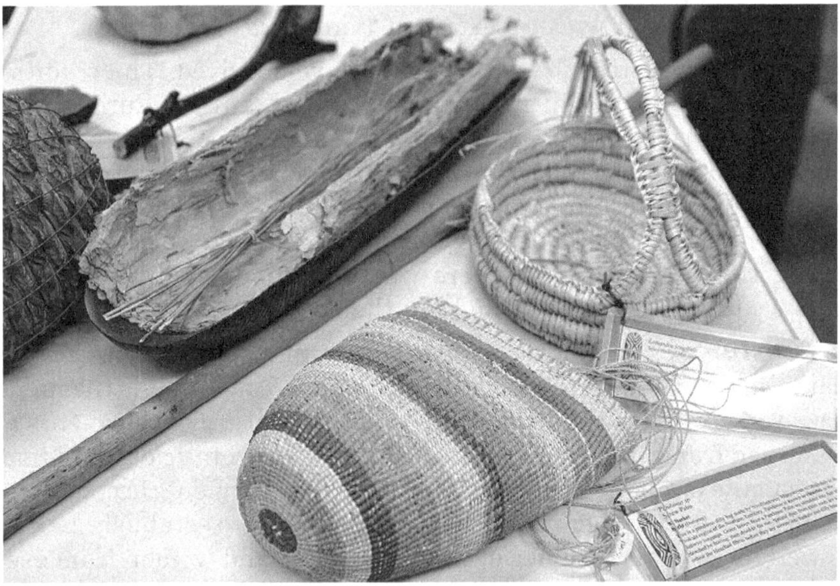

Figure: *Baskets were often made from twisted bark fibres*

Bark was used by many people across the continent. This technology is still used today to produce baskets, which are particularly popular in the tourism industry. Kurrajong bark is a popular bark, as is the bark of river wattles, sand figs, banyans, burney vines and peanut trees.

In the north, the more tightly woven styles were made, whereas in the south, a looser stringed bag, popularly known as a dilly bag was made.

Hair

Hairstring was an important textile traditionally made by Australian Aborigines.

People, particularly the women, cut their hair regularly using quartz or flint knives. This hair was never wasted. It was spun into long threads of yarn on a spindle rolled on the thigh and then plaited to about the thickness of 8 ply wool.

Purposes for the string were manifold. These included making the head ring for resting the coolamon, headbands to keep the hair off the face, spear-making (securing the head to the shaft), and even balls for ball games.

A general-purpose belt was made of the string, from which things could be hung, such as small game like goannas in order to free the hands on long walks and hunts.

Among some groups, including the Pitjantjajara, a small modesty apron was made of the string for young girls to wear when they reached puberty. People in Central Australia today may talk of a girl having her "string broken", which can mean sexual abuse, or having sex when she is not ready.

Among some tribes, adults wore a loincloth-like pubic covering, which also hung from the waist belt. This was made either of the string itself, or of other material, including paperbark. In the Kimberley region of Western Australia, the men wore pearl shells as a pubic covering, which they call *Riji*, and which are considered extremely sacred.

The string could be dyed various shades using dyes such as ochre.

Some string was only worn for ceremony, such as skirts worn by the women.

String Games

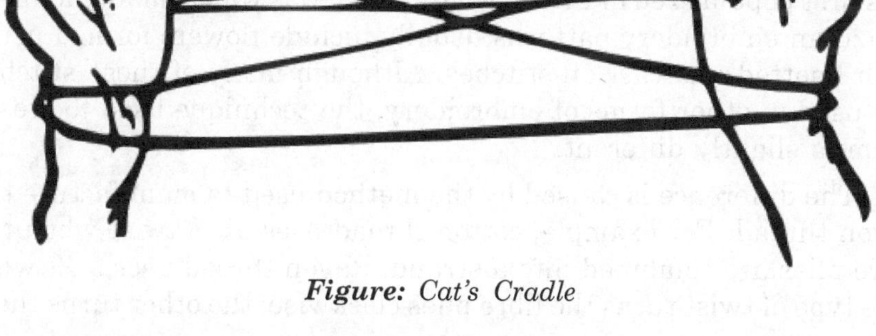

***Figure:** Cat's Cradle*

Many Aboriginal groups traditionally made many shapes out of the string (cat's cradle). A researcher once watched and photographed a young Aboriginal woman from Yirrkala make over 200 separate string figures.

Each one involved complicated movements of her fingers and thumbs. She was able to remember the correct sequence of finger movements for nearly every figure she made, with only an occasional mistake which she quickly corrected. As she made each figure she gave it a name. Some examples included *dangurang* — a lobster, *bapa* — lightning, *matjur* — an ibis flying into a tree and *gapu* — the ripples on a pool.

The Bangarra Dance Theatre's 2005 production of CLAN incorporated traditional desert string games into one of their performances, creating intricate patterns as they thread themselves through long, elastic strings.,

Grasses

Grasses were combined with the hair to create a tougher fibre. This varied depending on the area in Australia. In the arid areas, it was spinifex, whereas in the Top End, it was palms such as pandanus.

Pandanus and sand-palm are used in areas such as the Daly River region and Arnhem Land to weave carry baskets, dilly string bags, wall hangings, floor mats and fish-nets. The women of Peppimenarti and Oenpelli are famous for such weaving, however each community has their own distinct styles and techniques.

Textile Arts of Brazil

Brazilian Embroidery

Brazilian embroidery is a type of surface embroidery that uses rayon thread instead of cotton or wool. It is called "Brazilian" embroidery because the use of high-sheen rayon thread in embroidery was first popularized in Brazil, where rayon was widely manufactured. Brazilian embroidery patterns usually include flowers formed using both knotted and cast on stitches. Although many of these stitches are used in other forms of embroidery, the technique used to create them is slightly different.

The difference is caused by the method used to manufacture the rayon thread. For example, cotton thread uses an *S* twist when the fibre plies are combined into a strand. Rayon thread uses a *Z* twist. One type of twist turns the fibre plies clockwise; the other turns them counterclockwise. When forming the knots of Brazilian embroidery, the embroiderer must wrap the thread onto the needle in the opposite direction from that used in other types of embroidery. Otherwise the fibres of the thread will unravel and make the resulting stitches and knots unattractive.

Textile Arts of Central America

Maya textiles are the clothing and other textile arts of the Maya peoples, indigenous peoples of the Yucatán Peninsula in Mexico, Guatemala, Honduras, El Salvador and Belize. Women have traditionally created textiles in Maya society, and textiles were a significant form of ancient Maya art and religious beliefs.

Process

In woven textiles, the first step is preparing fibre, which can come from plants, such as cotton or maguey, or animals, such as wool from sheep. The loose fibres are spun into threads by hand, with spindles, a long stick-like device for holding the thread, and whorls, a weight held on the spindle to increase its motion. In the pre-Columbian era, Mayan women exclusively wove with backstrap looms, that use sticks and straps worn around one's waist to create tension.

After European contact, treadle looms were introduced, although backstrap looms continue to be popular. Bone picks were used before contact and were unique in that they had different designs for most families and were usually passed on from generation to generation with the elite having the most expensive and beautiful.

Materials

Ancient Maya women had two natural types of cotton to work with, one white and the other light brown, both of which were commonly dyed. The preparation of cotton for spinning was very burdensome, as it had to be washed and picked clean of seeds. Elite women were also given the opportunity to work with the most expensive feathers and pearl beads.

However, women of the elite not only had to prepare the best clothing for their families, but they also had to be talented in weaving tapestry, brocade, embroidery, and tie-dyeing for tribute to other families and rulers. Weavers had three different natural dyes to work with. Women also worked with maguey. Maguey was of major value as a cordage material used for horse gear, nets, hammocks and bags.

Pre Contact Attire

In the Maya civilization, a man's typical dress was a cotton breechcloth wrapped around his waist and sometimes a sleeveless shirt, either white or dyed in colours. A woman typically wore a *traje*, which combined a *huipil* and a *corte*, a woven wraparound skirt that reached her ankles. The *traje* was held together with a *faja* or sash worn at the waist. Both women and men wore sandals.

When the weather was temperate, Mayan clothing was needed less as protection from the elements and more for personal adornment. Maya clerics and other dignitaries wore elaborate outfits with jewellery.

Maya farmers wore minimal clothing. Men wore plain loincloths or a band of cloth winded around their waists.

Some wore moccasins made of deerhide. Women possessed two items of clothing: a length of ornamented material with holes made for the arms and head, known as a *kub*. Both genders wore a heavier rectangle of cloth, as a manta, that functioned as an overwrap on cool days, and as blanket at night. The manta also served as a blind across the door.

Huipil

The most prevalent and influential aspect of women's clothing in ancient times is the *huipil*, which is still prominent in Guatemalan and Mexican culture today.

The *huipil* is a loose rectangular garment with a hole in the middle for the head made from lightweight sheer cotton. The huipil is usually white with colourful cross-stripping and zigzag designs woven into the cloth using the brocade technique still commonly used today. The *huipil* could be worn loose or tucked into a skirt; this depends on the varying lengths of the *huipil.*

Huipils were important displaying one's religion and tribal affiliation. Different communities tended to have different designs, colours, lengths as well as particular huipils for ceremonial purposes. It was uncommon and often disgraceful to wear a huipil design from another community within one's village; although, it was a sign of respect to wear a community's *huipil* when visiting another village.

Although, women were not just limited to their community's design. Instead the design offered an outline for what women were required to have and within the community design women were allowed creativity to make theirs different from others often to express praise to different *kiuggkes* animals around the collar.

Hair Sash

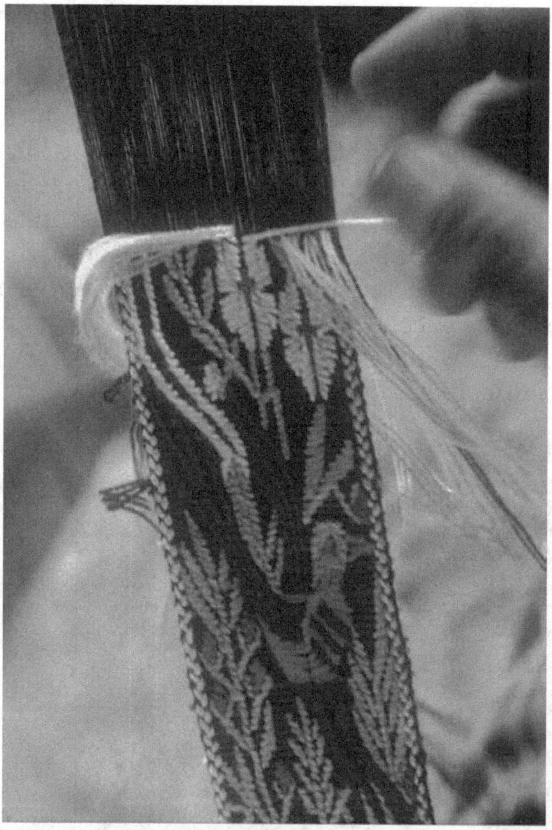

Figure: *Detail of hair sash being brocaded on a Jakaltek Maya backstrap loom.*

The hair sash is often the only part of the traditional outfit that is still locally woven by women on a backstrap loom. Each ethnic group not only has their own way of wearing the hair sash interlaced or wrapped around their long hair, but colours, motifs, widths, and the manner of setting up the loom and incorporating the geometric and figurative designs into the cloth are distinct. Elaborate hair sashes woven of finer thread with more complex imagery are worn on special occasions.

Ideological Aspects

The Maya believed that clothing could transform a person and a person could transform the garment and is expressed through it, so naturally clothing was of great cultural significance. They would often make textiles to enhance religious power; the most common way of doing this was dressing for the maize gods. Women and men would wear a net over-skirt made of jade, the colour of life, which represented their high place in society. In order to dress as a maize deity and manipulate the regeneration of the maize plant they would weave serpents onto *huipils* to symbolize lightning. The lightning god is the god believed to have created maize on the top of Mt. Sustenance. Mayan elite would also wear a shark shell belt and a jade-netted collar to the maize deity costume. Other significant costumes consisted of wearing many quetzal and eagle feathers on headdresses to represent and elite's power in blue and green tones, which represented the fifth direction, the centre of celestial, terrestrial and the underworld levels of the cosmos. Kings would also wear jaguar skin skirts, which signified their connection between the sky and the earth.

Oaxaca Art

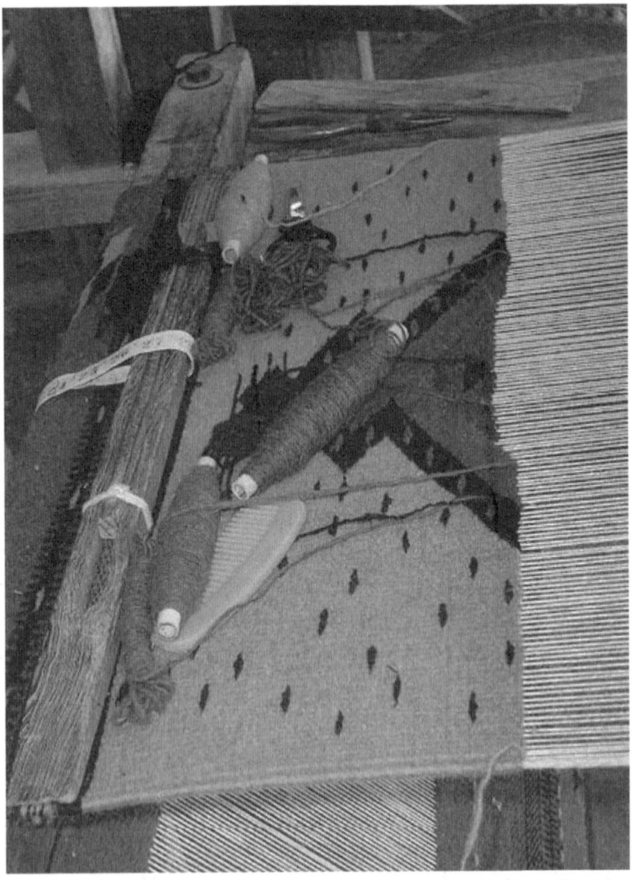

Figure: *A work in progress on a stationary loom.*

The state of Oaxaca in southern Mexico has a noteworthy tradition of finely crafted textiles, particularly handmade embroidery and woven goods that frequently utilize a backstrap loom. Oaxaca is home to several different groups of indigenous peoples, each of which has a distinctive textile tradition.

Construction

Oaxacan fibres may be hand spun from cotton or locally cultivated silk. Traditional dye sources include *purpura pansa* among the Huave, Chontal, and Mixtec people. The Chontal and Mazatec also utilize cochineal to attain bright red tones.

According to Alejandro de Ávila B., founding director of the Ethnobotanical Garden in Oaxaca, the region's biological diversity yields Mexico's greatest variety of fibres and dyes, and "the technical sophistication of Oaxaca's textiles is unparalelled in the country."

Traditional clothing items among the peoples of Oaxaca include the *huipil*, a women's blouse constructed from several panels; the *ceñidor*, a type of sash among the Mazatec; and the *paño*, a Chinantec head covering. Handcrafted Oaxacan textiles employ plainweave, brocade patterns, gauze weave.

Motifs

Mexican textile expert Irmbard Weitlaner Johnson associates pre-Christian spiritual traditions with the presence of butterflies in Mazatec textile motifs. "To this day the Mazatecs identify the butterfly as the soul that leaves the body. They believe that the souls of the deceased have permission to come to this world once a year on All Saints' Day and the Day of the Dead to visit their family. This is the period when butterflies are most abundant in the area and the Mazatecs consider it a sin to kill them."

Regional motifs without specific spiritual meaning, or for which disputed interpretations exist, include a class of stepped fret known as *xicalcoliuhqui*, which means "twisted ornament for decorating gourds" in the Nahuatl language; and the double spiral *ilhuitl*, whose name translates as "fiesta day." Pre-Colonial tradition associates colour with the four cardinal directions: yellow with east, red with north, blue and green with west, and white with south. Another shared motif among the region's indigenous peoples is a rectangular ornament below the neckline of the *huipil*. No specific symbolism is known, but it is a frequent theme in pre-colonial codices and surviving historic textiles that remains in popular use.

Huipil

Huipil ['wipil] (from the Nahuatl word *huîpîlli* is the most common traditional garment worn by indigenous women from central Mexico to Central America. It is a loose-fitting tunic, generally made from two or three rectangular pieces of fabric which are then joined together with stitching, ribbons or fabric strips, which an opening for the head and if the sides are sewn, opening for the arms. Traditional huipils, especially ceremonial ones, are usually made with fabric woven on a backstrap loom and are heavily decorated with designs woven into the fabric, embroidery, ribbons, lace and more. However, some huipils are also made from commercial fabric. Lengths of the huipil can vary from a short blouse-like garment or long enough to reach the floor. The style of traditional huipils generally indicates the ethnicity and community of the wearer as each have their own methods of creating the fabric and decorations. Some have intricate and meaningful designs. Ceremonial huipils are the most elaborate and are reserved for weddings, burials, women of high rank and even to dress the statues of saints.

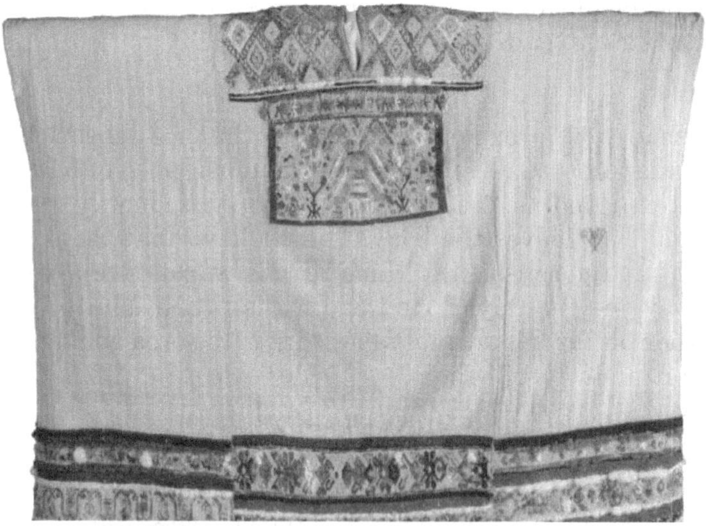

Figure: *The "La Malinche" huipil*

The huipil has been worn by indigenous women of the Mesoamerican region (central Mexico into Central America) of both high and low social rank since well before the arrival of the Spanish to the Americas. It remains the most common female indigenous garment still in use. It is most often seen in the Mexican states of Chiapas, Yucatán, Quintana Roo, Oaxaca, Tabasco, Campeche, Hidalgo,

Michoacán (where it is called a huanengo), Veracruz and Morelos . In Central America it is most often used among the Mayas in Guatemala.

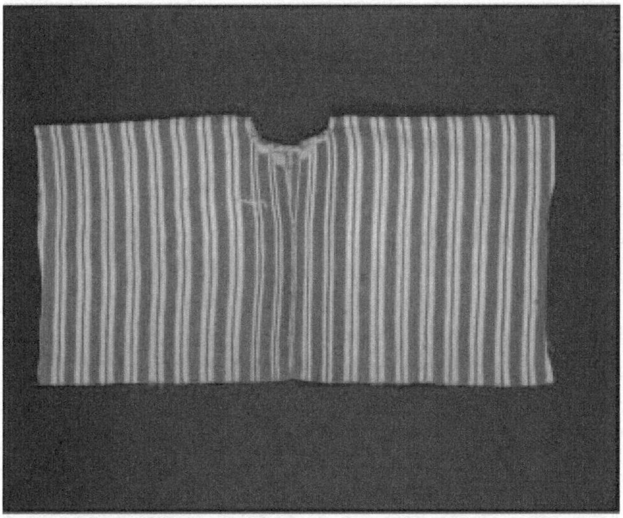

Figure: *Huipil, 1875-1890, Warp-faced plain weave cotton, Patzun, Guatemala (probably) V&A Museum no.T.23-1931*

After the Spanish conquest of the Aztec Empire and subsequent Spanish expansion, the huipil endured but it evolved, incorporating elements from other regions, European elements and even elements from Asia. One of the oldest known huipils in existence is the "La Malinche," named such because it was believed to have been worn by Hernán Cortés' interpreter as it looks much like ones in depictions of her in the Lienzo de Tlaxcala and the Florentine Codex. However, carbon 14 tests date it to the 18th century. It is exceptional not only for its age but there is none like it in any collection and it is larger than usual at 120 by 140 cm. It is made of cotton with feathers, wax and gold thread.

The design is dominated by an image of a double headed eagle, showing both indigenous and Spanish influence. It is part of the collection of the Museo Nacional de Antropología . Some huipils, such as those from the Isthmus of Tehuantepec show Asian influence due to cloth brought from the Philippines . In addition, the huipil began to be worn with other garments, especially European skirts, during the colonial period. This led to changes in the garment itself and how it was used. In some cases, the huipil became shorter, to function as a kind of blouse rather than a dress. In the same region, the huipil also evolved into a long flowing and sometimes voluminous head covering which frames the face.

To this day, the most traditional huipils are made with hand woven cloth on a back strap loom. However, the introduction of commercial fabric made this costly and many indigenous women stopped making this fabric, or making simpler versions. By the early 1800s, women began to wear undecorated huipils or European style blouses. By the end of the 19th century, most Maya women had forgotten the technique of brocade weaving entirely.

The huipil endures in many indigenous communities, if not as an everyday garment, as one for ceremonies or special occasions. When a woman puts on a huipil, especially a ceremonial or very traditional one, it is a kind of ritual. She becomes the centre of a symbolic world as her head passes through the neck opening. With her arms, she forms a cross and is surrounded by myth as between heaven and the underworld.

Creation

The huipil is a tunic-like garment made by stitching together anywhere from one to five pieces of cloth. The most common fibre is cotton, but there are those made from wool and silk as well. Most huipils are made from two or three pieces, which are usually the same size, with one exception being those from the highlands of Chiapas, where the centre piece is wider than the side ones. The panels are not sewn together in the normal sense with seams but rather they are joined using ribbons, small strips of cloth or complicated stitching which has the edges of the panels touching or almost touching. This adds a layer of decoration to the garment.

Most classic huipils are wider than they are long although there has been a reduction in width in recent years. Huipils can be as short as waist length or can reach to the ankles or anywhere in between, but most fall just above or just below the knee. Long or short, it is not designed to be a close-fitting garment. The neckline can be round, oval, square or a simple slit. Most are sewn on the sides, leaving an opening in the upper part for the arms to pass through. Some huipils are not sewn on the sides, especially the very short ones. While huipils today are made from commercial cloth, the most traditional are made from hand woven fabric made on a backstrap loom. The pieces to be used to make the huipil are woven to size and are never cut. Despite its simplicity, the backstrap loom permits more types of techniques and designs to be woven into the cloth than other types of looms. Most of the hand woven fabric have designs woven into them, especially cloth destined for ceremonial huipils. The decorative elements can signify history, cultural identity, something personal about the wearer and more. Since most indigenous come from agricultural societies, clothing designs generally relate to the natural world. The most complicated designs are generally known only to a few older master weavers. In addition to designs embedded into the fabric, other decorative elements can include embroidery, ribbon, feathers, lace and more.

The making of traditional huipils is an important cultural and economic activity for the Amuzgos, especially in Xochistlahuaca where most people still wear traditional clothing. Girls begin learning the craft when they are young, learning techniques and designs from their mothers and grandmothers. The weaving is an important source of income as agriculture is not enough to meet most families' needs. While they work on other items such as tablecloths and other items of clothing, the most popular and most valued remains the huipil. Amuzgo women have achieved a certain level of fame, with weavers such as Florentina López de Jesús winning recognition at the 2001 UNESCO handcraft competition for Latin America and Caribbean.

7

Textile Arts of China

Chinese Embroidery

Chinese embroidery refers to embroidery created by any of the cultures located in the area that makes up modern China. It is some of the oldest extant needlework.

The four major regional styles of Chinese embroidery are Suzhou embroidery (Su Xiu), Hunan embroidery (Xiang Xiu), Guangdong embroidery (Yue Xiu) and Sichuan embroidery (Shu Xiu). All of them are nominated as Chinese Intangible Cultural Heritage.

Chinese embroidery has a long history since Neolithic age. Because of the quality of silk fibre, most Chinese fine embroideries are made in silk.

Some ancient vestiges of silk production have been found in various Neolithic sites dating back 5,000-6,000 years in China. Currently the earliest real sample of silk embroidery discovered in China is from a tomb in Mashan in Hubei province identified with the Zhanguo period (5th-3rd centuries BC).

After the opening of Silk Route in Han Dynasty, the silk production and trade became flourishing.

In 14th century, the Chinese silk embroidery production reached its high peak. Several major silk embroidery styles had been developed, like Song Jin in Suzhou, Yun Jin in Nanjing and Shu Jin (‡&• Shu embroidery) in Sichuan.

Today most handwork had been replaced by machinery, but some very sophisticated production are still hand-made. The modern Chinese silk embroidery still prevails in southern China.

Genres

Major styles:

- Su Xiu — Suzhou embroidery is crafted in areas around Suzhou, Jiangsu Province, having a history dating back 2,000 years. It is famous for its beautiful patterns, elegant colours, variety of stitches, and consummate craftsmanship. Its stitching is meticulously skillful, colouration subtle and refined. Suzhou artists are able to use more than 40 needlework and a 1,000 different types of threads to make embroidery, typically with nature and environment themes such as flowers, birds, animals and even gardens on a piece of cloth.
    - o A rare subset is Su double-sided embroidery which requires ultimate skill and artistry. The front and back of the piece may have different designs, but the ends are not knotted but woven in so the back can't be distinguished.
- Xiang Xiu — Hunan embroidery comes from areas around Changsha, Hunan Province. It is distinct for its starkly elegant black, white and gray colouration. Its emphasis is on contrasts of light and shade that highlight the pattern texture to give a three-dimensional effect. Xiang embroidery composition combines void and solid imagery, utilizing empty space in the same way as Chinese ink and wash paintings.
- Yue Xiu/Guang Xiu — Guangdong embroidery is crafted in Chaozhou, Guangdong Province. It is composed of intricate but symmetrical patterns, vibrant colours, varied stitches and a defined weave. Its use of primary colours, light and shade are reminiscent of western paintings.
- Shu Xiu — Sichuan embroidery comes from areas around Chengdu, Sichuan Province. It is oldest known embroidery style in Chinese embroidery history. Its raw materials are satin and coloured silk, its craftsmanship painstaking and refined. The emphasis is on even stitching, delicate colouration, and local flavor. Sichuan embroidery is used to decorate quilt covers, pillowcases, garments, shoes and painted screens.

Other Styles

- Gu Xiu — Gu embroidery is rather a family style than a local style originated from Gu Mingshi's family during the Ming Dynasty in Shanghai. Gu embroidery is also named Lu Xiang Yuan embroidery after the place where the Gu family lived.

Gu embroidery ss different from other styles as it specialized in painting and calligraphy. The inventor of Gu embroidery was a concubine of Gu Mingshi's first son, Gu Huihai. Later, Han Ximeng, the wife of the second grandson of Gu Mingshi developed the skill and was reputed as "Needle Saint" (^"#W). Some of her masterpieces are kept in the Forbidden City. Today Gu embroidery has become a special local product in Shanghai.

Ethnic Styles

Other Chinese ethnic groups, like Bai, Miao, Zhuang and Tibetan people also have their own style of embroidery, which usually depicts a mythical or religious topic.

Yunjin

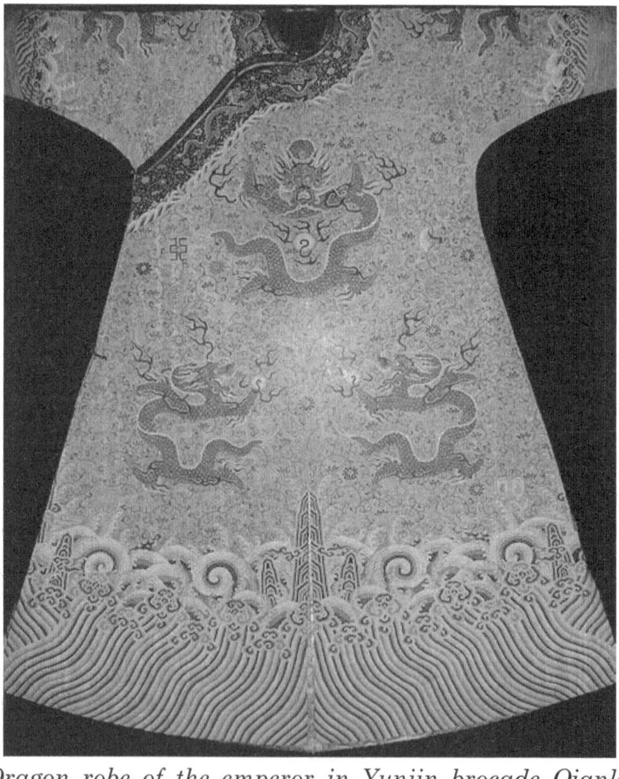

Figure: *Dragon robe of the emperor in Yunjin brocade Qianlong (1736-1796) at the Grassi Museum in Leipzig*

Yunjin, also called cloud brocade, is a traditional Chinese silk brocade made in Jiangsu since the end of the Song Dynasty, and based on weft-weaving techniques from both the Song and Tang dynasties. It is shuttle-woven, and often incorporates gold and silver threads with the coloured silks. During the Ming Dynasty the yunjin weavers developed a technique of swivel weaving that enabled them to weave colourful designs onto a base fabric in other weaves, such as satin.

Textile Arts of New Zealand

Maori made textiles from a number of plants, including harakeke, wharariki, tî kôuka, tôî, pingao, kiekie and toetoe—although the paper mulberry was introduced by Maori, who knew it as aute, it seems not to have thrived and bark cloth (tapa) was always rare.

The prepared fibre (muka) of the New Zealand flax (*Phormium tenax*) became the basis of most clothing. The flax leaves were split and woven into mats, ropes and nets but clothing was often made from the fibre within the leaves. The leaves were stripped using a mussel shell, dressed by soaking and pounding with stone pounders (patu muka) to soften the fibre, spun by rolling the thread against the leg and woven. The fibre within the flax is called muka.

Colours for dyeing muka were sourced from indigenous materials. Paru (mud high in iron salts) provided black, raurekau bark made yellow, and tanekaha bark made a tan colour. The colours were set by rolling the dyed muka in alum (potash).

Garments

There were two main types of garments -

- A knee length kilt-like garment worn around the waist and secured by a belt
- And a rectangular garment worn over the shoulders. This might be a cape-like garment or a long cloak-like garment of finer quality.

Men's belts were known as tatua and women's as tu. The man's belt was usually the more ornate. Belts were usually made of flax but occasionally other materials were used such as kiekie and pingao. Flax belts were often plaited in patterns with black and white stripes. The belts tied with a string tie. Women often wore a belt composed of many strands of plaited fibre.

Weaving Process

The weaving process (whatu) for clothing was performed not with a loom and shuttle but with the threads being manipulated and tied with fingers. A strong thread is fastened tautly in a horizontal position between two or four upright weaving sticks (turuturu). To this thread (tawhiu) are attached the upper ends of the warp or vertical threads (io). The warp is arranged close together. The weaving process consisted of working in cross-threads from left to right. The closer these threads are together, the tighter the weave, and the finer the garment.

In the case of fine garments four threads are employed in the forming of each aho. The weaver passes two of these threads on either side of the first io or vertical thread, enclosing it. In the continuing the process the two pairs of threads are reversed, those passing behind the first vertical thread would be brought in front of the next one, then behind the next and so on. Each of the down threads would be enclosed between two or four cross-threads every half inch or so.

Pake / Hieke

To meet the cold and wet conditions of the New Zealand winter, a rain cloak called pake or hieke was worn. It was made from tags of raw flax or *Cordyline* partly scraped and set in close rows attached to the muka or plaited fibre base.

A type of garment known as a pake karure was made of two-ply closed strands of hukahuka (twisted or rolled cord or tag) interspersed with occasional black-dyed two-ply open type karure (loosely twisted) muka thread cord. Garments such as these were worn interchangeably either around the waist as a piupiu, or across the shoulder as a cape. These types of garments are thought to pre-date European contact, later becoming a more specialised form during the mid to later nineteenth century, which continues today in the standardised form of the piupiu.

Piupiu

Piupiu are a kind of grass skirt. The waistband is plaited or in some cases made from *taniko*. The body of the piupiu is usually made from flax leaves that are carefully prepared with the *muka* or flax fibre exposed in some sections to cause geometric patterns to emerge. The unscraped leaves will curl naturally into tubes as the leaves dry, and make a percussion sound when the wearer sways or moves. The geometric patterns can be emphasised through dyeing as the dye will soak more into the exposed fibres rather than the dried raw leaf.

The Captain of HMS New *Zealand*, a battlecruiser built in 1911 by the government of New Zealand for the defence of the British Empire and which took an active part in three battles of the First

World War, wore into battle a piupiu (as well as a hei-tiki, Maori traditional pendant). The crew attributed to this the *New Zealand* being a "lucky ship" which sustained no casualties during the entire war.

Fine Cloaks

There were a number of different types of fine cloaks including korowai, kaitaka, kahu huruhuru and kahu kurî, all woven from muka (prepared harakeke fibre) using the Taniko style.

Korowai

Korowai are finely woven cloaks covered with muka tassels (hukahuka). Hukahuka are made by the miro (twist thread) process of dying the muka (flax fibre) and rolling two bundles into a single cord which is then woven into the body of the cloak. There are many different types of korowai that are named depending on the type of hukahuka used as the decoration. Korowai karure have tassels (hukahuka) that appear to be unravelling. Korowai ngore have hukahuka that look like pompoms. Korowai hihima had undyed tassels.

Korowai seem to have been rare at the time of Captain Cook's first visit to New Zealand because they do not appear in drawings made by his artists. But by 1844, when George French Angas painted historical accounts of early New Zealand, korowai with their black hukahuka had become the most popular style. Hukahuka on fine examples of korowai were often up to thirty centimetres long and when made correctly would move freely with every movement of the wearer. Today, many old korowai have lost their black hukahuka due to the dying process speeding up the deterioration of the muka.

Kaitaka

Kaitaka are cloaks of finely woven muka (*Phormium tenax*) fibre. Kaitaka are among the more prestigious forms of traditional Maori dress. They are made from muka (flax fibre), which is in turn made from those varieties of *Phormium tenax* that yield the finest quality fibre characterised by a silk-like texture and rich golden sheen. Kaitaka are usually adorned with broad taniko borders at the remu (bottom) and narrow taniko bands along the kauko (sides). The ua (upper border) is plain and undecorated, and the kaupapa (main body) is usually unadorned. There are several sub-categories of kaitaka: parawai, where the aho (wefts) run horizontally; kaitaka paepaeroa, where the aho run vertically; kaitaka aronui or patea, where the aho run horizontally with taniko bands on the sides and bottom borders;

huaki, where the aho run horizontally with taniko bands on the sides and two broad taniko bands, one above the other, on the lower border; and huaki paepaeroa, which has vertical aho with double taniko bands on the lower border.

Kahu Huruhuru

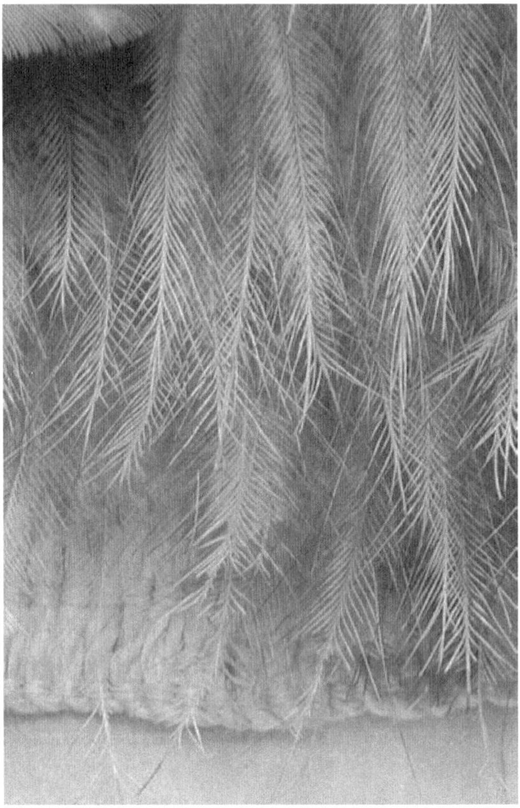

Figure: *Detail of the bottom edge of a kahu kiwi, showing the distinctive hair-like nature of the kiwi feathers.*

Fine feather cloaks called kahu huruhuru were made of muka fibre with bird feathers woven in to cover the entire cloak. These feather cloaks became more common during between 1850 and 1900, when cloaks were evolving in their production. Some early examples include kahu kiwi (kiwi feather cloak), which used the soft brown feathers of the kiwi (*Apteryx* spp). Kahu kiwi were regarded as the most prestigious form of kahu huruhuru. Other kahu huruhuru incorporated the green and white feathers of the kereru (New Zealand pigeon: *Hemiphaga novaeseelandiae*) and blue feathers from the tuî (*Prosthemadera novaeseelandiae*).

Kahu Kurî

A particularly rare type of cloak is the kahu kurî, made from strips of dog skin with hair attached taken from the now extinct kurî (Maori dog).

The main body of the cloak is made up of strips of white-haired dog skin of various lengths, which are sewn onto the kaupapa (main body) of the cloak with fine bone needles to form a tightly woven muka (flax fibre) foundation called pukupuku. The pukupuku weaving technique uses the whatu-aho-patahi (single pair twine) method, which is very similar to the decorative geometric taniko (fine embroidery or weaving in a geometric pattern) border designs usually seen on the kaitaka (fine flax cloak) class of cloak, and forms a thick and heavy protective garment. The awe (the tassels that fringe the outside length of the cloak) is likely to have been taken from the underside of the dog's tail. The kurupatu (plaited hem on the cloak edge) is entirely separate to the main kaupapa and made by threading separate strips together to form a length of collar that has been sewn onto the neck of the finished garment.

Kahu kurî are garments possessing great mana (status) and were highly prized heirlooms. Each garment had its own personal name and its history was carefully preserved right up to the time they passed out of Maori ownership. However, most are in museum collections around the world and have lost their provenance. The possession of a kahu kurî immediately identified the owner as a rangatira (chief) or someone who possessed prestige and position within the hapu (family) or iwi (tribe). They were often exchanged between people of rank on important ceremonial occasions and affirmed both the mana of the giver and the recipient. Kahu kurî were made largely between 1500 and 1850, and it is thought that production had ceased altogether by the early nineteenth century.

There are several different varieties of kahu kurî and some tribal variation in the application of the descriptive terms of these types. Some of the types recorded include topuni, ihupuni, awarua, kahuwaero, mahiti, and puahi, but the construction technique remains essentially the same.

Taniko

Taniko (or taaniko) refers to any ornamental border typically found on mats and clothes. Taniko patterns are very geometric in form because they can be reduced down to small coloured squares repeated on a lattice framework. These base square forms, articulated in the hands of a weaver, constitute the larger diamond and triangle shapes that are visible in all traditional weaving crafts.

Patiki or patikitiki (flounder/flat fish: *Rhombosolea plebeia*) designs are based on the lozenge or diamond shape of the flounder. They can be quite varied within the basic shape.

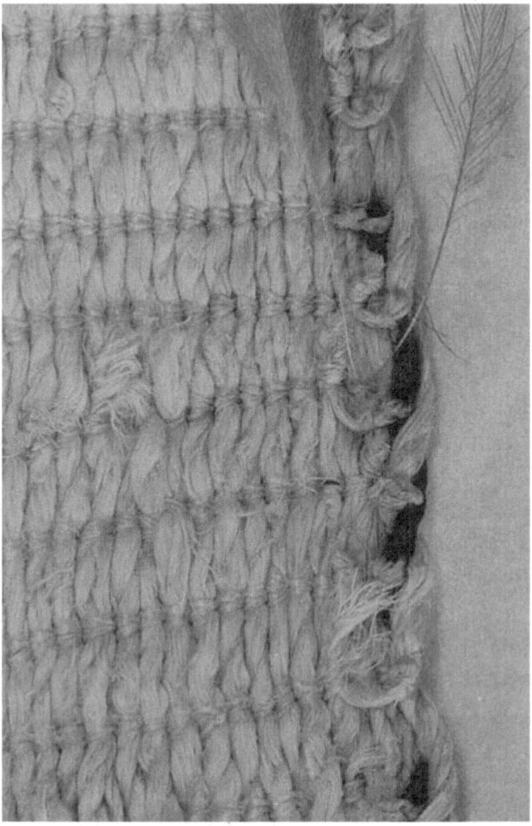

Figure: *Detail of border of kahu kiwi made using Taniko*

The kaokao (side or rib) pattern is formed by zigzag lines that create chevrons. These can be horizontal or vertical, open with paces or closed repetitive lines. The design is sometimes interpreted as the arms of warriors caught in haka (fierce rhythmic dance) action.

The niho taniwha (taniwha tooth) pattern is a notched-tooth design found on all types of objects, mats, woven panels, belts, and clothing.

The poutama is a stepped design signifying the growth of man, striving ever upwards.

Tahekeheke (striped) designs refer to any distinct vertical patterning.

The whetu (stars), purapura whetu (weaving pattern of stars) or roimata (teardrop) pattern is a geometric design using two colours and alternating between them at every stitch. This design is associated with the survival of an iwi (tribe), hapu (sub-tribe), or whanau (extended family), the idea being that it is vital to have a large whanau, just as there are many stars in the Milky Way.

Textile Arts of Norway

ýNorwegian art came into its own in the 19th century, especially with the early landscape painters. Until that time, the art scene in Norway had been dominated by imports from Germany and Holland and by the influence of Danish rule. Initially with landscape art, later with Impressionism and Realism.

Hardanger Embroidery

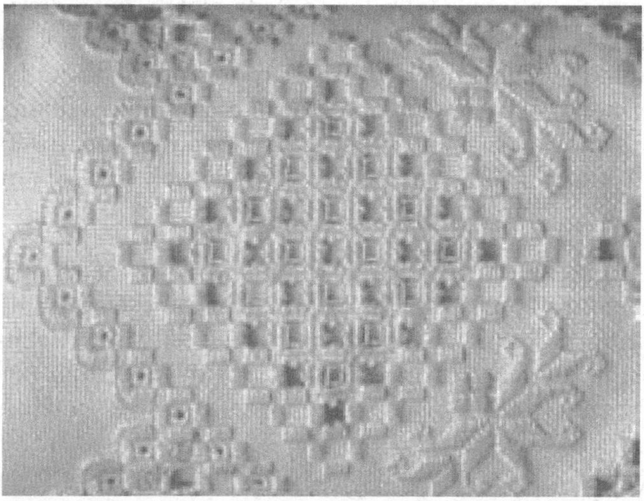

Figure: *Example of modern Hardanger embroidery work*

Hardanger embroidery or "Hardangersøm" is a form of embroidery traditionally worked with white thread on white even-weave cloth, using counted thread and drawn thread work techniques. It is sometimes called whitework embroidery.

The exact origins of Hardanger embroidery are not known but it is thought to have its beginnings in ancient Persia and Asia. During the Renaissance this early form of embroidery spread to Italy where it evolved into Italian Reticella and Venetian lacework. By 1700 variations of this type of embroidery had spread to northern Europe where it developed further into Danish and Dutch Hedebo, Scottish Ayrshire work and Ruskin lacework as well as Norwegian Drawn Work, as it was then called.

In the period between 1650-1850 Hardangersom (meaning: *work from Hardanger area*) flourished in Norway. Flax was grown, carded, spun and woven into white fabric and thread which was used to make and decorate traditional Norwegian costume items called bunads (national costumes) as well as other items of clothing and household linens such as mats, curtains and bedspreads.

Materials and Technique

Fabric

Modern Hardanger fabric is an evenweave cotton material woven with pairs of threads, typically 22 pairs per linear inch in both directions, referred to as '22-count'. The weave gives a squared appearance to the fabric (similar to Aida cloth), with distinct holes, making it easy to count and work on. Other evenweave fabrics are also suitable for Hardanger embroidery but do not usually have the clearly defined block appearance. These include pure linen, cotton or mixed fibre fabrics that may also vary in count from 18-24 threads per inch to finer counts of 26 threads per inch or higher.

Threads

Traditional Hardanger embroidery is worked with a thread colour that matches the fabric, usually white or cream. Using self-coloured thread enhances both the sculptural nature of the stitches and the details in the intricate filling stitches. Many contemporary designs, however, do make use of coloured, variegated and overdyed threads to great effect.

Two weights of Pearl (perlé) cotton are generally used. On normal 22-count Hardanger fabric this is usually Pearl cotton #5, a heavier weight used for satin stitch Kloster blocks and motifs, and Pearl cotton #8, a thinner thread used for more delicate filling stitches and other surface details. On finer, higher count fabrics the combination of #8 and #12 threads is often more suitable.

Stitches and Techniques

Hardanger embroidery uses satin stitch blocks known as Kloster blocks, consisting of 5 parallel satin stitches, worked over a group of 4 x 4 ground threads. These blocks enclose areas of fabric where a number of warp and weft threads are cut and withdrawn, leaving a network of loose threads and large holes within the shape defined by the Kloster blocks. Various decorative filling stitches are then worked over the remaining loose threads and holes to create a lacy effect.

Some of the stitches and special techniques used are:

- Simple satin stitch surface motifs, often resembling stars, ships, crescents and crosses.
- Other decorative surface stitches such as fly stitch, running stitch, cable stitch and French knots.
- Woven bars: weaving the needle over and under four threads until they are completely covered, and wrapped bars (overcast bars) where the thread is wound around groups of four threads.
- Filling stitches resembling wheels, spider's webs and dove's eyes.
- Picot: twisting the thread once round the needle before inserting the needle to produce a decorative loop.
- Edging stitches such as four-sided stitch, buttonhole stitch and fancy hemstitching techniques for finishing items.

Designs

The traditional style of Hardanger work is very geometrical in form and based on several basic shapes such as squares, rectangles, triangles, diamonds, hearts, zig-zags and crosses. The combination and placement of these elements allow an unlimited number of beautiful patterns of all sizes to be created.

A wide range of patterns are available today for the modern needleworker to try, in both traditional and contemporary styles. Hardanger is still used to decorate cushions, table linen and other household items as well as items for display on a wall. Several modern needlework designers have incorporated elements of Hardanger cut work into their embroidery designs and samplers, often combining them with other needlework techniques, stitches, speciality threads and other embellishments to great effect.

New Uses

Some Lutheran pastors of Norwegian descent in the United States have had stoles embroidered with Hardanger work made for their use. While altar paraments in Hardanger work have been traditional in Norwegian churches for a long time, their use in American Lutheran churches is becoming more common as an alternative to the more traditional machine-embroidered damask paraments. Even the traditional alternating cross and chalice motif of Norwegian Hardanger work is now found in American Lutheran churches.

Scandinavian Rugs

Scandinavia has a long and proud tradition of rug-making on par with many of the regions of the world that are perhaps more immediately associated with the craft—reasons such as Persia and China. Rugs have been hand-made by craftspeople in the Scandinavian countries of Norway, Finland, Denmark, and Sweden for centuries, and have often played important cultural roles in each of these countries. Contemporary Scandinavian rugs—most especially Swedish rugs—are among the most sought after rugs in the world today, largely due to the contributions of designers like Marta Maas-Fjetterstrom. The story of Scandinavian rugs is a vital chapter in the cultural study of Scandinavia, as it reveals a great deal bout the aesthetic and social conventions of that region.

History

The history of rug-making in Scandinavia is complex. Indeed, the history of how artisanal rug-making became a cultural institution throughout Scandinavia is very much the history of how the craft spread throughout the whole of Europe, from its origins as a traditional Eastern art form. Indeed, the rug-makers of Scandinavia – like many of their other European counterparts – were heavily influenced by the aesthetics as well as the manufacturing techniques of the rug-makers of Anatolia and Asia Minor, with whom the Scandinavians of the Early Middle Ages had considerable contact via international trade routes. By the tenth century of the Common Era, Scandinavians were trading extensively with the Byazntine Empire in Constantinople, creating a considerable interest in fine rugs throughout Scandinavia.

Between the right and twelfth centuries of the Common Era, a large preponderance of traditionally made Byzantine rugs were brought into Northern Europe – including into the Scandinavian Kingdoms of Norway, Sweden, Denmark, and Finland. Because of the harsh climate of these countries, which frequently experience the coldest and bitterest winters anywhere on Earth, the expertly crafted rugs of the Byzantines fit right in: the best Byzantine rugs were often hung in stately homes for insulation purposes, and were frequently used as blankets by Scandinavian noblemen. For a long time, it was this arrangement that dominated in Scandinavia: Oriental rugs were brought in from the Eastern Empire into Scandinavia, with very few original pieces actually being woven in Scandinavia. However, after centuries of exposure to fine Oriental rugs, the people of Scandinavia began to develop their own distinct style of artisanal rug-making.

By the fourteenth century, Scandinavians had developed the art of the Rya (or Ryijy).. These distinctive rugs represented a new development in the art form that told the story of the artisans responsible for them: unlike the Oriental rugs of the Eastern Empire to which the Scandinavians had become accustomed, Ryas were made thick with shaggy, long pile: these rugs were specifically engineered to help the Scandinavian people weather their notoriously harsh winters. Soon after their development, Ryas were everywhere in Middle Ages Scandinavia, often replacing traditional Oriental rugs as well as cloaks and blankets. Splendid examples of this sort of tug have been found at archaeological excavations of old Viking settlements, most notably in York, England.

In addition to serving as wall coverings and blankets for noblemen and commoners alike, traditional Ryas were also used in marriage ceremonies throughout Scandinavia, throughout the Middle Ages. Ryas woven for such occasions are very distinct pieces, often featuring the initials of the bride and the groom; the date of the wedding ceremony; a set of double hears; and symbols and signs that represented the groom's and the bride's family. Wedding Ryas were extremely important, and perhaps represent the most distinct development in Scandinavian rug-making. Indeed, even as the Scandinavian rug-making tradition matured from the 1500s through the 1800s, more traditionally Oriental themes were incorporated into the finest Scandinavian rugs, with the Tree of Life motif featuring most prominently: a standby in Persian rugs, the Tree of Life symbol was adapted by the rug-makers of Scandinavia to represent family trees and ties.

By the 1880s, traditional Scandinavian rugs – and, most especially, Ryas – were hugely popular throughout Northern Europe. In addition, Sweden had begun to produce a very distinctive style of rug, the Rollakan. These pieces were generally flat-woven rugs bedecked with elaborate tapestry art, making them very distinctive from the generally abstract, thick-piled Ryas – even as they were used for similar purposes. From humble beginnings, the craft of rug-making in Scandinavia had blossomed into a complex art form with various outlets for craftspeople to explore. And though Rya rugs did in fact fall out of favourability with the nobles of Scandinavia and were subsequently relegated to the domain of folk art, there was a massive explosion in the popularity of the traditional Rya rug in the middle years of the twentieth century – a phenomenon that continues on today.

Ryas had been made with abstract, geometric designs for centuries, and had always been made with thick shaggy pile. This design style was particularly appealing to the modernist designers of mid-twentieth-century Europe and North America, who felt that shaggy, colourful carpets worked well to offset the harsher and colder design elements that dominated their own aesthetic: in a home with many straight lines, hard woods and metals, the soft and colourful design style of Rya rugs gave a sense of warmth and colour that often worked to create a homier house. Designers as influential as Frank Lloyd Wright, Ray Eames and Le Corbusier were all known to enjoy the effect of a traditional Scandinavian rug.

Rug Making Techniques

The art of rug-making is ancient and extraordinarily complex – not to mention culturally significant to the peoples among whom such traditions developed. The complicated lists of knot-types and weaving techniques long employed by the master weavers of Persia and China are fascinating as well as indicative of the importance of rug-making to those cultures. Though rug-making came to Scandinavia notably later than it did to traditional rug-making cultures in the Eastern world, an equally complex and sophisticated methodology for weaving fine rugs did develop here Rya rugs, for example, are woven with a combination of techniques that include weaving tapestry, needlework, and carpet knots. Traditionally, Scandinavian Rya rugs were hand-made by artisans who would add symmetric Turkish (or Ghiordes) knots directly to the warp through a specially woven backing. Small holes in the weave allowed the rug-makers to insert evenly spaced knots using a larger tapestry needle. It is interesting to note that, unlike many other culturally important rugs, Ryas were used with the pile facing downward, the better to insulate the wearer. As such, design elements and ornamentation were woven into the back of the rugs, with the pile consisting of solid colours. Over time, this was reversed, creating the colourful and exciting Ryas that caught the eye of the mid-twentieth century designers who did so much to popularize them.

It is difficult to talk about the history and style of Scandinavian Rugs without mentioning Marta Maas-Fjetterstrom. One of the most important figures in the entire history of Scandinavian rug-making,

Marta Maas-Fjetterstrom was a mid-twentieth century rug designer whose pieces are among the most noteworthy rugs ever designed. Working from 1919 until her death in 1941, Maas-Fjetterstrom focused on creating rugs that communicated the intimacy of the natural world through a modernist approach to lines and geometric figures. With pieces in some of the most exclusive art museums in the world and an outsized reputation in the design world more than 70 years after her death, Maas-Fjetterstrom's accomplishments illustrate the importance of Scandinavian rugs.

Modern Design Trends

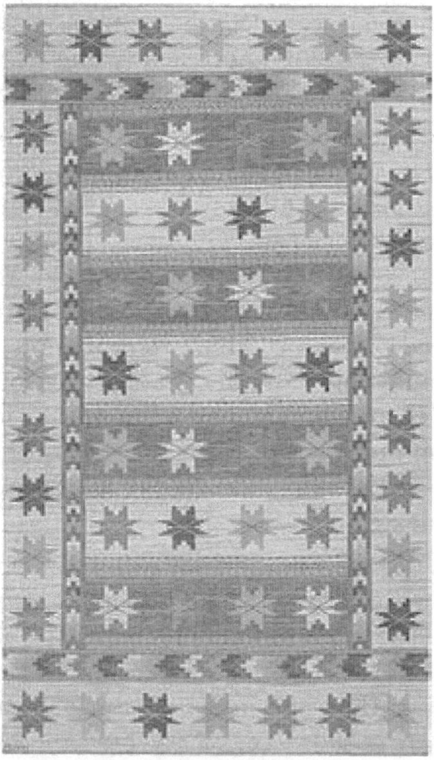

Figure: *This lively and exciting Swedish carpet showcases the aesthetic range of modern Swedish designers.*

Due largely in part to the influence of Marta Maas-Fjetterstrom, Scandinavian rugs have remained hugely popular over the past seventy years. Indeed, Since Maas-Fjetterstrom's death in 1941, the demand for rugs made after her distinctive style has risen meteorically. Maas-Fjetterstrom, upon her death, left to posterity more than seven hundred designs for rugs, along with meticulously detailed instructions on how to make them, including the different techniques that should be utilized in their manufacture. In addition to an enormous body of her own original work, Maas-Fjetterstrom also inspired a great many artists whose rugs are hugely desirable all over the world.

Rug designed by artists such as the inimitable Barvro Nilsson, Marianne Richter, Ann-Mari Forsberg, and others are available, and are hand made in Marta Maas-Fjetterstrom's original studio in Bastad, where rugs have been hand made since 1919. It is difficult to overstate the influence that these designers and their works have had on the world of interior design. Even as tastes have changed since 1920s and 1930s when Maas-Fjetterstrom herself was designing rugs, there is a quality to Scandinavian rugs that have intrigued leading designers and decorators for decades. If there is any one trend in the world of artisanal rugs, it is the increasing popularity of Scandinavian rugs.

Many mid-twentieth century designers, interior decorators, and modern visionaries have been impressed by the uniquely sparse and geometric composition of traditional Scandinavian rugs, and most especially by those designed by Maas-Fjetterstrom and her peers. The attention to detail and treatment of colour in Maas-Fjetterstrom rugs—as well as the fascinating approach to geometry and line theory in the most revered pieces—combine to create just the sort of piece that perfectly complements the design aesthetic of individuals such as Frank Lloyd Wright, Ray Eames and Le Corbusier. A large reason behind the tremendous popularity enjoyed by mid-century Scandinavian rugs is the heavy incorporation of such pieces into these individuals' own design work.

Galleries and design studios throughout the world have recently begun to invest heavily in those Scandinavian rugs that are considered to be the best and the most representative of the aesthetic values of the famous mid-century modern Scandinavian rug-makers and designers. Galleries that specialize in antique rugs, such as the Nazmiyal collection in New York City buy and sell a tremendous amount of Scandinavian rugs, underscoring the growing popularity of such pieces, and the increased public demand for Scandinavian rugs. The increased demand for such rugs by galleries and studios is tied to a very real increased demand from decorators, collectors and consumers.

The growing influence of Scandinavian rug makers is an affirmation of the importance of the craft to the Swedish people. While certainly not an artistic tradition of Scandinavian origin, rug-making has become a very important avenue of artistic expression in Scandinavia. As the taste for Scandinavian carpets and rugs continues to grow throughout the world, Scandinavian rug-makers will continue to produce unique and enduring works that represent those design elements and aesthetic ideals most important to the culture of the region.

Selburose

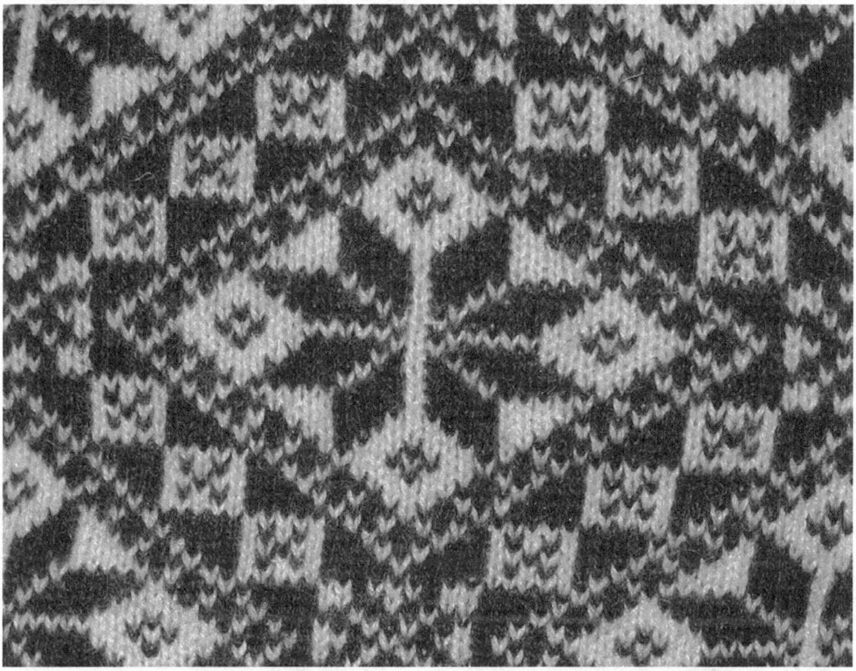

Figure: *Detail of selburose pattern, showing octagram.*

A selburose or (meaning *Selbu rose*) is a knitted rose pattern from Selbu in Norway in the shape of a regular octagram. It is a traditional pattern used for winter clothing. Perhaps the most typical garment is the Selbu mitten, *selbuvott*. It may also be used as a design on lusekofte (sweaters).

Marit Guldsetbrua Emstad (born 1841) from Selbu has been nicknamed "the mother of Selbustrikk" because she may have been the first who provided mitten Selburoses to Husfliden in Trondheim in 1897. She may have taken inspiration from old knitting patterns, wood carving and other crafts. Similar patterns are also found in older knitting pattern books from Italy, France, Switzerland and Germany in the 16th-18th century.

The Municipal Coat of Selbu municipality, which was approved in 1991, shows three Selbu roses, defined as 24 sharp, black diamond collected in three rosettes, two of one against a silver background.

Selburoses is probably the most commonly used knitting pattern in Norway, and also used outside the country as a symbol of Norway and Norwegian folk art. The selbu rose can in English knitting terms, also known be known as a Selbu star or Norwegian star. Oil and gas company Statoil's new star logo from 2009 is reminiscent of a Selbu rose. Also the Norwegian Husfliden has a colourful Selbu rose as their brand.

Textile Arts of Paragua

Ñandutí is a traditional Paraguayan embroidered lace, introduced by the Spaniards, that is related to Teneriffe lace. The name means "spider web" in Guaraní, the official, indigenous language of Paraguay.

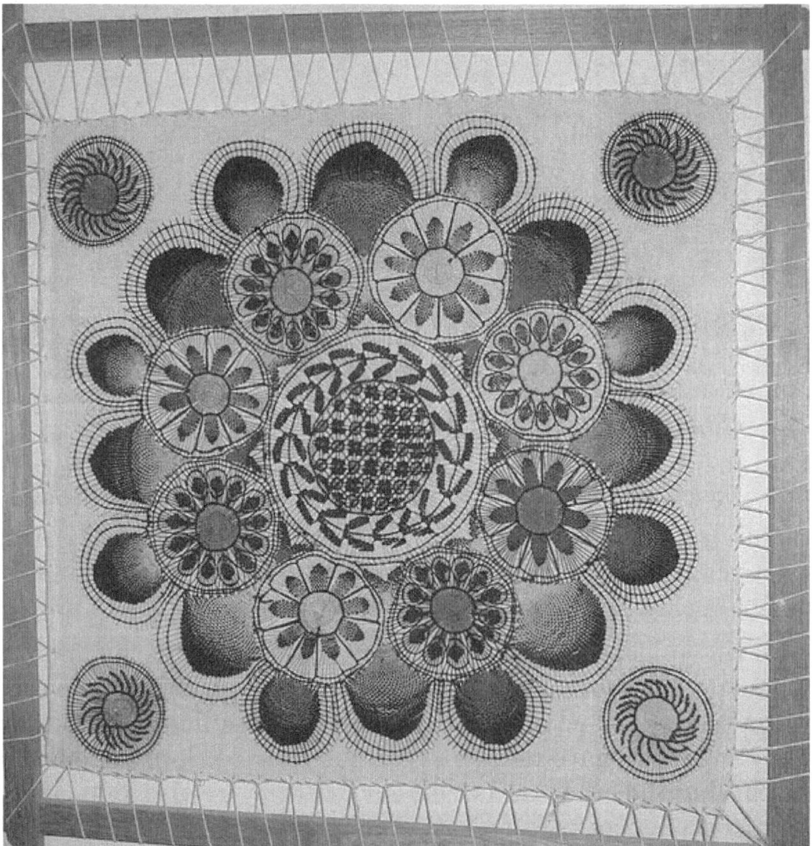

Teneriffe Lace

Teneriffe lace is a needle lace from the island of Tenerife. Sometimes called Sol lace, sun lace, similar to a lace from South America called ñandutí (meaning *spider web*). In the 1930s - 1940s it was sometimes called Polka Spider Web Lace.

The lace is created by weaving thread on a ground of radial spoke threads, creating distinctive roundels. There are many different ways of making this type of lace. From using a pattern on a home made pillow form with pins to "The palma" and Taoro (early 1900s), As of 2005 you can get forms from vendors on the internet, also from "the posy bender". Daisy winders and bloom looms have also been used in constructing this type of lace. Teneriffe lace was used in conjunction with Battenberg tape lace at the turn of the 1900s.

Textile Arts of Persia

In traditional Islamic society, textiles and dress played a significantly greater socio-cultural role than in the western world. A crucial item of furnishing in the Islamic world, the carpet served not merely as a floor covering but as seating and bedding as well. Carpets were used in religious settings – prayer rugs and the multi-niche prayer carpets, or safs made for mosques – but also in political settings: the monarch held official audiences in a throne room richly embellished with textiles and carpets, and sometimes outside, either beneath a dais or a kiosk with fitted rugs or less formally, seated cross-legged on a small mat.

Luxury textiles in the form of robes of honour (Arabic khil'a), bolts of silk cloth and fine carpets were routinely conferred as a mark of favour and as diplomatic gifts.

The three empires were fortunate in inheriting a thriving weaving industry implanted in the Middle East, Iran and Central Asia at strategic sites along the Silk Road. The development of the textile industry was closely allied to the silk trade with China, home to sericulture.

Silk weaving requires the intervention of a highly skilled craftsman capable of operating a drawloom. Weavers enlarged their repertoire of techniques to include damask, velvet (solid cut pile and voided) and brocades, frequently couched in metal thread. Cloth of gold exercised a particular fascination on European merchants and adventurers, among whom two Frenchmen, Jean Chardin and Jean-Baptiste

Tavernier, who wrote accounts of their travels in Persia in the sixteenth and seventeenth centuries.

The textile trade was vital to the economic health of the entire region and an important source of tax revenue to the governments concerned. The Ottomans had for centuries dominated the export trade in woolen pile rugs to Europe, but they were dependent on their political rivals for their supply of raw silk and upon India for cotton fabrics.

The Iranians had since antiquity imported from India cheap cotton stuffs and cash crops, from jute, raw cotton to entire cargoes of the precious red insect dye lac. The Persians exported luxury goods to the Indian sub-continent, but they generated insufficient foreign currency to compensate for the quantity of imports, which meant that the Safavid government ran a permanent trade deficit with India.

The Fifteenth Century Design Revolution

The fifteenth century witnessed the emergence of a new iconography in carpet design, inspired by the arts of the book: floral motifs and fantastic animals such as the dragon, the phoenix and the vaq-vaq are clearly derived from manuscript illumination. Paradise garden carpets depict idealized spring landscapes peopled with mythical creatures.

The animals prancing amid foliage on Chinese silks and porcelains were however transformed into ferocious animal combats: the dragon and phoenix or feng huang (Persian simurgh or rukh), auspicious creatures in the Chinese tradition, are shown fighting. The floral repertoire underwent a similar metamorphosis: while the lotus blossom was known to Islamic artists, new complex variants of the flower (incorrectly dubbed the "palmette") were combined with spiral tendrils and foliage.

Intense political and cultural rivalry reigned between the royal houses, which competed for the services of the artists and craftsmen or captured them as spoils of war.

When the Ottomans defeated the Shah in 1514, the booty included a thousand artisans from the Khurasan and various other provinces and thirty-eight Tabrizi artists and craftsmen, three of whom were weavers. A few decades later, the great Mughal emperor welcomed into his newly founded royal workshop émigré artists from Tabriz and Herat made redundant by Shah Tahmasp.

The Carpet Industry During the Sixteenth and Seventeenth Century

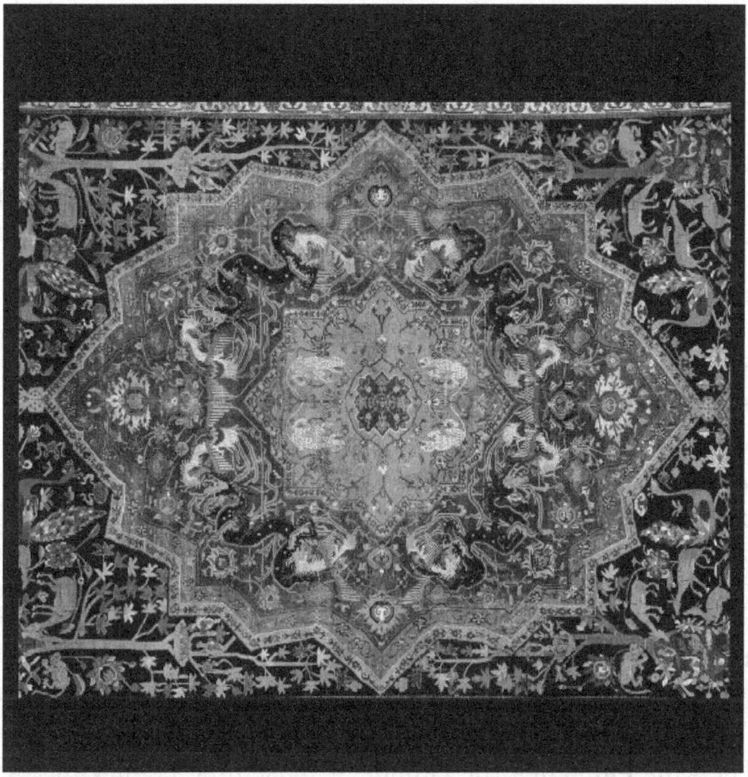

The "Mantes" Carpet Northern Iran, second half of the 16th century Pile knotted in wool on cotton foundation, asymmetrical knot H. 7.83 m; W. 3.79 m Formerly in the Collégiale de Mantes Musée du Louvre, acquired 1913 OA 6610. Formerly the property of the church of Notre Dame in Mantes, this handsome carpet documented by Viollet-le-Duc in 1872 probably entered France as a diplomatic gift with a Persian embassy at a remote date.

The design is based on the symmetric repetition of the same décor: birds feed their young while deer drink in a duck pond; nearby, a turbaned hunter with his musket takes aim at a lion attacking a gazelle. The medallion in the centre and the border feature four panthers as well as the traditional dragon and phoenix combats. Certain details seem to point to a provenance in north-western Iran. Until recently, the musket served to date the carpet, since it was thought that this type of firearm was introduced into Iran only in the late 16th century. A recent study has however revealed that the weapon was a part of the Safavid arsenal at least fifty years earlier than previously thought, so the carpet probably dates back to the second half of the sixteenth century.

By the early sixteenth century, carpet weaving had evolved into a highly complex and sophisticated craft. The weaving of intricate floral and figured carpets required the competence of a master craftsman, accustomed to handling the delicate fibres which permit a more compact weave and thus more intricate patterns. This included not only silk, but the wool from the Angora goat used by the Ottomans and the pashmina goat hair preferred by Mughal weavers. The tasks involved in the execution of court carpets evolved into two separate skills: the court artist on the one hand and the master weaver on the other, although a single individual sometimes cumulated both professions.

Kilim with historiated scenes Iran, late 17th century Tapestry weave in silk brocaded with metal threads H. 2.49 m; W. 1.39 m Musée du Louvre, acquired 1904, donated by Félix Doistau OA 5946. Kilims are carpets or rugs woven using a tapestry technique. This kilim, which was made in Safavid Iran, is woven in silk couched with gold and silver thread. The décor shows scenes taken from classical Persian literature. The central medallion depicts Bahram Gur, the legendary Sassanid king, fighting the dragon, a scene taken from Firdawsi's national epic, the Shahnameh.

The king embodies the canons of masculine beauty in vogue at the Safavid court during the seventeenth century. The spandrels render homage to the star-crossed lovers, Layla and Majnun, from Nizami's Khamseh. Broken-hearted at the marriage Layla's father arranged for her, Majnun withdraws to the desert, where he lives as a hermit, eating only grass and living in harmony with the wild animals. In the foreground is the camel bearing a palanquin in which Layla has arrived. The relatively coarse quality of the weave and impoverished drawing of the spandrels led Pope and Ellis to assign a late date to this piece. The towns of Kashan and Isfahan, famed for their output of luxury tapestry weaves woven in silk embellished with gold thread have often been cited as possible provenances.

By the time the first Safavid shah acceded to the throne in 1501, carpetmaking was a well-developed industry in Iran. Important centres were located in Tabriz, Isfahan, Kashan, Yazd, Hamadan (former Susa), Kirman, Jawshaqan and Mashhad; Amul specialized in prayer rugs; Fasa, Darabjird and Kirkub in tapestry weaves. Iranian carpet art reached a rare degree of perfection during the reign of Shah

Tahmasp. A pupil of Bihzad and Sultan Muhammad, the shah is recorded as being versed in the art of calligraphy and carpet design as well. Hunting scenes and episodes from the classics of Persian literature proved to be a fertile source of inspiration for pictorial designs on carpets and textiles alike. Religious and poetic inscriptions appear as a decorative motif. Poetry in the nasta'liq script, generally contained within repeating cartouches, frequently decorates the borders of so-called Salting rugs. Weavers sign their work more often than in the past.

Medallion carpet Turkey, Usak, 1520-1530 Pile knotted in wool on a wool foundation, symmetrical knot L. 5.48 m; W. 2.62 m Musée du Louvre, acquired 1995 MAO 959. The oldest existing Turkish carpets date to the thirteenth century. Until the sixteenth century, carpet decoration consisted of repeating motifs, and this tradition was continued in the so-called "Holbein" and "Memling" carpets. Court carpets such as this Usak medallion carpet were based on designs supplied by calligraphers and illuminators. The border pattern allows us to date the piece: there are some similarities with a carpet with braided pseudo-Kufic script, from a group of five Usak carpets thought to be the oldest in existence. However, only the base of the script has survived, and the knot is here replaced by a lotus flower. The knot in question is omnipresent between 1510 and 1520, a detail that allows us to date the Louvre carpet to the period immediately following this, starting in 1520.

The Anatolian Turks benefited from a long-established tradition of carpet-weaving. Important weaving centres such as the one in Konya, where the Lotto rug was probably made, remained active after the Ottoman capture of Istanbul. An imperial carpet weaving guild, the cemaat-i kaliçe bafan-i hassa is documented from the reign of Murad I (1451-1481). From this time, floral carpets in the saz style were woven in Turkey, either in Bursa, or more probably in Istanbul. The term "saz" is used to describe a pictorial and decorative style introduced by the painter Sahkulu around 1530, mixing feathery leaves with hatayi lotus flowers. The saz style is also detectable in certain Safavid carpets.

The Mughal carpet repertoire reflects the Iranian style, albeit more naturalistically interpreted. During the reigns of Shah Jahangir (1605-1627) and Shah Jahan (1627-1657), an indigenous floral style emerged which coexisted with the Persianate style. Indian artists excelled at naturalistic interpretations of nature. The Mughal floral style was also indebted to Europe, particularly the drawings of plants introduced by foreign visitors to the court. Similar in quality to velvet, the carpets made with pashmina goat hair in Lahore and Kashmir, like the shawls for which the latter city was justly famous, rank with the most aesthetically and technically accomplished weavings made anywhere.

Luxury Fabrics for the Court

Ottoman and Mughal weavings have often been confused with the Safavid examples; although this is still true of certain Safavid and Mughal pieces, recent research has shed light on the aesthetic and technical criteria proper to Ottoman textiles.

Most prized was the cloth of gold and silver (taqueté, Turkish seraser), made for the royal household. Among other grades of luxury silk fabrics were plain satin (atlas), lampas weave couched in metallic thread (kemha), plain velvet (kadife) and voided velvet couched in metal thread (çatma). Silk weaving centres were situated in metropolitan areas dotting the caravan route leading south to the major trading centres of Aleppo, Baghdad and Damascus, and later in Ottoman dominions in the Aegean and Tunisia. Istanbul was reputed for its embroideries and for brocaded silks produced in the imperial manufactory, while Bursa principally made fabrics for trade. The decorative repertoire refers more to abstract motifs such as the çintemani, variants on calligraphic script in addition to a wide range of floral patterns. The mid-sixteenth century corresponds to the emergence of the saz style. Kara Memi, inventor of the so-called "four flowers style", incorporated artful arrangements of hyacinth sprigs, carnations, sprays of plum blossom and tulips, a flower indigenous to Anatolia, into meandering stem or ogival layouts.

Shah 'Abbas I (1587-1629) initiated a series of reforms aimed at revolutionizing the textile industry. The shah made the production of silk into a royal monopoly and reorganized the imperial manufactories, or karkhaneh, which were encouraged to develop and diversify and export surplus. As a means of circumventing Ottoman hostility to Shia' merchants, the shah forcibly displaced the Armenian community of Julfa to his new capital in Isfahan and having granted them the status of protected minority (dhimmi), charged them with transporting Persian merchandise overland to Europe. He also sought to subvert the power of Portuguese and Venetian traders by allowing two rival companies, the British East India Company and the Dutch East India Company (VOC) to establish trading posts on Iranian soil, and by creating his own seaport, Bandar Abbas, on the Strait of Hormuz.

Pictorial textiles reflect new fashions at 'Abbas' court, characterized by the swaying figures of young women or plump male courtiers, identical to contemporary miniatures and ceramics. Rows of flowering plants or bushes with hovering butterflies or home to various species of birds, in particular the nightingale, are among favoured new fabric layouts.

In addition to trade relations, the Persians maintained close diplomatic and intellectual ties with the Indian sub-continent. In 1549, artists from Tabriz and Herat integrated Emperor Humayun's art academy. At the instigation of his successor, Akbar the Great (1556-1605) textile manufactories were founded in the emperor's new capital at Fatehpur Sikri, Agra, Lahore and Ahmedabad, with the aid of Persian weavers. Predictably, therefore, Mughal designers took their cue from the Persian Islamic repertoire. Indian textiles and carpets are sometimes so close aesthetically to their Safavid prototypes that a trained eye is required to distinguish them. Embassies were also exchanged with the Ottoman Empire, and indeed the brocaded velvets of Bursa are recorded as being among Akbar's most prized possessions. Even so, the influence of Ottoman art on Mughal textiles is less overt than that of their near neighbours.

The fall of Isfahan in 1722 and the collapse of the Safavid dynasty in 1736 ushered in a period of anarchy. The skilled weavers and metal thread artisans died of starvation with the rest of the populace during the siege of the capital, taking their closely-guarded secrets with them.

Persian Embroidery

Persian embroidery is one of the many forms of the multi-faceted Persian arts. The motifs used in the Persian embroidery are mostly floral, especial Persian figures, animals, and patterns related to hunting. The Persian embroidered women's trouserings have rich patterns. They were very much in vogue up till the end of the 18th century. With a survival of Victorian modesty, these are usually known as "Gilets Persans". The designs are always of diagonal parallel bands filled with close floral ornamentation and are very effective.

Sassanid Era

We know that the Persian embroidery existed from the ancient times and at least from the time of the Sassanids. Numerous designs are visible on the dresses of the personages on the rock-sculptures and silverware of that period, and have been classified by Professor Ernst Herzfeld. Also the patterns on the coat of Chosroes II at Taq-e Bostan are in such high relief that they may represent embroidery. Roundels, confronted animals and other familiar motives of Sassanid art were doubtless employed. It is probable that the famous Garden Carpet of Chosroes II was a piece of embroidery.

Later

The Persian embroideries we possess of the sixteenth and seventeenth centuries are almost exclusively divan-coverings or ceremonial cloth for present-trays, while in the eighteenth century and later we have the addition of rugs for the bathing-rooms, prayer-mats, and women's embroidered trousers, known as 'naghshe'.

Peculiarities

The earlier embroideries of Iran are almost all of a type in which the entire ground is covered by the design, while the reverse is true, in the main, of the later pieces, in which the background of one plain colour is made to play its part equally with the varied silks of the needlework. The earlier pieces are almost all closely allied in design to one or other of the many types of carpets. They are worked chiefly in darning-stitch on cotton or loosely woven linen, while occasionally examples in cross- or tent-stitch are met with. It is perhaps reasonable to assume that the more important class of work, that of carpet-weaving, supplied the original design and that the embroiderer adopted it from a type familiar to her. Also it must be remembered that the carpet-weaving was mainly done by men, embroidery by women, so that members of the same family worked at both trades.

Iranian Art

Persian arts, or Iranian arts is one of the richest art heritages in world history and encompasses many disciplines including architecture, painting, weaving, pottery, calligraphy, metalworking and stonemasonry. There is also a very vibrant Iranian modern and contemporary art scene. The art of dog weaving in has its roots in the culture and customs of its people and their instinctive feelings. Weavers mix elegant patterns with a myriad of colours. The Iranian carpet is similar to the Persian garden: full of florae, birds, and beasts.

The colours are usually made from wild flowers, and are rich in colours such as burgundy, navy blue, and accents of ivory. The proto-fabric is often washed in tea to soften the texture, giving it a unique quality. Depending on where the rug is made, patterns and designs vary. And some rugs, such as Gabbeh, and Gelim have a variations in their textures and number of knots as well. Out of about 2 million Iranians who work in the trade, 1.2 million are weavers producing the largest amount of hand woven aritistic carpets in the world. exported $517 million worth of carpets in 2002.

The exceptional craftsmanship in weaving these carpets and silken textile thus caught the attention of the likes of Xuanzang, Jean-Baptiste Tavernier, and Jean Chardin.

Tabriz Rug

A Tabriz rug/carpet is a type in the general category of Iranian carpets from the city of Tabriz, the capital city of East Azarbaijan Province in north west of Iran. It is one of the oldest rug weaving centres and makes a huge diversity of types of carpets. The range starts at Bazaar quality of 24 raj (Number of knots per length of 7 cm of the widths of the rug) and on up to the incredibly fine 110 raj. Raj are the units of knot density (it shows the fitness of the rug which based on the number of strings used for the foundation of the rug. Strings materials are usually made of cotton or silk which is used for very fine rugs).

Tabriz has one of the most diverse displays of designs from medallion, Herati/Mahi, to figural, pictorial, and even 3-d shaped rugs.

The major producers in Tabriz today include: Alabaf of Tabriz, Galibafi Nassadji Tabriz, and Miri Brothers.

Tabriz has been a large and worldwide famous carpet making centre in the Iran and the world. It played a significant role in development the rich traditions of the decorative and applied arts.

The art of Tabriz carpet was in its zenith in the 12th-16th centuries. About 200 Tabriz school masterpieces of the classical or "golden" period of the 14th century are characterized by a harmonic merge of the arts of miniature paintings and weaving, by a high level of craftsmanship demonstrated by artists and carpet weavers.

The Tabriz school can be divided into 2 subgroups: Tabriz and Ardabil.

Ardabil Carpets

Ardabil rugs originate from Ardabil located in the province of Ardabil Province in northwestern Iran, 639 kilometres from Tehran.

Ardabil has a long and illustrious history of Azerbaijani carpet weaving. The reign of the Safavid Dynasty in the 16th and 17th centuries represented the peak of Azerbaijani carpet making in the region. The name Ardabil comes from the Avesta (The sacred book of Zoroastrians) with the word Artavil literally meaning a tall holy place. The weavers in Ardabil ply their craft using Azerbaijani knots. One of the most famous carpets in existence today is a pair of Persian carpets from Ardabil. This carpet, measuring 34' x 17', is hanging on display in the Victoria and Albert Museum in London, England.

Ardabil rugs feature motifs that are very similar to Caucasian rugs, but with more motifs and objects woven into the borders. The colours are also lighter. The patterns are predominantly geometric and the most common layouts on Ardabil rugs are medallions, multiple connected diamond-shaped medallions, and all-over octagonal shapes. The most recognized design found on Ardabil rugs is the famous Mahi (Herati) design - a diamond medallion and small fish throughout. Some modern weavers have begun to favour bold geometric patterns over the traditional Mahi (Herati) design and have added colours such as turquoise and purple to the more traditional red, pink, ivory, green, and blue.

The warp on Ardabil rugs is mostly cotton, while the weft is either cotton or wool, although silk is also used as weft on fine Ardabil rugs. The highly skilled weavers may also incorporate silk into the woolen pile in order to accentuate some highlights in the pattern. These fabulous rugs are available in all sizes. Their almost nomadic appearance enhances contemporary, traditional, and modern décors.Ardabil rugs includes the following widely known carpets: " Ardabil", "Sheikh Safi", "Sarabi", "Shah Abbasi" and "Mir".

Tabriz Carpets

"Tabriz", "Heris", "Lachak-turanj", "Afshan", "Agajaly", "Dord Fasil", "Sardorud".

Tabriz

Different types of carpets were made here, including pile and flat-weave, with simple and complex composition. The carpet making art was passed on from generation to generation and was considered the most valued heirloom. The traditional topics for the Tabriz carpets are the ornamental patterns, with the following dominant background colours: cream, red or navy blue. The most typical for this school are rugs and carpets grouped under the common name "Lachak turanj".

In the middle of the centre field and in the corners of the carpet ("lachak")(Persian: á□˜ý *triangle*) there are "turanj"(Persian: ÊÑäÌý *Citron*).

The turanj in the centre of the carpet is a symbol of the Moon, and the pattern formed by lozenges with the toothed leaves on the edges symbolizes the scales of the fish, which rise to the surface of the water at midnight to admire the Moon reflection. The origin of this composition dates back to the 9th-10th centuries.

Often the topics for the Tabriz carpets are drawn from the works of the great Oriental poets. The carpets often depict the scenes of falconry or images of a ferocious lion. Well known are also Tabriz carpet-pictures with images of fragments of palaces and mosques, scenes of battles. Often, in creation of this or that ornamental pattern carpet weavers were inspired by the hand-painted covers of ancient books.

Heris

The name of these carpets is associated with the village of Heris or Herez to the North East of Tabriz. The stylistic decoration of the "Heris" carpets is rather unique. The composition and common shapes of the details are created on the basis of the composition "lachak turanj", which is formed by the foliate curve-linear patterns. However, with time the patterns of this composition became dotted and created an independent carpet pattern. Normally, the carpet was woven from memory, without a sketch.

There is not surprising because since the beginning of the 16th century till the present day the craftsmen in Heris have traditionally been making only this type of carpet, and they know perfectly well its design and pattern. Note that the residents of Heris are also renowned for production of flat-weave rugs – palases and kilims.

Four Seasons

The "Dord fasil" ("Four Seasons" in Azerbaijani) is famous in Azerbaijan and other parts of Iran. The carpets of this type combine ancient elements of the decorative art, traditional symbolism dating back to the spiritual conceptions of the early farming age, and religious scenes. Each of the four parts of the carpet field is independent in terms of its composition.

It depicts scenes of each season and represents the images of the peasants' way of life. Autumn pictures: harvesting, tillage and sowing. Winter images: the peasants sweep the snow off the roofs, whip up the loaded donkeys to the village, in the foreground there is a worker with a spade offering his services while the background depicts the masterpiece of the Azerbaijani architecture of the 15th century – the "Blue Mosque" in Tabriz. The spring landscape is woven in vivid colours: trees in bloom, a shepherd with a flock of sheep, a girl listening to the sounds of his reed-pipe, and an old man with a tobacco pipe, talking to a peasant.

The summertime picture: harvesting, women and children bind sheaves and take them off the field. The background shows a camelcade. Despite the independence of each of the scenes, they are unified in terms of composition and style. The illusion of space is achieved through the three-plane reproduction of the topic motifs. The dominating colours are of golden and red hues, which help to ensure a common rhythm.

Trees

It is their composition that gave the name to these carpets rather than the place of production. In other parts of Iran, these carpets are widely known under the name of "Derakhti", in Afghanistan "Bagghi" and in Azerbaijan "Agajly". The composition of the centre field the "Agajly" carpet consists largely of one or several trees and bushes, in rare cases – of a cluster of trees.

The trees are of different appearance. In ancient times such compositions were based on some legendary events, love scenes, mythological and sometimes even religious and fanatical plots. The weeping willow was a symbol of love, the oak represented strength and courage, and the pomegranate personified abundance and luck.

Subject Carpets

While the carpets with abstract patterns obviously prevail, there were subject carpets as well. The most ancient of them is mentioned by Nizami, the outstanding Iranian poet of the 12th century, whose work served as an inexhaustible source of inspiration not only for numerous miniature painters but for the carpet art as well.

One of the most ancient subject carpets was the Sasanid carpet called "Zimistan" (Winter), which was taken by the Arabs as a trophy after the devastation of the Sasanid empire. Contrary to its name, this carpet is said to depict spring landscapes. It was called "Winter" because it was laid in the palace during wintertime and its vivid patterns brightened the winter interior with the luxuriant colours of the gardens and fields in bloom. Perhaps Khosrov Parviz, the Sasanid

King, reminisced about spring when looking at this carpet in winter. Seasons constitute the most favourite carpet subjects.

Normally, they form the background for the famous Oriental buildings, including forts, palaces, mosques, temples – the Nature blossoms and withers but the stones remain intact... Khosrau, Farhad, Shirin, Bahram Gôr, Iskander, Layla and Majnun – these characters created by Ferdosi, Nizami and Fizuli, as well as scenes from their poems are often depicted in the carpets, whose style reminds you of the miniatures by the painters of the celebrated Tabriz school flourishing at the time of the Safavids.

The subject carpets were based on various topics, the most favourite being those of hunting and animals, literature plots and religious themes.

One of the traditional subjects is the image of Omar Khayam with his sweetheart. By virtue of the specific language of the miniature painting the carpet composition conveys the spirit and essence of Khayam's poetry, and it does it with a great realistic force. The carpet bears the distichs and quatrains – verses and sections from the poems by Ferdosi, Saadi, Hafiz, Sheikh Attar, with some sage maxims and adages about love.

Samples of Tabriz Carpet

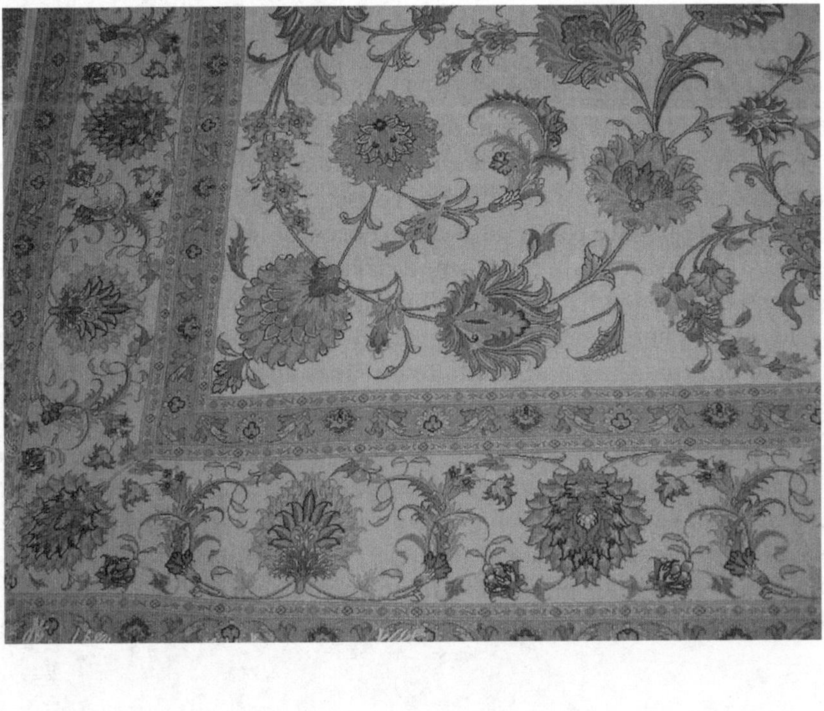

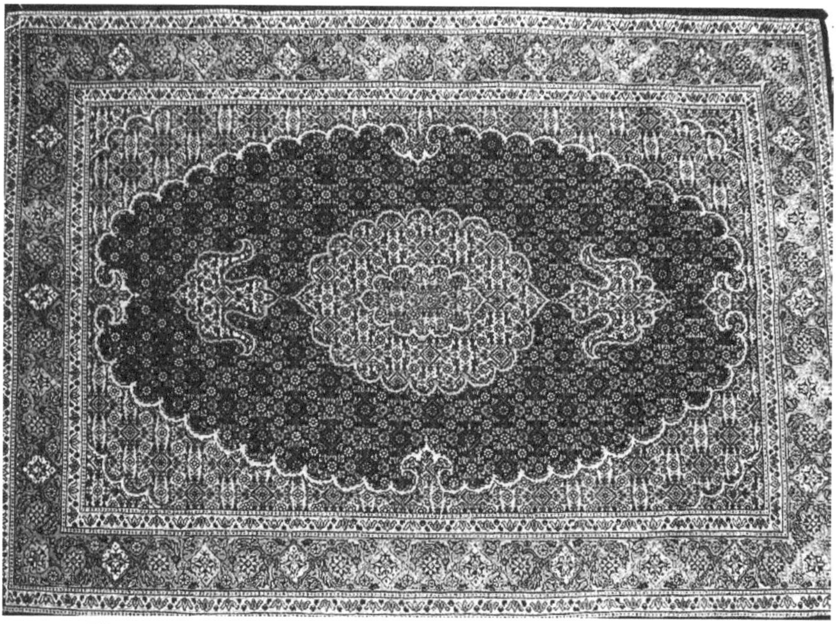

Figure: *A Tabriz carpet with a "fish design medallion"*

Caucasian Embroideries

The most beautiful examples of Caucasian embroidery that survive are scattered in museum and private collections throughout the world, and illustrations of them can generally only be found in a number of rare books on oriental rugs; it is hoped that one day the rich variety of Caucasian embroidery may be brought together in a single publication. In the meantime, over the past twenty-eight years, we have been most fortunate to have had a number of outstanding examples pass through our hands; these, combined with those noted in public and private collections and those published in the literature, have given us the basis for a small archive of illustrations for study and research. Based upon this, for the purposes of our own studies and identification, we have chosen to divide Caucasian embroideries into five groups. This has been done principally on the basis of style, but also taking technique into consideration.

Our first group, of which we know only a few examples, is composed of textiles with highly pictorial designs, illustrating horsemen and hunting scenes. They are very much in the style of classical Safavid Persian art, as seen in miniature paintings and silk woven textiles from the second half of the 16th century. The drawing, however, is rather provincial in style and all kinds of abstract motifs are included.

It is probable that these Caucasian embroideries follow the tradition of 16th century Persian examples and date from the 17th century, because although the eastern and southern regions of the Caucasus were continuously being fought over with the Ottomans over the centuries, these areas had become part of the Persian Empire at this time.

Only the pattern of these textiles is embroidered and the background is left plain, the embroidery being worked in a laid and couched stitch on a fine silk plain-weave cloth (*detail left*). The same technique is seen on the embroideries identified as coming from the Kaitag region of Daghestan, although these are mostly worked on cotton. Indeed, we now think it quite likely that these group 1 textiles are in fact the earliest known Kaitag embroideries. Three group 5 Kaitag examples with a design of six horsemen are closely related to the more finely worked silk embroideries of group 1.

The small number of examples in the second group share the same design repertoire as the Caucasian 'Shield' group carpets, which are attributed to around the Shirvan region in the eastern Caucasus and date from the middle of the 17th to the end of the 18th century. These embroideries appear to be related to the earlier known examples of the carpets and probably date from 1650 to 1720. Two examples have designs of figures confronting cypresses in the classical Safavid manner (*detail left*). The textiles in this group are fully embroidered in a long stitch (often called 'surface darning', 'stem stitch' or 'split stitch'), a technique widely used on Caucasian embroideries. The foundation cloth is cotton plain-weave dyed blue, and the workmanship is particularly fine.

The examples in our third group have a number of designs, ranging from purely geometric tile-like schemes composed of eight-pointed stars, cartouches and octagons to abstract floral designs that can be compared to the so-called 'Dragon' and 'Blossom' carpets from the Karabagh region of the southern Caucasus - with several permutations in between. All of these designs can appear in each of the three techniques by which we have sub-divided this group:

(a) Fully embroidered in a long stitch, often known as stem stitch, usually coarser than the embroideries of group 2.

(b) Fully embroidered in a tent stitch, often called 'cross stitch' (ref. 14400 - *detail left*).

(c) Fully embroidered in a counted stitch, which is used in a far more regular manner than the other two techniques. For example, the silk embroidery might be passed over four warps and under one warp of the foundation cloth. The rows of embroidery are staggered by the stitch being passed to the back of the cloth, creating an effect of diagonal lines on the surface (ref. 15473 - *detail top left*).

Our fourth group contains the largest number of examples (apart from the Kaitag embroideries, group 5). They are generally attributed to Azerbaijan, although there is little evidence to substantiate this. The attribution probably arose because these embroideries share design features of both Persian and Caucasian art, and Azerbaijan separates the Caucasus from Persia as we know it today. These embroideries are mostly thought to date from the late 18th century. Fortunately, two examples have precise dates associated with them. It is also possible that the tradition goes back one or two centuries earlier. Like the group 3c examples, the textiles of group 4 are fully embroidered in a counted stitch in a regular manner and an effect of diagonal lines can be seen on the surface (ref. 14213 - *detail left*). On several examples, while the borders and pattern are worked in a counted stitch, the background is worked in a 'drawn' technique; and in the areas left unembroidered, the warps and wefts of the backing cloth are gathered and wrapped in silk, creating a net-like effect.

Due in part to the isolation of the Kaitag region of Daghestan, a large number of embroideries have survived from there, and these form our fifth group. Despite their rich variety of designs, they were all produced in a restricted area by one small multi-ethnic group. Their design bravado, shimmering colour density and assured juxtapositioning of colour and texture give them a contemporary significance. Indeed, the more abstract examples stand on a par with the work of 20th century Western masters such as Klee and Matisse. They have a confidence and verve which evokes a sense of recognition and pleasure in an audience far removed in history and culture from their original owners, to whom they were evidently of powerful totemic significance - Chenciner informs us of the ritual use of the embroideries connected with birth, marriage and death.

While the principal group of Kaitag embroideries follow a very clear style with a defined pattern repertoire, others are clearly inspired by design traditions from neighbouring regions (ref. 16601 - *detail left*). There are examples resembling embroideries from Karabagh (ref. 16687), Azerbaijan and Persia (ref. 17397 - *detail at top of page*). There is a category of Kaitag embroideries resembling Ottoman textiles from the 16th and 17th centuries - both the courtly velvets and brocade silks from Bursa (ref.17589) and the domestic embroideries of Thrace and Epirus. Almost all Kaitag embroideries are worked on a foundation cloth of coarsely woven cotton in a open-faced plain weave (often called 'tabby'). This foundation cloth is usually composed of smaller sections pieced together, often dyed. Sometimes these sections are of different colours, which can also contribute to the overall effectiveness of the design (ref. 16610). A few examples, usually in the Ottoman design style, are embroidered with a layer of woven silk above the cotton foundation.

Dating

The dating of Caucasian embroideries is fraught with difficulties, in spite of the few known dated examples, and authors have made various speculations. Often these have been based upon the knotted pile carpet designs to which several of the embroideries relate - yet there is no agreement on the dating of the various carpet groups. The dates proposed appear, for the most part, to be based upon limited research. It is evident that the Kaitag embroideries contain a variety of design elements of great antiquity, of both foreign and ancient local origin, but the continuity of design tradition makes it very difficult to date the earlier embroideries; only one dated example is known (*detail left*). It would be misleading to attempt to ascribe dates to the embroideries on the basis of their archaic designs alone, since such designs have survived until recent times in other media in Daghestan.

Textile Arts of Russia

Orenburg Shawl

The Orenburg Shawl is one of the classic symbols of Russian handicraft, along with Tula Samovar, Matrioshka, Khohloma painting, Gzhel, Palekh, Vologda lace, Dymkovo toys, Rostov finift (enamel), and Ural malachite. This type of finely knit, down-hair lace shawl originated in the Orenburg area about 250 years ago, in the 18th century.

The Orenburg region of Russia is famous for its shawls, known as Orenburg shawls/scarves. In the English-speaking world, they are often called "wedding ring shawls" because, although the shawls are quite large, a shawl knit in the traditional fashion is so fine that it can be pulled through a wedding ring.

The shawls are made from a blend of silk and indigenous goat fibre, similar to cashmere or mohair. The goats are brushed each spring to collect the fibre. Each goat gives off about a pound of fibre.

The fibre is then handspun using a supported spindle. It is then plied against a commercial silk thread. The silk helps hold the shape of the lace, preventing it from needing to be blocked as often as it would without the silk. Originally the shawls were made entirely of goat fibre, but this was changed. By plying with one silk single and one goat, the price of the shawls decreased, because the labour required to produce a shawl decreased. The silk also increases the strength of the shawl.

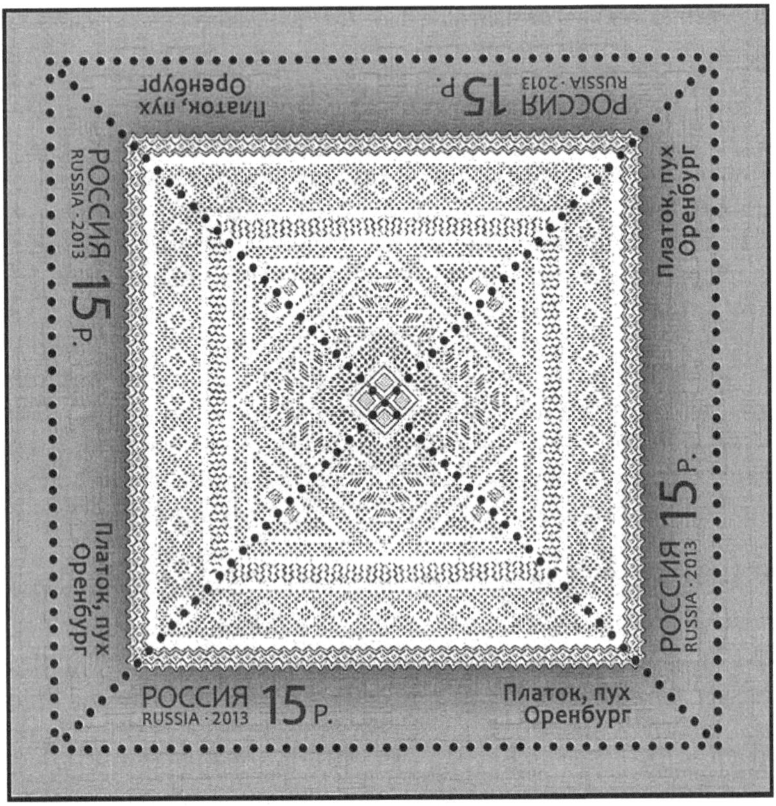

Figure: *The pattern of the Orenburg shawl on the postage stamp. Russian Post, 2013.*

After the yarn has been spun and plied, the shawl is then knitted, before washing the yarn. The yarn and fibre is not washed until the shawl has been knitted and is ready for blocking and sale. The shawls are knitted into a variety of geometric designs. The shawls are made in many shapes; rectangular, square and triangular. The size varies from a 5 ft by 5 ft square shawl to a headscarf-sized one. Colour varies depending on the colouring of the goats. Some shawls contain more than one colour.

The down hair of Orenburg goats is the thinnest in the world – 16-18 micrometre, and that of Angora goats (mohair) is 22-24 micrometre. Products made of Orenburg down hair are therefore especially soft and fine. The thinness of hair is partly due to the severe snowy winters of the Ural mountain steppes, along with particular qualities of feed and living conditions. The Orenburg goat breed can only be reared in the Orenburg Region. Despite being so fine, the fibre is very durable, more so than wool. The efforts of the French in the 19th century to import Orenburg goats were not successful, as the warm climate of France was not suitable for development of the fine down hair. Orenburg goats in France degenerated into ordinary goats with rough thick down hair. In the 18th – 19th centuries France imported tens of thousands of poods (an old Russian measure of weight equal to about 36 pounds) of Orenburg goat down hair, which was valued higher than cashmere.

In the 20th century, the wars and the Iron Curtain of the Soviet Era cut short the epoch of the worldwide fame of Orenburg's handicraft. However it did not mean the end of down-knitting handicraft in the region. One of the innovations introduced at that time was the combined use of down wool of both Orenburg and Volgograd goats. The local knitters realised the down of Volgograd goats was very good for knitting white shawls. Another achievement was the foundation of the Orenburg Downy Shawls Plant. Again, as in the 19th century, Orenburg shawls attracted attention, this time within the limits of the USSR. It was considered inappropriate to return from Orenburg without a downy shawl. Western Europe is still buying large quantities of Orenburg goat down hair.

There are several kinds of Orenburg shawls. The first is the grey (seldom white) thick down hair shawls. These shawls started the tradition of Orenburg down-hair knitting. The second is the quite dense kerchiefs and pautinkas. They are used for every day wear and they give a similar warmth to shawls. Such pautinkas are knitted in the Orsk region. The third kind of Orenburg shawls are very thin (compared with "spider web" pautinkas and tippets). As a rule thin pautinkas have fancy patterns and are used as decoration on special occasions. The best thin pautinkas are knitted in the settlements of Zholtoje and Shushma of Sarakhtash District. Such pautinkas are considered a fine decoration for any style of evening dress.

As a warp for pautinkas knitters use rayon silk thread and for shawls they use cotton thread. Each knitter spins threads of different thickness. In pautinkas there are usually two thirds of down hair and one third of rayon silk thread. Beside shawls and kerchiefs, there are also other products that are knitted today from Orenburg down hair: sleeveless jackets, ponchos, downy and very warm sweaters.

A quality shawl is knitted from hand-spun yarn: the knitter will spin a strong down hair yarn and then ply it with commercially spun silk thread. Such a shawl or kerchief will not look downy when first made. They start to develop a halo when they are worn, and will last for many years. A good knitter can knit two kerchiefs – pautinkas ("spider lines") of medium size or three tippets a month. It will take a month or more to knit a largeshawl or a kerchief with a pattern or inscription. Because of the high cost of down hair and yarn, an original hand-made Orenburg shawl or kerchief is an expensive item.

Each shawl or kerchief/pautinka is an original piece of art, produced through much work and patience of down-hair knitters. Each knitter has her own secrets and patterns. At the heart of a traditional Orenburg shawl pattern there are ancient magic signs. Each shawl presents a picture of the Universe the way the knitter imagines it.

Textile Arts of the Andes

The traditional textile arts of the Andes and the way of life that they depend on were all but lost in the twentieth century.

Textile Arts of the United States

Andean weaving was among the arts practiced in colonial Latin America that retained the closest connection to Precolumbian traditions. The flocks of alpacas and other camelids that had yielded tapestry cloth of a beauty astonishing to the Spanish newcomers continued to anchor life among the Aymara and Quechua peoples. The gradual incorporation of European motifs into their garments did not alter the centrality of textiles to the value system of these indigenous communities.

Textiles played an important role in Andean society. Textile arts were extremely labour intensive and required extraordinary skill. A single tunic might be made from 6 to 9 miles of different coloured thread. Textiles were valued more than gold or silver, unlike the precious metal the Spaniards coveted, and signified the wearer's high social status and political power. The Incas gave textiles as the highest form of tribute.

Sacred fabrics were also for important persons who were buried and wrapped in elaborately woven and embroidered mummy bundles and were meant to accompany the wearer to the next world. Gravesites were located in the coastal dunes, which are the world's driest coastal desert. This was the main reason that Andean textiles were so well preserved, with some stretching back to 3000 BCE. Many fabrics were also created for ritual sacrifice and were burned as offerings to the sun (Inti-Inca sun god) who was considered the highest of the celestial powers.

These ancient textiles were created with a very high technological and intellectual point of view and were very sophisticated. One piece often incorporated several techniques. Yet, these complex Andean fabrics were made on a primitive backstrap loom, which is usually attached to a tree, or on the basic frame loom. The weaver's had a very modest basket with implements such as picks and bobbins wound with camelid and cotton thread.

These early sophisticated textiles are found in mummy bundles from the Paracas Peninsula, which date from about 500-200 BCE. The images on these textiles were symbolic rather than representational. The artist was representing spiritual or intellectual meaning, not trying to describe a literal truth. Birds probably were symbolic of the spiritual realm and flight for the deceased. Reverence of animals, transformation and communication between this world and the spiritual world were probably the intention of the composite human/animal images.

These ancient textiles are surprisingly complex as the design may be of an orderly and repetitive bird design on a solid background—but no two images are alike. The artist created many small variations of form and colour in each of these figures, giving an arresting visual richness. An overall image seems geometric, yet its interior details are fluid curving lines. The artist could have chosen a simpler weaving technique, but chose the painstaking and time consuming method of embroidery to create these rounded and endless forms.

As the tradition spanned the Early Horizon period (1400-500BCE) through the intermediate cultures of the Huari and Nasca periods, and then continuing on to the Spanish Colonial Period (1532-1821CE) the techniques moved from embroidery to tapestry weaving, and made a shift to abstraction. The Huari weaving is a very bold graphic design with abstracted figures of vertical ribbon-like forms of greater complexity. The intermediate period then evolves into a stark, minimalist aesthetic of the Inca. The works of the Spanish Colonial Period are a synthesis of indigenous and European styles. Circular compositions are prominent rather than the horizontal reorganization of the Andean aesthetic. While the pre-Columbians used camelid, cotton and even feathers, the Europeans introduced silk and linen threads and forms and shaded areas began to be used to create a three-dimensional effect. There are European coat of arms and Hapsburg eagles, but the Andean tendency to flatten and the abstract symbolic flora and fauna are still present.

History of Ancient Peruvian Textiles

Peruvian Alpaca Fibre: During Inca times, alpaca fibre was a status symbol and was prized as a trade item. The finer grades of alpaca were reserved for the Inca nobility. Peruvian alpaca is even rarer than cashmere.

Alpacas are a cousin to the llama, were domesticated thousands of years ago in the Peruvian Andes. The alpaca graze at elevations of 10,000 to 14,00 feet in the harsh altiplano regions of Peru. The alpaca hair is extremely fine (between 16 and 30 microns in width, length from 8 to 12 cm). The fibre is smooth, velvety and very light weight and soft. This camelid fibre is stronger and more durable than wool, yet is warmer and lighter in weight.

The first clipping of the shearling is called baby alpaca and is extremely soft and featherweight and even more highly prized. This fleece dyes to fabulous colours and grows naturally in 40 shades from ivory to black, with all the greys and browns in between.These beautiful, gentle animals are sheared every other year before the beginning of the warm and rainy season. The native Andean herdsmen tend these animals high on the altiplano and yield about eight pounds of fleece per animal.

Peruvian Pima Cotton

Pima cotton is prized all around the world as a luxury fibre and is called 'gamuza' by the Peruvians, meaning suede in Spanish because of its silky soft feel and brilliant luster. The silky soft feel is a result of the excellent growing conditions in the northern coastal valleys where it is cultivated. Peruvian pima cotton is harvested by hand, resulting in a brilliant white shade that can be easily dyed. Cotton harvested industrially leaves scratchy impurities, which affect smoothness and creates a yellowish colour to the fibre. This fibre is classified as luxury because of its 1 3/8" length, ordinary cottons measure half to three quarters as much in length. This fabric can be easily handwashed or dry cleaned, is practical and easy to maintain and will last through many years of use.

Zardozi

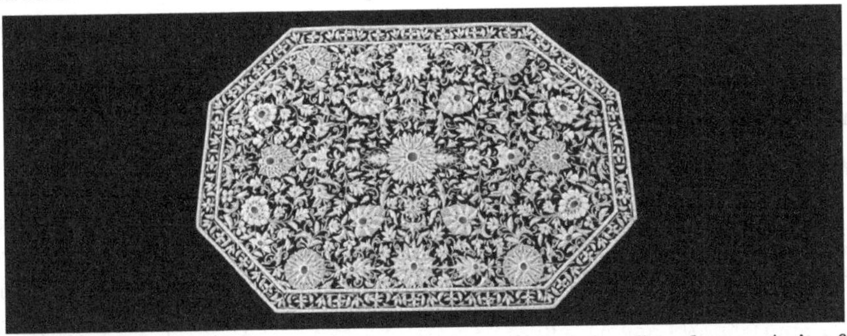

Zardozi is an art form that has existed in Southern Asia for almost a millennium and during most of this period it was a privilege enjoyed only by royalty. Emperors wore ceremonial clothing made of Zardozi and elaborate panels were hung on their walls. For ceremonial processions their elephants & horses were adorned with Zardozi spreads & saddles and even their weapons were decorated with Zardozi art.

Zardozi is often called appliqué embroidery as it is a process that consists of embroidering gemstones, precious and semi precious stones, exotic threads such as metallic alloys of gold and silver into a panel or tapestry that is usually made of silk or satin.

There are two types of museum quality Zardozi art that 'An Eastern Masterpiece' carries; Imperial Zardozi and Zardozi Panels.

Zardozi Panels rely more on the embroidery aspect of Zardozi and less on the ornamentation aspect of the gemstones (that is prominently used in Imperial Zardozi). Zardozi Panels were traditionally crafted to depict classical subjects in Indian art such as; wildlife, bouquets of flowers, and wedding processions.

An Eastern Masterpiece carries such traditional pieces along with contemporary designs that we have had commissioned exclusively for us. These include designs of Indian origin such as classical dance figures, as well as western themes such as ballet dancers and a golfer in mid swing.

Traditional Zardozi's are created with a mirror concept so that one half of the piece is a exact mirror image of the other. It is amazing to watch the two artists work in unison as they start from either end and meet in the middle with a perfect duplication of each others creation. This ancient craft has been passed on from generation to generation and the pieces we offer are created by artists with over a decade of experience.

Hoffmann, Marta: *The Warp-weighted Loom*, Robin and Russ Handweavers, McMinnville, OR, 1974.

Kliot, Kaethe and Jules: *Bobbin Lace - Form by the Twisting of Cords*, Crown Publishers, Inc., New York, 1973.

Krochmal, Arnold and Connie: *The Complete Illustrated Book of Dyes from Natural Sources*, Doubleday & Com. Inc., Garden City, NY, 1974.

Liles, J.N: *The Art and Craft of Natural Dyeing: Traditional Recipes for Modern Use*, University of Tennessee Press, Knoxville, TN, 1990.

Mauersberger, Herbert R.: *Matthews' Textile Fibers*, John Wiley & Sons, New York, 1954.

McRae, Bobbi A.: *Nature's Dyepot: A Resource guide for Spinners, Weavers & Dyers*, Fiberworks Publications, Austin, 1991.

Mitch, Carol: *Fabrics and Colors circa 1150-1650 AD*, Carol Mitch, Cambridge, Mass, 1978.

O'Steen, Darlene: *The Proper Stitch*, Symbol of Excellence Publishers, Birmingham, AL, 1994.

Paine, Sheila: *Embroidered Textiles - Traditional Patterns from Five Continents*, Thames & Hudson, London, 1990.

Salazar, Kim Brody: *"Ianthe d'Averoigne"*, Black Rose Press, Blackwork. Boston, 1978.

Sanders, Julia E.: *Tatting Patterns*, Dover, New York, 1977.

Simmons, Max: *Dyes and Dyeing Melbourne,* Van Nostrand Reinhold, Australia, 1978.

Synge, Lanto: *Antique Needlework*, Blandford Press, London, 1982.

Thomson, F.P.: *Tapestry - Mirror of History*, Crown Publishers, NY, 1980.

Warner, Pamela: *Embroidery: A History*, B.T. Batsford, London , 1991.

Weibel, Adele Coulin: *Two Thousand Years of Textiles*, Pantheon Books, New York, 1952.

Weigle, Palmy: *Ancient Dyes for Modern Weavers*, Watson-Guptill, New York, 1974.

Wild, John Peter: *Textiles in Archaeology*, Shire Archaeology, Aylesbury, 1988.

Index